ADRIENNE VON SPEYR
My Early Years

ADRIENNE VON SPEYR

My Early Years

Edited and with a Preface by
Hans Urs von Balthasar

Translated by Mary Emily Hamilton
and Dennis D. Martin

IGNATIUS PRESS   SAN FRANCISCO

Part One, which was originally written in French,
has been translated from the French text:
Adrienne von Speyr: *Fragments autobiographiques*
© 1978 Dessain et Tolra, Paris

Part Two, which was originally written in German,
has been translated from the German text:
Adrienne von Speyr: *Aus meinem Leben:
Fragment einer Selbstbiographie*
© 1968 Johannes Verlag, Einsiedeln
Second edition 1984

Cover design by Roxanne Mei Lum

CONTENTS

My Early Years

PART TWO

ILLUSTRATIONS

FOREWORD

Adrienne von Speyr would not, on her own initiative, have begun to write this partial autobiography. However, since she liked to tell stories about her childhood and youth, and because the events of her life before her conversion seemed indispensable for an understanding of her extraordinary existence, somewhere around 1945 I asked her for a written description of her life that would at the same time make her inner development comprehensible. I do not know how long she spent writing the manuscript that is presented in this book, but she probably worked at it intermittently until the early 1950s, placing the large sheets of paper in her desk drawer when they were finished. Since she probably never reread them as a whole, occasional minor repetition in content and unevenness in style remain. Some of this only becomes apparent if one compares the present work with the other autobiography she wrote later.[1] None of it affects the overall picture that emerges from these two complementary portraits of her early life. Moreover, one is astonished at the freshness and precision with which this woman of fifty years of age recalls the events of her youth, and one marvels at her facility at extracting the meaning and significance of these events within the broad scope of her life as well as their import when viewed in retrospect.

The first part of the manuscript, which covers her youth up to the point of her entry into the Basel girls' secondary school [*Basler Töchterschule*], was written in French. Adri-

---

[1] *Geheimnis der Jugend* [The mystery of youth], vol. 7 of her posthumously published writings; see also Hans Urs von Balthasar, *First Glance at Adrienne von Speyr* (San Francisco: Ignatius Press, 1981), 17–18, 108–10.

enne wrote the second part of the book, dealing with her life in Basel, in German, a language that, like the Basel dialect, she never managed to master effortlessly. For this reason, a few minor adjustments in style have been made by the editor. The book's content was never altered at all; the editor's concern was simply to remove a few Swiss idioms and, here and there, to simplify the syntax. Her vivacious way of expressing herself is evident in a charming chapter that she dictated rather than wrote down, which has been added here as an appendix: "Grandmother's House". The editor is also responsible for adding a few headings to break up what otherwise would have been excessively lengthy sections.

As we have seen, the author's concern lay primarily with inner development, with the way that both pleasant and difficult experiences became significant for later decisions. This is in fact the main thrust of the entire work, and the reader soon becomes aware that it must be read in this light. Two themes weave their way like a scarlet thread through the labyrinth of her earliest years: an unshakable determination to become a physician (note her frequent "doctor" role-playing games as a child as well as her description of a visit to the national exposition in 1914) and an equally unshakable determination to belong to God alone, to place her entire existence unreservedly at God's disposal. Only as a negative aspect of this second theme can one grasp her otherwise almost incomprehensible antipathy toward the conventionally bourgeois, relatively superficial yet firmly anti-Catholic Protestantism of her surroundings.

In her childhood, Adrienne had no possibility of contact with Catholics, to say nothing of Catholic clergy, yet, as both autobiographies reveal, she manifested already in her earliest years a rare and penetrating knowledge of certain facets of things Catholic. Moreover, she gave public evidence of this in school recitations. For this reason the editor has thought it indispensable to insert as a fifth chapter her short account of an encounter, on a steep lane in La Chaux-de-Fonds on Christmas Day 1908 between the six-year-old girl and a man she later clearly recognized in visions as having been Saint Ignatius of Loyola. In connection with the writing of her second autobiography, she told me this story; I asked her for a written account of it, which she gave me. It has been inserted here at the proper place chronologically.

To some degree this brief chapter constitutes a digression in this first autobiography, since Adrienne, who never made anything at all out of her supernatural experiences, omitted mention of other similar events from earlier or later periods of her childhood and youth (at the Waldau mental hospital during Holy Week in 1911, she experienced a vision of the Crucified One). Her account of the vision of the Mother of God that took place in November 1917 is the only exception here, and this she reports in a succinct and unselfconscious way (omitting details that would later prove to be significant), as if it were, though certainly a beautiful and blessed event, not really anything extraordinary. When Adrienne comments elsewhere on the theory of mysticism, one often finds that she made no effective distinction between specifically mystical vision and experience and the normal "vision" of the mysteries of the faith granted by grace and the indwelling Holy Spirit to anyone with living faith. Still, the insertion of this short chapter does no harm if it makes the reader aware of the special quality of the life that is described here, if it helps make clear that more than mere obstinacy directed this girl's resolute yet uncompleted search for her place in the world and in God's kingdom, if it illustrates how much importance such minor and apparently tangential experiences may acquire for other Christians as well.

One of the most beautiful aspects of this book is Adrienne's precise way of reading the fundamental principles of Christian love of neighbor out of the examples and models that were given in her experience—in other words, how the religious dimension unquestioningly shines forth from the ethical. One example of this is found in her description of her father's personality, as also in her description of her cousin Charlotte Olivier, and even more so in the portrait of her beloved teacher, Professor Hotz. Finally, this characteristic takes on almost lyrical proportions in her account of the "asceticism" of the nurses in the operating room under the spiritual leadership of Hedi Hotz. Here she finds, basically, the realization of the ideal she has always sought. She sees in their anonymous but perfect and faithful service a kind of model for what she wanted to see accomplished by the members of the secular institute she founded after her conversion: total forgetfulness of self in service to one's neighbor, out of love of the God who loved us in Christ.

We have to employ the term "model" here, since the picture of the operating room lacks some of the hues required by her fully developed ideal. Contemplation is missing as well as the prayer in all its forms and dimensions that graced her from her earliest youth, prayer into which she was led steadily deeper through an unbroken sequence of suffering, disappointments, setbacks, lonelinesses. Over time prayer would take all possible shapes: verbal and wordless prayer, prayer as uplifting contemplation, as returning gratitude, as petition, as self-sacrifice for people, as mute existence with a silent God, as active offering in service of neighbor. She became well practiced in each of these, one after the other, like an organ in which new stops are installed, until in the end the full-voiced instrument stands ready for the Master to play with pleasure. The present volume does not reveal this full performance; for that one must consult the many other volumes of Adrienne's writings that have already been published.

This book gives memorable voice to many things, but it also leaves much unsaid. Indirect illumination hints at the depths veiled by individual words. In her *Allerheiligenbuch* [Book of all saints], Adrienne was able to reveal the souls of the saints in a marvelous way, and she never intentionally covered up anything about her own soul, for she knew no deeper joy or greater need than sacramental confession. Yet she was an extremely reserved person. "Deeds without words", the von Speyr family motto, was not only one of her favorite phrases but something she confirmed often in deed. Her face was turned toward God, and one never knew what sort of reckless courage she repeatedly showed to her Lord when she offered herself up for friend and stranger alike or, in simple total abandonment, placed herself at the disposal of God's requirements. Abandonment was such a normal aspect of gratitude for her that she would have been embarrassed to have made a great affair out of it. Adrienne possessed the inner characteristics of a refined spirit: an instinct for the pure and noble wherever she encountered it; a willingness to serve in any manner; a greatness of soul that gives without counting the cost. It would be useless to try to calculate how much of these qualities she had "by nature" and how much "by grace". It is possible that it was precisely the Protestant effort to distinguish these two spheres (the sinner and the blessed) that repelled and increasingly alienated her from Protestantism. She wanted to belong to God indivisibly, without reflecting at all on herself, on "mine" and "thine".

That is why, on nearly every page of her autobiography, one observes the intertwined organic growth of the two main concerns of her life: her medical ethos and her Christian ethos. Much of what she relates here comes across as a prelude to her many notes about "physician and patient", writings that will be published at a later point. Other things written here seem to have provided training for her ecclesial task as a mystic. In many small strokes she gathers together here the elements that she, in the end, integrated into the complete picture offered by her personality. May that image be a source of enlightenment and guidance in this time of confusion in the Church.

— HANS URS VON BALTHASAR

PART ONE

The von Speyr Family portrait.
Adrienne standing behind her parents

WE, THE CHILDREN

My father was ten years older than my mother; he was German-Swiss, serious and quiet; he always made me feel awed beyond measure and represented absolute authority as far as the whole family was concerned. My mother, who was French-Swiss, had married very young and had in a way taken on her husband's personality; she asked his advice on everything, to the point that she almost acted as if she were his daughter; she made her schedule fit in with her husband's, she was always at home waiting for him when he finished his consultations or came back from the hospital, and she would sit down next to him with some work or a book, making herself sit there quietly; it was often quite a sacrifice for her because she was by nature very lively and vivacious. My father spent his leisure time reading medical journals or Greek or Latin texts; he loved ancient languages with a true scholar's passion and also spoke several modern languages.

There were four of us children, two girls and two boys. I was the younger of the two girls, and the boys were born at rather long intervals after we were. Our lives were rather far removed from our parents'. We had a governess and a huge playroom, where we spent most of our time.

My first clear memories do not go back very far. They are memories of two disappointments. One day, I must have been about three years old, I was sitting astride my toy bear, a big plush bear with stout legs on wheels, and I had put on a pair of trousers; I was convinced that I'd transformed myself, that I was now a boy, and I was singing at the top of my lungs: "My name is Adrien! My name is Adrien!" My father would have none of this game and explained to me that I was still a girl; not even my tears could make him change his mind.

About a year later, I followed my sister to school one day. The bell had not yet rung. The teacher sat me down at my sister's desk, and I began to read her a story from my sister's book; of course it was only a primer, but I read the last pages to her. The teacher paid me compliments, but, even so, she did not feel obliged to keep me in her class; she had to use not only reason but force to make me leave before the class began, and I remember sobbing bitterly in the dark corridor, feeling that I had suffered an inexplicable injustice: since I knew how to read, surely I had a right to stay in school! My sister was in school, and all she could do was read by spelling out the words!

On weekdays, we saw our parents only at luncheon, and in the evenings, when we were put to bed, they would come to tell us good night; at the table, we were not to speak unless spoken to. In the evenings, my mother came in after she had heard our governess' report on our misbehavior that day, and then she would give us a lecture suited to the list of naughty things we had done. I did not mind those times, because I had a distraction that held my attention completely and kept me from hearing what Mama had to say: I would count the minutes on the white clock, painted with nursery scenes, that hung on the wall in front of my bed. Since they put us to bed very early, it seemed to me that the later they turned out the lights, the more grown up they considered us to be; and my mother's lectures were the only possibility of delay. So, I liked the lectures all the better for their length, but I very rarely wasted time on their content. And then, if I had torn my stockings when I fell down, I would also have skinned my knees, and if I had torn my pinafore, I would not have failed to pick up some scratches; so it seemed to me I had already paid for my mistakes with my own skin and that they no longer had much to do with my mother's reprimands. Besides, if they scolded me at the very moment, I understood and repented; but if they waited until bedtime, it was absolute indifference.

On Sundays we had our breakfast with our father. Instead of the usual milk, there was hot chocolate; he made it himself, and, since the governess was not there, we would make our own toast like big girls. Then, we would go with Papa to the hospital or to the clinic, and we would tell him lots of stories; at the hospital, he would take us to visit the sick children or leave us with one of the deaconesses until he had finished his rounds.

In the afternoon he would take us for long walks, or, if the weather was too bad, we would play with my mother and father at those family games that I did not like very much but that my father and my sister seemed to enjoy. As for me, I preferred my dearly loved dolls or reading. Once the little Sunday-girls were put to bed—no lectures on Sundays, usually—we would become once again the little weekday-girls with their life far removed from their parents'.

LES TILLEULS [1]

An old farmhouse converted into a country house in the middle of a large garden: it was paradise for us, and Grandmother gave a charm to it all that I have never found any-

---

[1] The few recollections recounted here are more fully developed in the Appendix entitled "Grandmother's House"—ED.

Adrienne with her mother and sister

Around 1907

With Grandmother

where else. We used to spend whole afternoons with her, and, when evening came, it was a bit hard for us to go home again. It was at Grandmother's house that I learned, while still very young, about silence and recollection. How many times, when I had only just arrived, did I ask her, after giving her a kiss: "May I be quiet, Grandmama?" She always said Yes. When she was alone, I would sit down by a window, and I would do a thousand different things or nothing at all.

Grandmother never intervened by suggesting something else to do: she left me in peace to solve or to try to solve my problems. Sometimes I spent whole hours with my nose to the window, watching the snow fall; I think there was no other place in the whole world where it snowed as much as it did in the garden of Les Tilleuls. The snow fell solemnly, enlarging the silence; it came straight down from heaven, bringing an inexplicable mystery. Now and again a flake or two would alight on the windowpane, and those flakes were like little stars filled with light; other snowflakes would fall on the windowsill, slowly covering the crumbs that had been put out for the birds. I would ask: "Grandmama, would you tell me some things about heaven too?" And Grandmother would say: "Why do you say 'too'?" "Because the snow comes from there, and it seems to be telling me that everything in heaven is white." And Grandmother would tell me stories about heaven, but she would also tell me many childhood memories and stories about old mills and enchanted forests; she knew a lot of stories, both serious and joyous, and she did not have to be begged to tell you about all the pranks played by her cousin John—a true fairy-tale character —and about the old ladies I knew who had been little girls when she was. Sometimes she sat down at the piano and sang old songs, or else she would teach me to knit and to sew, or show me how to make dresses for my dolls, helping me with the difficult parts. There was no question I could ask her that would make her lose patience, but she, too, loved silence.

Sometimes, when other children were there too, we would play games in the hall or play hide-and-seek all over the house, which was full of subtle but incomparable smells. But the best thing about it was still the silence. Often, when I arrived, Grandmother would say, "I've fixed up your little corner for you." She would have put out my favorite books, my handwork and my tea-time snack at the end of the hall by the warm stove, and I could curl up there.

In the summers there was always the garden, but it was not as nice as the house; and in the back of the garden there was a big meadow, called the pasture, where one could take long walks, play games, swing, or read on the grass. Sometimes we would eat outside, under a big fir-tree, and, to call the serving-maid, we would ring a cowbell.

Grandmother did not come to our house very often, but she expected us at hers; and we went there as often as we possibly could. She spent her days at her worktable facing the window, doing sewing for the poor and for her numerous granddaughters' dolls. She did not read much, but she prayed a lot.

My grandfather would come back to the house for meals; we did not know him very well because we never went to Les Tilleuls on Sundays. Besides, I was a little afraid of him: he wanted us to be able to give the names of the plants and animals, and this was precisely what I did not know.

One winter evening, Mama did not come home. The governess told us that she was staying with Grandmother, who was ill. On Christmas morning, 1913, it was snowing. We went up to Les Tilleuls with Papa; Hélène and I stayed in the big kitchen with its gleaming copper pots. As the cook was preparing dinner, I said to her: "Well, if Grandmother is to drink all of that, she's doing much better then", and I saw big tears fall from the cook's eyes right into the coffee. Papa came to get us and took us in to see Grandpapa; he was sitting in the middle of the sofa, and Papa sat us down, one on his left and one on his right, and he told us in a very hoarse voice: "You have lost a very good grandmother."

I do not know exactly what happened right after that, but when Hélène and I went back into the house, we said: "We shall have to ask for Grandmother's Bible so we can read it together from beginning to end." That very evening, I was singing as loudly as I could in the playroom, and Mama asked me, "Why are you singing like that?" "Because it's Christmas and Grandmama's in heaven." Mama said, "You're really unbearable."

A few days later, I had done something or other that was naughty, and that evening, at the time she usually gave us our scolding, Mama said to me: "At last, Grandmama can look down from heaven and see what a bad girl you are; she often told me I scolded you too much; how astonished she must be now to see that it was I who was right!" I did not look at the clock but began to sob inconsolably; but soon sleep came and I grew calm.

A few weeks later my grandfather met his second wife in Paris; she was not interested in seeing us, and Les Tilleuls became paradise lost and was sold a few years later.

Even now, when I go back to La Chaux-de-Fonds, I go to look through the iron fence at Les Tilleuls, and when I have a lot of courage, I open the gate and walk around a little in the garden; on the outside, the house has not changed, and the gravel makes the same little noise underfoot.

WILLY

Willy was born in 1905 and Théodore much later, in 1913, when Hélène and I were already big girls. So Théodore did not share in our children's games, although Willy was rather good at going along with our whims. He was the father of our dolls, but we had to pay dearly for the privilege of having him as a husband. Every day, it would begin all over again; Hélène and I would give him an eraser, a little, well-sharpened pencil, a picture—we outdid each other in finding gifts to make him agree to play the husband. The victor looked down her nose just a little bit at the other one, whose dolls were left fatherless. I do not remember ever really having played dolls with Willy. I remember only the incredible haggling that preceded the games until the day finally came when I no longer consented to "buy" my children a father and preferred playing dolls by myself. I had quite a collection: I loved the old ones tenderly, the ones that were all faded or damaged; I cared for them, I bandaged them, I operated on them. There, I had a problem. To make the operations bearable for them, some anesthetic was necessary. It was impossible to be their surgeon and their anesthesiologist at the same time: I needed an assistant. So I had to ask Willy, who was busy being my sister's husband; he came along without too much begging and turned out to be a very able anesthetist. Sometimes we operated on the bear; his case was not quite so critical, but we could pull out the stuffing from his tummy and put it back over and over again, even hide candy inside him, neatly sew him up, and go into ecstasy at the next operation over all that was found in his enormous entrails.

We each had our own corner in the playroom, where we

each had our own table or desk. I had a kitchen table, painted bright green. On my afternoons off from school, I would remove the drawer, turn the table upside down, and it would become my boat where I would install myself with books and provisions for long hours. The four table legs served as masts with one or two of my dolls' bedsheets attached as sails, and I went off to discover the world. Hélène and Willy had elaborate desks that would not have survived being turned upside down, so sometimes Willy came to join me. He did not have a very imaginative mind; I had to explain to him what countries we were passing or to read him a few pages from *Robinson Crusoe*, adapting it to the circumstances.

One day, when I was all of nine years old, I explained to him: "Now we are getting too old to conquer only countries with our boat. We are going to conquer God." Willy thought I was most presumptuous, and I explained to him at length why it really was necessary, how everything would go from bad to worse until the day the Lord came back to earth again, and that probably he was having to wait until God [the Father] gave him permission to come back. So our primary task must be to reach God; that done, the rest would be quite easy. Willy found all that entirely too complicated. He needed more direct realities. First of all, was I sure the Lord would come back, and how would we know it when he did? I was sure of it; the first point seemed to me to be sufficiently resolved by my conviction alone. As for the second, I thought that we would be so struck, so affected by the coming of the Lord that no doubt would remain. Willy did not seem wholly convinced. The end of the world announced by this appearance would be terrible, worse than death. I tried to reassure him, but when all was said and done, the more I said to him, the more uneasy I saw him. He wanted details; I had hardly any, but I thought the Lord would come at a moment when most people were not expecting him; perhaps we would see a small black speck through the window, far away, dimly visible but always getting bigger; we would think, Look! it's a mouse; no, it's a bird, and then someone; and all of a sudden we would know: it's he! Willy asked immediately: "Do you see anything? Is that something?" He pointed at a defect in the windowpane. I comforted him: "No, that's not anything." Then he asked: "You're very sure it's *not* today?" No, I was not sure; I admitted I knew absolutely nothing about it: all I knew was that some time, maybe only thousands of years from now, he would really be there, surely. And it was being sure that was important, not knowing when.

That evening, after he had been put to bed, Willy began to howl. He was afraid that the Lord was coming. And Mama came to scold me: I had upset the little fellow. All I could say in reply, and I can still feel the distaste that overwhelmed me, was: "I don't like being in a family where you can't even talk about the Lord." And Mama answered: "You can talk about him to your parents." But that was just what I did not feel in the least like doing; I knew that they would not understand the kind of anxiety that tormented me; they would have had to share it in order to understand it.

Willy was very strong-willed, and I admired him for that. We used to call him "Bubi". One day, as we were taking a walk along the rue Léopold-Robert, while we were looking at the window display of a store, he said to me all at once: "From now on I shall not answer when somebody calls me 'Bubi'; I want to be called by my real name." And, despite our unwillingness, we all had to do it, for he stuck to it, and if ever anyone slipped, he would remain absolutely silent and pay no attention to us; I don't believe he betrayed himself even once.

One day, at teatime, on the lawn at my grandparents' house, our governess was serving us some slices of bread and butter that she had brought, with some raspberries that we had picked; I ate raspberries only when I absolutely had to because I could not stand the worms that never failed to hide inside. Willy suddenly said to me: "I can eat the worms even without the raspberries." And he spread a whole collection of worms on his slice of buttered bread and swallowed them without the least grimace; he was very proud of that for a long time and spoke about his exploit to anyone who would listen; I almost found it difficult to maintain my affection for him, and my distaste for raspberries grew still more pronounced.

PRIMARY SCHOOL

School never brought me anything but joy. I do not believe I was ever bored there; I loved the lessons as much as recess; it all enchanted me, I went from discovery to discovery. For the first year, I was in a private school; I do not remember what I might have learned there, because I already knew how to read and write when I started; but I was happy to go there, I liked all my little schoolmates; they were very diverse.

There was one named Maurice, whose fingers and copybooks were always stained with ink: the teacher made him show the class all his stains, and she explained to us what a very bad example he was for us. I admired him for managing to be so dirty and especially for possessing a real penknife with which he peeled his ten-o'clock apple, while we others had to eat ours as they were. With the elastic bands from his stockings and the buttons he tore off his clothes, he made a stunning sort of top; and, to crown it all, he did not come to school on Saturdays, and he was learning Hebrew. His sister Marthe had red hair and a green dress, while all the other girls had brown or blonde hair and big aprons with sleeves, and I think we all envied Marthe for not wearing a smock. As for Willy R., he wore a little starched white collar and parted his hair very straight; he never ran, and his good behavior was exemplary. Mama told us: "Be kind to Willy. His mother is a widow, and she's a dignified woman of much merit." From then on I have never separated the idea of widows from the idea of dignity, and as for Willy, whom I still run into now and then, if he no longer wears his little white collar over his black smock, he still always looks like a very well-behaved little boy. Marthe and Maurice met their deaths in a German concentration camp. Hélène B.'s parents had a dairy, and she used to give out little cheeses to her girl friends; she received twenty centimes every day when the cash-register receipts were counted; that seemed an unbelievable sum to us, for we never had any money. Anything that was different from what we had at home made a big impression on us: up until then, we had had no contact to speak of with other children, so we had thought everyone else's family was just like our own.

I have forgotten both the classes and the playtimes at Mademoiselle Robert's school. I remember only the children I liked so much and to whom I used to bring whatever I was allowed to take from home, and probably more besides. I do not think I joined in their games very much;

I think it was fully enough for me to watch and listen to them. There were sometimes less than favorable remarks on my Saturday report card. "Chatters." And when my father would ask me, before giving his required signature, "Why do you chatter, you are so quiet at home?", I would explain, "I don't talk, but I ask." And my father would continue his inquiry: "Well, what do you ask them, then?" My answer was short: "Everything." Really, I think I was insatiable; I had to know all their likes and dislikes and everything about their brothers and sisters; and when Lilly told me that she was an adopted child, my fondness for her knew no bounds —which did not keep me from asking her sweetly one day, "Would you like some sugar?" and then shoving a spoonful of salt into her mouth.

My sister Hélène and I both entered public school on the same day. We were in the primary school, where the corridors smelled awful. Hélène's teacher was Mademoiselle Vermot, whose brother was a priest. It was impossible to find out what a priest was; the big question was whether their God was the same one as ours, but there was no one to tell me. Hélène claimed she knew, but not for anything in the world would she explain it to me. One day, after I had asked I don't know how many children—my parents were out of the question—I plucked up my courage and sought out Mademoiselle Vermot in her classroom. I remember that, even though I was only eight, I was as tall as she was; and then, instead of coming straight to the point, I first asked her: "Do your students always realize that you are the teacher?", and then very quickly and a little lower: "Is it very difficult to be a teacher when one is the sister of a priest?" I do not remember anything of her answer, but she did not hold my indiscretion against me, because sometimes she allowed me to spend recess with her.

My own teacher was named Mademoiselle Hammel, which amused my father.[1] She taught me to sing a scale by reading the notes. I have never come across a single one of my little schoolmates from the primary school, but I became acquainted with the illness of others, which reinforced my idea of becoming a doctor, and with my own, which always seemed a little improbable to me; it seemed to me a very special courage was needed to admit that one is ill.

Jean had diabetes; he was supposed to refuse all sweets, and that cost him terribly. I was passionately fond of sweets; yet, when I saw him eating something that would make him ill (often after having begged it from the others), it really distressed me; so I proposed to him: "Maybe it would be easier for you not to eat chocolate if you knew that I wouldn't eat it anymore?" He did not understand very well, but he seemed delighted all the same. He asked me, "How long will you go without chocolate?" I said, "For as long as we are together at school." From that day on, he would hide from me when he ate it; I felt a kind of tearing apart when I realized it. After a while he did not come to school anymore, and, the day he was buried, our whole class gathered in front of his house to sing a goodbye-song as they carried his coffin into the hearse. Suddenly I burst into tears. I had eaten chocolate that very morning.

Mademoiselle Hammel suffered from asthma. She was short and stout, really very homely; she had to come to school very early to recover from her shortness of breath before beginning her class; she spoke very softly, for as soon as she raised her voice, she would have an attack. And since we liked her very much, we always kept very quiet so as

---

[1] "*Hammel*" means sheep. According to the faculty roster preserved at the school, her name was E. Hamm—ED.

not to make her wear herself out for nothing. One day I proposed to her, as if it were the simplest thing in the world: "I could give the lessons for you"; at first she was somewhat skeptical, but then she accepted my offer. From then on, I did my best to help her, and I would read aloud, give the dictations, correct the slates; these things suited me perfectly; I was having great fun, and, to show that I was not taking the whole thing very seriously, during recess I would play all the boisterous games that I did not enjoy much, and I would let myself be caught a little too easily.

As much as I exerted myself at school, I was equally quiet at home; as soon as I got there, I would sit down at my table and read, or I would make things for the poor or play dolls, that is, I would rock one of my dolls in my arms while softly telling her a story or, rather, daydreaming.

I had an impossible inclination toward moralism. When I read "Les petites filles modèles" [Model girls] or "En vacances" [On vacation], it seemed to me desirable to become like the heroines in my books, and I worked hard at any kind of good behavior, convinced that being good was an end in itself.

Even the route I took to school was strewn with joys; in the winter when there was deep snow, I had a fine time not walking on the shoveled street but jumping from one pile of snow into another; my father's barber informed on me to my parents and it earned me the punishment of being sent to bed without any supper, but it did not stop me from doing the same thing again soon, maybe even the next day.

MEETING SAINT IGNATIUS[1]

At home, we always celebrated Christmas on the 24th; that
year (it was 1908) Hélène had a party in the small private
school she was then attending, which was run by the Misses
Loze, who seemed to us infinitely old and must have been
between thirty and forty. Aunt Jeanne had come from the
Waldau to spend the day with us; she came very seldom;
apart from Christmas in 1917, this was the only time she
came to La Chaux-de-Fonds in the winter. Aunt Jeanne and
I were to pick up Hélène at her get-together; Mama had
given me strict instructions: on no condition—"and you
know very well what I'm talking about"—was I to accept
anything to eat from the Misses Loze; they were too poor
for it to be permissible to take any of their sweets, but they
were so gracious that they would not fail to offer me some;
it was a matter of being firm and refusing. Fine, at six years
of age I thought nothing of it. It was snowing a little bit,
in languid flakes; they had put a big red woolen cap on my
head that formed a sort of collar on the shoulders and came
to a point on top. So Aunt Jeanne and I went on our way.
When we came to the end of the rue Jaquet-Droz, I suggested to my aunt: "You could go up the usual way by the
rue de l'Arsenal and I'll make a little detour by the steps
at the end." Aunt Jeanne could find no reason to object
to that. As I climbed the steps that went alongside a sort

[1] The episode inserted here is not a part of the autobiographical notes
as originally written. It was written separately, at my request. For fuller
details, see vol. 7 of the *Nachlassbände* and my reference to it in *Erster Blick
auf Adrienne von Speyr*, 17, 77 [English trans.: *First Glance at Adrienne von
Speyr* (San Francisco: Ignatius Press, 1981), 21], where the same episode is
reproduced in part 2, 102f. [English trans.: 116–18]—ED.

of lumberyard, a man was coming down the steps toward me. He was short and rather old, and he had a slight limp. He took my hand, and at first I was really frightened, but I began to look at him. He said, "I thought you would come with me; don't you want to?" I said, with a kind of fear (was it good to say No to a poor person?): "No, Sir, but merry Christmas." He let go of my hand immediately; I thought he looked a little sad. I continued on my way, and throughout the days that followed I said to myself: "Perhaps I should have said Yes, but I really had to say No." When I told Aunt Jeanne what had happened, she was very alarmed and forbade me to leave her side. When we got to the Misses Loze's place, everything went very badly; the students had finished eating, and there were still whole plates of meringues left, and they literally obliged me to take some. I ate one, with the feeling that it really would have been too rude to refuse—besides, when I consulted Aunt Jeanne, she approved. And I know for a fact that I did not disobey Mama out of a desire for sweets but so as not to offend the "old" ladies. When we arrived at our house again, I was roundly scolded by Mama, who asked me right away if I had eaten anything and learned from my aunt the story about the man. In those days, I cried easily, and I had not yet succeeded in drying my tears when Mama rang the bell for the Christmas tree.[2]

---

[2] Adrienne tells that, when the man disappeared, she felt perfectly sure that he was not the same as other men; he was not of this world, yet, at the same time, "he completely belonged to my world." As a young girl, she said to herself: "One does not go with a stranger", but then she asked herself immediately, "Is he a stranger, then?" "An extreme poverty and, at the same time, something very simple, very touching, radiated from him. If I had had to guess what his profession in life had been, I would have said at first: he is a poor man." On returning home, she wrote in a little

THE YEAR 1911

Only with difficulty can I place many of my childhood memories, and I must remember what grade I was in at the time in order to date them. The year 1911, however, began for me in such a memorable way that it is almost wholly etched in my memory.

On New Year's there was always a family dinner at my great-grandmother's. I do not know why, but we called her "Grandmother-on-the-other-side". That year I was wearing for the first time a red coat that I thought wonderful. As I was being helped on with it, I was strongly advised to take good care of it: it was not a question of taking it along on my usual climbing adventures, but of showing that I was a big girl now, worthy to deserve to wear such a fine coat. I do not know why, but my mother sent me on ahead to meet my grandparents and accompany them to my great-grandmother's. Fortified with my mother's advice and very determined to be good and to take care of my coat, I returned a few minutes later spattered from head to foot, unrecognizable for all the dirt and mud. My mother's indignation was justified. I tried to explain: at the corner of the rue Léopold-Robert, a horse pulling a sleigh had knocked me down, horse and sleigh had both run completely over me, leaving me only the quick vision of a noisy catastrophe; when I came to amid the shocked cries of passers-by, I was slightly dazed but unhurt. A large crowd had gathered, and it was only with difficulty that I succeeded in returning home by myself, because everybody was offering

---

notebook, "I said No to the man, but I would have liked to say Yes." Much later, in numerous visions, she saw and recognized Ignatius—ED.

to carry me home, convinced that I had been seriously injured. Finally I managed to escape by running away, fearing more than anything the scandal this strange accompaniment would have produced at home. Mama did not believe a single word of my story and scolded me terribly for lying that way. Confused, ashamed, and wearing my old everyday coat, I went along with my parents to the family dinner. The story went around the table, and my uncles really made fun of me. Why not just admit to everyone what had really happened? I did not dare utter another word or repeat the story of my adventure; it didn't occur to me in the least to defend myself. Then the storm quieted; I recited some poems I had learned for the occasion and played with my sister at some of those strange, quaint games that filled the game cabinet; those games were nothing like the ones we had at home. There were whole boxes of cardboard flowers that you were supposed to arrange in bouquets on a sort of mother-of-pearl table; there were dolls, but their heads were made of wax: they were Japanese, and they wore silk kimonos.

We never had much fun visiting Grandmother-on-the-other-side; my aunt Marie would choose the game to which we had to devote ourselves, and a kind of constraint prevailed, so Hélène and I found a way to amuse ourselves better: we would whisper a story that we had begun years ago and that we continued every night after they had put us to bed, before we went to sleep. This game was called "Heini and Valy", after my father's physician and his wife. Hélène was the teacher, and I rather think I was the gardener and maid-of-all-work; we ran a boarding school, and we were waiting for the arrival of our students and the ardently longed-for visit from Heini and Valy. I do not think we ever played our game out to the point where either of the

awaited persons actually arrived; it was all taken up with the
numerous descriptions of the necessary preparations. But on
this particular New Year's Day, even "Heini and Valy" had
lost its charm; I was still a bit upset from the morning's
adventure, and the game seemed only a sort of respite until
my mother's scoldings were resumed at home. But what a
surprise when we returned! The newspaper reporters had
telephoned to see how I was, one old gentleman had sent
flowers, and my parents spent their evening answering numerous telephone calls and repeating how happy they were
that I had come through that experience safe and sound.
When they put me to bed, they saw that my abdomen was
all black and blue, and, when my father asked me why I had
not told them I had had pain in my stomach, I had to admit
that I had been afraid of being scolded all the more. Then
Papa said to me, in his nice, serious voice with his slight
German-Swiss accent: "You can always tell me everything."
A brief notice appeared in the newspapers the next morning;
they would not let me read it because there was something
in it that was not suitable for me to read. Only years later
did I learn what that something was: the papers referred to
"the charming little von Speyr girl", and my mother was
afraid the term "charming" would have a bad effect on me.

We were, moreover, forbidden to read newspapers: yet,
only a few days later, they began, almost ceremoniously, to
present the daily paper to my sister, pointing out to her the
passage she would be permitted to read. I burned with curiosity to know what it was all about. But Hélène knew
how to keep secrets in an almost absolute way. All kinds of
stratagems had to be used to induce her to talk. The whole
town was astir over a tragedy that involved my sister's gymnastics teacher, and, doubtless because her whole class was
talking about it, my parents allowed her to read the news-

paper accounts of it. A woman had determined to poison her husband with arsenic so that she would be free to marry the gymnastics teacher. To let him know each day the amount used and the results obtained, she would hang socks on her terrace; the number and color represented prearranged signs. On the death of the husband, the whole story was exposed. When Hélène finally told me about it, I had the bad luck to say, as my sole commentary on it: "Instead of first knitting the socks, I would have used the skeins of yarn." Little did I suspect that this business of the skeins of yarn was in a way, and for a long time, to make me a kind of slave to my sister. Indignant at my cynicism, she explained to me how guilty I was for having ideas which could be used in carrying out a murder and threatened to tell everything to my parents. From then on, whenever I was doing something that did not absolutely suit her, Hélène had only to say the magic word "skein", and I would obey very quickly and without hesitation, convinced that I had committed a crime, at least unintentionally, and imagining some sort of atrocious punishment my parents would inflict on me when they found out. At first all this was not such a great tragedy, for I knew I had committed a fault whose importance I did not exaggerate too much. With the years, however, it grew in importance until one day, when I couldn't stand it any longer, I confessed the "skeins" to my father, who had no idea what I was talking about and asked, "And then what?" I was dazed at being released at this point by my confession, but I no longer remember which made me happier: the end of my inner distress or quite simply the complete cessation of my sister's tyranny. Now that she was deprived of her treats, she had no more power over me.

That last Christmas, I had received a doll that at first had struck me with horror; I had never seen anything like it:

it looked amazingly like a monkey, so much so that I initially thought it was some kind of joke and that it would be
changed very quickly and replaced with a regular doll. Nothing of the sort; it was a new model, which they called a "nature baby", which was gradually going to capture the hearts
of little girls. I really felt sorry for my doll because she was so
homely and became extremely attached to her. She became
my constant companion. I christened her Blondinette, after
a little girl in a story that I had very much enjoyed reading,
and I went to work to sew her a very complete layette. On
February 1, returning from school, I felt quite miserable,
and, without asking permission, I went to bed, putting my
doll to bed beside me. My grandmother happened to drop
in (she rarely came to visit us), and she asked me what I was
doing in bed; since I felt less ill in bed than standing up, I
explained enthusiastically to her that I had just given birth
to Blondinette and therefore I had to stay in bed. Whereupon there was a consultation with my mother, who was
somewhat put out with my independence; I had to get up,
and my mother called me into her boudoir to have a word
with me. She told me that it was now time for her to speak
to me about certain things, that I was old enough to know
how babies come into the world, but that first she needed
to find out how much I already knew. On that point I told
her proudly: "I know everything." My mother went on,
"And where did that come from?" I responded in a very
self-assured tone that brooked no contradiction: "I know
that in the Bible it says, 'and Mary conceived a son'; and I
think that is quite enough." And with that, I fled the room,
refusing to continue the conversation. Needless to say, I
knew absolutely nothing and went to find my doll again
with an unwavering confidence in my maternal knowledge.

The next day, returning from school, I felt quite miserable again. On the way I met a girl whom I did not know, who was eating a huge slice of bread spread with plum jam. With each mouthful, the jam dripped down her chin, and I thought: "Oh, how much better I would feel if only I could have a bite of that slice of bread." But since I was unacquainted with the girl, I could not ask her to share it with me. On returning home from school, I turned down the slice of bread that was already prepared for me and asked for some plum jam on it. My father said to me, "You are ill." And I said, "Yes, I should not have had to get up so soon after Blondinette's birth." They put me to bed. I had scarlet fever. The next six weeks were utterly delightful, like a beautiful dream. My brother was in Basel and stayed there for several months; my sister had been spending the day with Grandmother, and she stayed there. The playroom was made into a disinfection room, where my parents disinfected their hands and slipped on white smocks, without which they never appeared in my room. No more governess, no more maid—just my parents; I had never seen so much of them. In the mornings, my father would bring me my breakfast that he put together in a rather strange way: cocoa, bread, and cheese. It was as good as it was unexpected. And he would always tell me a story about when he was a boy, and I would tell him a story about when I was grown up and a doctor like him. It was Mother who made my bed and did my room; she too would tell me stories. At noon, my father reappeared with my dinner, and it was also he who brought me supper. In the afternoon, on my father's orders, Mother would go out for a walk and each day bring back a surprise for me, usually pictures to color, often sparkling white pages that became richly colored pictures when you passed a moistened paintbrush over them. At other times she brought me books. Hélène wrote me letters and made puzzles for me; she never mentioned skeins; the only time I was worried was when I was opening a letter from Hélène. I had to make sure right away that the fatal word was not in it so I could read it to Mother without fear. Except for that I was perfectly happy, surrounded by flowers and treats, with a very well-behaved Blondinette and parents who had become really visible.

I made my first outing with my father to go and see a hotel that had burned down a few days before; Hélène used to cry when there was a fire; she was terribly frightened of fire. The hotel, black and completely ruined, stark against the spring morning, made a rather strong impression on me, for I found it both beautiful and frightening at once. Besides, I considered myself a big girl now; my independence no longer blossomed only when I was out of the house; I was beginning a real life. I said as much to my father, in words that were perhaps slightly confused, but he seemed to understand, for he approved, took me to a bookstore, and let me choose two books. I asked him to help me pick them out, but he answered: "No, I am here simply as a purse." I did not immediately grasp this, but he took the trouble to explain to me his function, thus stripped of all those he filled in my eyes, and told me that, precisely to help me in my wish to become independent, he would have to begin by not helping in my choice. Even though I did not yet fully comprehend these words, they made me positively feel that I was visibly growing up. I took the books, whose titles I do not remember, out of the shop as if they were a real treasure, tokens of my independence.

I had a bit of trouble on our way home; I had a very bad backache. During the next few days, I really had trouble dragging myself around. The disorder was pronounced to be the aftereffects of the scarlet fever, and so I was going to stay at the Waldau, at my uncle and aunt's, where we were dispatched for all our vacations and after all illnesses. I spent long hours on a chaise longue. Every day, several doctors examined my back; as long as I was lying down I felt fine, but I did not do well when I stood on my legs. I did not much like talking about it.

After a few weeks I returned home and went back to school. It was a new school, and it did not really smell bad like the old one. The teacher's name was Mademoiselle Schmutziger. At the ten o'clock recess, she used to send a student out to buy her a penny roll. One day, I asked her if she knew she was spending more than eighteen francs a year that way. "Yes, it is expensive", she admitted, and I thought she meant that the rolls were really beyond her means. She gave private lessons, and I asked at home if I might take some. My parents were surprised: "What sort of lessons do you need, then?" I did not really know; I suggested drawing lessons; they cost one franc an hour. I began indefinitely to draw cuckoo-clocks and paint red tulips, and at the end of every lesson I was happy; I was thinking: that makes twenty rolls for the teacher.

At the time, schools still gave prizes. One day, the teacher presented me with an illustrated edition of *Robinson Crusoe*, which was my prize for the last class; Mademoiselle Hammel had not had a chance to give it to me herself since I had never returned to her class. The new book was so different from my old *Robinson* that I just couldn't like it; it remained foreign to me.

It must have been about this time that I gave a talk about mental reservations and the value of truth, basing what I had to say on the teachings of Saint Ignatius. I had gathered some older schoolmates around the teacher's desk, reserving her chair for myself, and from that position I explained, with fervor apparently, what I considered important. I no longer remember it; one of my schoolmates, who was several years older than I and who subsequently became a Catholic, told me this story recently, saying that this was the first she had heard about Saint Ignatius and wanting to know where I had learned what I was then recounting. I do not know myself, for I do not believe that I possessed even the least little theology book or the shortest life of a saint.[1]

One June day, when I was wearing a white dress with blue polka dots and a red sash, I got caught in a thunderstorm right after school let out. Nadine, who lived quite near the school, invited me to her house. There, I went from surprise to surprise: at Nadine's, life was spent in the kitchen; it was there that her mother welcomed us; she buttered the bread right on the loaf, spread the jam on it, and only then did she cut the slice. And they bit into the slices of bread without either plates or knives. It was great. Suddenly Nadine's father appeared, ate his toast the same way, and we all drank our tea out of cups with no handles; the tea was sweetened with crushed sugar. The most astonishing thing was that Nadine's father was a real postman just like the one who brought us letters and packages, and he had children, a family; as he came in, he had deposited his dripping-wet cap right in the middle of the table, turned his jacket inside out over the back of a chair, and now he looked just like anybody else. I couldn't get over my surprise. Suddenly he

[1] When Adrienne wrote this autobiography, she no longer had a vivid recollection of her meeting with Saint Ignatius at Christmas in 1908 (an account of which has been inserted above). It was only at the time she wrote her second autobiography—since she was transported, by virtue of obedience, to the days of her youth—that she recalled this meeting and put it in writing, as reproduced here. For the same reason, the present autobiography contains no mention of the little girl's encounters with the angel —ED.

said to me: "I'm going to fix you a slice of bread the way Nadine likes it", and instead of jam, he put sugar on top of the butter. It was so good and I was so awed by everything I saw that I could hardly manage to swallow. They told stories and talked like old friends. All of a sudden somebody said, "That is as wrong as the Mass [*la Messe*]", and Nadine's father explained, "No, you must say, 'as wrong as the plague [*la peste*]' ". I asked, "What is Mass?" He answered, "It's the Catholics' worship service." At that moment, I forgot everything: the cap on the table, the sugar on the bread, and the slightly unreal and very awesome presence of a real postman in his kitchen. I began almost to shout with joy, "You are Catholics!" "No," he said, "thank God, no, but it is necessary to understand them, and it's not right to mock their Mass." I asked him question after question: he answered them with the authority of a real postman. I asked him what a priest was, and he said to me: "They don't have wives, but that's their business." "Why don't Protestants have a Mass?" "Because they no longer know how to sing, they have become stern." "If I sing a hymn, that isn't a Mass, is it?" "No, because you aren't a priest." It was as clear as spring water, and Mademoiselle Vermot was not so bad off, being the sister of a priest. Just to make sure this was really so, I asked Nadine's father again; he told me that, on the contrary, among the Catholics, everything was for the priests and so, too, for their relatives. I was delighted. Finally, I also asked him why he had said "Thank God, no", since from what he had been telling me, being a Catholic did not seem so bad. Then he said: "I said 'thank God' without thinking." Then, he drank a glass of white wine, put his jacket back on, gave his cap a final shake, and left. Through the window, I saw him starting off again, with big postman-steps, through the rain, which no longer had anything of a thunderstorm about it. Then I went home. Disdaining the marked paths, I walked through the fields of wet daisies and arrived home drenched. A severe scolding awaited me, but I was too happy to mind and kept everything to myself, not even speaking to Hélène about it.

I believe it was after my visit to Nadine's house that I acquired a great fondness for thunderstorms; they seemed to me just made for opening new perspectives, for giving life a more forceful charm. I often scanned the sky to see if some big black cloud might not offer itself, like a promise. Yet, I never went back to Nadine's house, and I never saw the postman again. I do not even think I had any particular desire to see him; I felt that he had probably told me everything he could, and I had plenty to think about for a very long time. What had also particularly struck me was that one could enter right into such a discussion, and as a family. At our house, while I was ill with scarlet fever, I had thought that might become possible; I had had high hopes, but they were not realized. Life went back to its usual course, and with it came that kind of constraint that we could feel almost everywhere in our apartment except the playroom. When we were in the parlors, my mother was a little uneasy about our presence and the improvisations of our flights of fancy; in the hallways, we were supposed to be very quiet so that we would not disturb my father's consultations; at the table, we were not to speak unless spoken to. There was never any general conversation, and it never would have occurred to us to speak about anything that was really close to our hearts or that really interested us.

At school, I would have dearly loved to know who was a Catholic and who wasn't, but since we had no religion classes there was no visible division. One day, I found out that Anita and Carlo were Catholics; now Anita was dirty, although elegant, and probably the worst student; I wasn't anxious to get closer to her. As for Carlo, I liked him very much, but the first time I asked him a question, he said: "Mama has forbidden me to talk about things like that because we're living in a lost country now, but when we are home in Italy, I will tell you everything; you shall come with me." So, there was no way to insist.

BELLEVUE

When summer vacation arrived, I was first invited to spend a few days at Bellevue, on a family estate located a short distance outside the town. A great-uncle who was a surgeon in Lausanne always spent the summers there with his family. He had five children and a lovely wife who was lively and full of the unexpected: she was my grandfather's sister. Together, they made an unusual family, not at all like ours; they all smoked, even my aunt, and they were croquet fanatics. We regarded Bellevue with a mixture of wonder and dread. We generally spent one or two Sunday afternoons there every summer. After we had exchanged the customary greetings on arriving, my cousin Maurice would round up Hélène and me, along with his sister Friquette, and take us to the tool shed. Then he would lock us into the shed, with a key. He would come and get us at tea-time, only to lock us in again until it was time to go home. He used to threaten us with unimaginably frightful torture, with a slow, shameful death, if we told on him. Friquette would assure us that Maurice was not cruel at all, and I really wanted to believe her, but still. . . . When we reappeared, my aunt would say: "These little ones are truly good, you don't hear a sound out of them." If we had screamed in that shed, nobody would have heard us. When, that summer, my aunt invited me to spend a few days with her, I was not too keen to accept her invitation. But Maurice said to me: "Say Yes, and I give you my word of honor, I won't lock you up." It was my parents, however, who accepted for me.

That vacation bore no resemblance whatsoever to any of my previous vacations. All of us were allowed great freedom; my uncle and aunt never interfered. We were expected to be on time for the two main meals of the day, but we disposed of the rest of the day and indeed even the night as we pleased. It was an exceptionally hot, very dry summer that year. Friquette said to me: "We'll make night out of the day." I was a bit disconcerted but full of good will. About two or three in the morning, Friquette woke me up, we got dressed without making any noise and tiptoed down to the pantry to see what we could find; we were allowed to help ourselves. We took some cold roast—the roasts at Bellevue were of astonishing dimensions because the household was always elastic, and they had to provide for the unexpected—some cheese, some bread, and some fruit, and then we left, wandering off through the woods. It was still pitch dark, but Friquette knew all the paths; she was perhaps about eleven, while I was not yet nine. I shivered with cold until the sun came up, even though we were walking, but I was very careful not to complain. We had a splendid walk, we saw the sunrise by watching the sky between the branches of the pine trees or watched it appear from behind the hills; and we saw the colors that emerged from the morning greyness. It grew warmer as it got lighter, and it always seemed that it was first the sky that became brighter and that the earth came alive afterward, awakening smells. Friquette spoke little; from time to time, she would explain, "This is Ramuz' farm", or "The Pelletiers have four cows and three children", or else she would call my attention to the grass in a meadow or the bark on a beech tree. About six or seven o'clock, when the day had definitely settled in, we breakfasted on the provisions we had brought with us. Then she read aloud, with the greatest seriousness, as if the text demanded it, some chapter of the *Imitation* [*of Christ*], a book she always had with her. Then we had serious discussions. One day I got up the nerve to ask, "Friquette, do you know any Catholics?" She replied, "Don't mention those people, they're awful." Her tone precluded any reply; I looked up to her too much ever to have had the courage to broach such a thorny subject again. But she had planted a kind of doubt and hesitation in my soul. Did I have to believe what Friquette said? Maybe so. Then again, maybe not. But still?

This doubt that crossed my mind at times may have lowered Friquette a bit in my estimation, but it did not keep me from enjoying my vacation and its strangeness. We got back to Bellevue toward the end of the morning. We were tired; it was very hot, and we lay down in the big hammocks suspended between the ancient trees in the garden, and we slept until we heard the dinner bell. It was a cowbell, which my aunt rang herself at the same time as she called everyone. This double summons was just one more oddity. At the table also was my great-grandmother, with Aunt Marie beside her. Aunt Marie had a fixation that got worse as she grew older: she had to win whenever she played. I do not know if I would ever have noticed it all on my own. This mania about winning was irritating for those who observed it, and once Friquette had warned me about it, I had to overcome a genuine loathing for playing with her. Besides, the only game they played was croquet, and the grownups admitted the presence of children only when it was obviously neces- sary, such as when there were too few partners, or when my uncle, shocked by his sister-in-law's little cheating, dropped his mallet and called one of us to take his place in the match already in progress.

We spent part of the afternoon asleep in our hammocks; it was hot, our half a night's sleep demanded completion, and we were thirsty. Now the drought was so great that the well had run dry. The farmer and Maurice went to the town fountain every morning to get water in a cart laden with every vessel capable of containing liquid. When they came back, Aunt Marie, who was in charge of the household dur- ing vacations, made lemonade with lemons and limes, and everyone received his share, which was a whole bottle each. At first Maurice contented himself with swiping one bottle out of the two that Friquette and I were given. One day, he explained to us that if we had water, it was thanks to him because he was the one who went to get it; if we refused to give him both our bottles, he would no longer go to get it, and all the rest of the family would have to go without too; for us, it would amount to the same thing: in either case, no more water; but to deprive the rest of the family of water, out of mere stupidity, no, he did not expect that of us. Although his argument was groundless—it was the farmer who went to get the water and was merely being kind to take Maurice along—he succeeded in convincing us, and it was then, I think, that I learned what it really means to be thirsty.

Friquette and I had children's nightgowns with long sleeves. One night, Friquette told me she wanted to sleep in the shirt she wore in the daytime because it was definitely too hot; I did not want to be outdone, so I did the same.

When her mother came to tell us good night, she asked me if I was in the habit of sleeping like that, and if my mother had already given me permission. I told her "Yes", in a firm voice, and I felt my face turning red; I had lied shamelessly. I would have admitted my lie right away, but I could not bear the thought of losing face twice over in front of Friquette, by being a liar, and, in addition, by being obliged by her parents to sleep in a nightgown no matter how hot it was.

The walk at dawn was not much fun; I had not slept well; after we had gone a few steps, I sat down in the darkness and admitted to Friquette that I was too tired to go very far and, moreover, that I had lied. Friquette told me in confidence: "I lie whenever it is necessary, but only then." I asked her, "Then why did you tell me that Catholics are terrible people? Was that necessary?" Friquette explained, "It's the truth. Do you want me to swear to it?" No, I did not want her to swear. Since I either could not or would not walk any farther, we stayed, shivering with cold in the darkness, on the trunk of a fir tree. I did not understand why it felt so very cold, for in a few hours the heat would again be overwhelming. Finally I suggested that we go home and go back to bed. Friquette agreed. That day my parents came to see me and found me sick. They immediately began to wonder what foolish thing I might have done. In front of the entire family, the story of the nightgown was talked about and, along with it, the lie I had told. My father decided to take me back home. In the train, my teeth chattering, I asked my father if what I now had was the illness of the lie. He thought, rather, that I had German measles; we would know for sure in the morning. That was what it was. It was rather serious for nearly a week. The only clear memory I have of that time, except for my obsessive fear of the lie, which filled my fever with painful dreams, is that I was not eating anything, and my father asked me if I would like some ice cream. Ice cream was my favorite treat. When it was brought to me, I found it unbearably awful, and I was truly relieved as I watched it disappear into the mouth of the maid, who strongly recommended that I ask for it every day without admitting it was she who was eating it. But I had had enough of lying and secretiveness.

I went to join my brother and sister at the Waldau; every year on August 1 they had a celebration there, with Japanese lanterns and fireworks. That afternoon, my aunt was afraid that a shower might keep them from having the celebration in the garden. I stationed myself on the swing, and, as I swung back and forth, I studied the sky. On one side, it was almost blue, and, on the other, there were big, black clouds. While swinging very hard and very high, I felt as if I were being thrown from good weather into bad. This was the first time I noticed how clouds travel and change shape; it was a real discovery. I ran to tell my family about it, but they were not the least bit interested; I felt a certain disappointment, but I waited for a more propitious moment to talk to them, thinking that they had not understood very well. I resumed my post on the swing. I did not know what I would prefer: the storm that might bring surprises or the good weather that would permit the fireworks. Toward evening the storm broke, bringing with it a gale-force wind that made the greengage plums fall like veritable rain.

I was still often having severe back pain, so they sent me to a specialist in Bern. He was not able to come to much of a decision. When I returned to La Chaux-de-Fonds, a chaise longue was permanently installed in the playroom, and I spent several hours every day reclining on it. I spent almost all my free time there. It was only several years later that an X ray revealed that three vertebrae had been affected by a slow spondylitis. Since I could no longer play in my boat, the table reassumed forever the role that nature had granted it, at least until the day when it became the operating table. We had some young cousins who came to play with us sometimes in the afternoons; since these little girls were somewhat younger than we were, it was not easy to find games suitable for them that would not be too boring for us. The idea occurred to me one time that it would be much more fun to operate on our cousins than on our dolls. So when they came, Hélène and I, with a power of persuasion we had perhaps borrowed from Maurice, would explain to them all the benefits they would derive from an operation performed on them by us. We carried them to the operating table, not without giving them some little present to make them more docile, and we rigged them up with dolls' bedsheets, babies' blankets and whatever else that looked as if it might play a useful role. Then we would decide on which limb to repair or to amputate, and we applied endless dressings. We found all this very amusing, my cousins perhaps somewhat less so, except for one of them who took such delight in the little presents that she would gladly have endured more than an hour or two of forced immobility just to grow rich with candy, chocolates, or colored pencils. Besides, I frankly think that at the time we were so caught up in our game that we assumed our patients were enjoying it every bit as much as we were.

I do not really know what I learned in school. I liked going there, I admired Mademoiselle Schmutziger very much, but my admiration ceased very suddenly the day I saw her thrash two boys in my class for not knowing their homework; I was convinced that they would surely have much preferred to have learned it but that it was really too difficult for them.

Henri and Carlo had asked for and received girls' toys for Christmas: Henri a little cook-stove and Carlo, if I remember correctly, a little iron and laundry utensils. Their mothers, to whom the boys had confided in expressing their wishes, telephoned my mother to tell her that their sons had asked for gifts that would permit them to invite me to come to play with them. My mother was indignant and flatly refused to let me go, even though she must have known she was depriving my two little playmates of a pleasure that, it seems to me, had cost them quite a lot, for they had received nothing else. It was only after we went back to school that I learned about this, for my mother had taken good care not to mention it to me; I did not want to believe it, and I went home to ask about it. My mother explained that I was really too big to play with boys and that some day, when I had daughters of my own, I would be grateful to her for having been firm. I had no idea what she was talking about, and I did not know what to make up to get Henri and Carlo to forgive me; but Henri very promptly consoled himself by inviting another girl.

SUNDAY SCHOOL

On Sunday mornings at eleven, the "independents" had Sunday school in the oratory. Protestants in Neuchâtel were divided into two camps; the National Church was attached to the State, while the "independents" were not. That was the whole difference. The oratory was a small, dark chapel, lost on a dead-end street. Basically, it was a meeting room, large enough to hold about one hundred fifty persons. Before leaving, Hélène and I had to recite our verses to Mama, and we would each receive from her ten or twenty centimes for the Pagan Baby. The Pagan Baby was placed at the front of the room on a table and would nod its head as a sign of thanks for each offering. Some young girls, monitors, would gather about ten small children around them and have them recite their verses, explain to them the verses to be memorized for the next time, and distribute the Sunday-school leaflets to them, little folders containing a Bible story followed by several verses. Then the pastor would drop in and give a sermon that was easy to understand, and we would sing hymns. I was passionately fond of Sunday school. It seemed even finer than weekday school to me. I had all sorts of adventures there. One day I took my little cousin Madeleine along with me—she was about two years old, exactly six years younger than I—and I begged the pastor if he would please baptize her secretly, since her parents had refused to have her baptized. I could not comprehend why he refused, and it was with sobs that I insisted. With a heavy heart, I took Madeleine back home again, and I thought it unworthy of the pastor to be an accomplice of the wishes of parents who had strayed. This was the very same pastor who had explained to us how necessary it was to baptize the Pagan Babies, and now he claimed to know some other weight and measure. I did not grasp the consequences baptism implied, and so this problem tormented me for a long while. But again, as I always did when something was troubling me, I was careful not to ask the grownups about it. It always seemed to me that whenever it came to something really deep, they saw things from another angle; they did not seem to take seriously what might be hidden within a child's question.

Sometimes we could tell the pastor or the monitor which hymn we wanted to sing. I always said the same one and cried out as loudly as I could: Number 285!

Entends-tu l'appel du maître? Il te veut pour moissonneur.
Réponds-lui: oui, je veux être, ô Jésus, ton serviteur.[1]

And every time it seemed to me that I was committing myself anew to something that expanded me completely, almost took my breath away, and made me happy. And yet, I was not too sure exactly what I was committing myself to. To some service, surely, but what? For a long time I thought it would have to do with being a missionary; but I never gave up the idea of being a doctor. Willy, when I confided in him, had a good laugh. "A missionary!" No, he did not believe it, and we made a bet. If I became a missionary, he would buy me a Prague ham, but if I didn't, it was he who would have a good meal. He got the idea of the Prague ham —I have never known exactly what that refers to—from a book in which this specialty was described as being the finest thing in all the world. Perhaps Willy even today bears me the tiniest grudge for not having offered it to him, for every once in a while he reminds me: "Don't forget, you owe me a Prague ham."

For my tenth birthday, I received a five-franc piece from my godfather. I think that until that day I had never possessed more than twenty centimes at one time. I debated for a long time whether to buy a book or a paintbox; but that very evening the brilliant idea came to me: the hundred sous would be for the Pagan Baby. So, that Sunday, I tried to drop the coin into the slot, which turned out to be too short; it would not go down. Whereupon I quickly picked

---

[1] "Do you hear the Master's call? He wants you for a reaper. Answer Him: 'Yes, O Jesus, I want to be Your servant.' "

up the Pagan Baby—very embarrassed to be taking so long
—and I slipped the coin under the Pagan Baby itself. Would
they really have found it there? I do not think the idea that
I was making some kind of renunciation ever entered my
head for a moment.

One Sunday, the monitor was absent, and they asked me
to take her place. I did so with true joy. Then it became a
custom; I always substituted for one of those who were not
there, and then I had my own little group. Later, I realized
quite clearly that something was not in order; I lost my joy.
I liked the children very much, but it became painful for
me to tell them the stories from the New Testament. And
one evening, I understood why: all these stories lacked a
mother; they were like orphans, and, from the next Sunday
on, I said I did not want to tell stories anymore. Of course,
I kept on going to Sunday school regularly. I do not think
I minded listening to the stories, but I did not want to tell
them myself anymore. The idea of a real conflict that had
pierced me through so painfully went away rather quickly.
Now it is difficult for me to understand why it was only
speaking that was difficult for me; even with the perspective
that time affords, I do not understand how such a distinction
had imposed itself and why I was abruptly stopped short on
a path that appears to me to have been already rather clearly
established at that time. I would have to walk thousands of
steps before the path would appear clearly indicated to me.
There were whole years during which it seemed really lost
forever.

Once each year, a missionary returning from the field
came to speak to us; sometimes we were allowed to ask
questions. So, one day, I dared: "Don't the Pagan Babies
need a mother, too, beside the Savior?" The missionary
tried to reassure me: "Why, yes, there are the missionaries'

wives and the teachers as well." Obviously, he had not understood anything at all. A doubt came to me: maybe this need for a mother didn't in truth exist for other people. It was impossible to find an answer; I gave up and kept completely silent in Sunday school.

MY FATHER

My father was a serious man. He spoke little and almost seemed to weigh his words. Obviously he enjoyed an indisputable authority at home; perhaps that was itself reinforced a little by the fact that he was a doctor and therefore used to wielding a certain, very necessary authority in his profession. When he made a decision about something, probably all anyone could do was to comply. Once, I no longer remember exactly why, I tried to reverse a well-established order. I was perhaps four, maybe even five years old. It was always my father who ran the baths, because the gas apparatus that heated the water was thought to be dangerous; we were bathed in the evening on certain fixed days. Early one afternoon, I went to find my father in his room to explain to him that I wanted a bath. A first vague refusal on his part. Repeated if not very convincing explanations on mine: I was a bit dirty, I liked to play with the little boats in the water, I was quite capable of washing myself all by myself. My father no longer refused, but he looked surprised. I insisted again, perhaps even with some new arguments. Finally my father gave in and went to draw the bath. After a minute, he came back and announced to me with a big smile that everything was all ready. And then I said to him, very sweetly, very nicely, but with the strength of an irrevocable decision: "No, thank you, I have changed my mind; I won't take a bath after all." As to what happened after that, my memory fails me completely; but I think that was perhaps the day I found it somewhat painful to sit down in the hours that followed. Above all, what I don't know is what it was that gave me the nerve to be so obstinate in my untimely request and in my unthinkable refusal that so ill repaid my father's kindness. That was, I think, the only time our wills clashed and probably the only disagreement we ever had, and certainly through my fault.

We always felt a very great tenderness in my father, but it was not expressed easily; it was apparent, for example, in the tone he used when he introduced us to his acquaintances. He would say: my little girls, although we were already taller than he was, and he was not short.

There were several times when he thought he was going to lose me, and sometimes he spoke of the difficult hours he had spent then. At the time of my birth, it seemed that I was absolutely refusing to appear. They had to anesthetize my poor mother three times and try to force me to come in the end; my mother's life did not seem to be in any danger, but mine certainly was. After my birth, I was pale and blue for several hours, and they had to keep bringing me back to life.

Then, several weeks later, I had a serious digestive problem, and my father concocted some sort of food that he himself gave me in a bottle. He would get up several times a night, with the devotion of a wet-nurse, to see whether his younger daughter needed anything.

As for his care at night, I particularly remember the time we had whooping-cough. At every fit of coughing he would be there, redoing our bed, giving us something to drink, and he would stay with us until we went back to sleep. My mother was away, taking care of my brother, who was ill too, and my aunt Jeanne came to look after us. One day, as he was leaving for the hospital, my father told her that the druggist was going to deliver a new prescription and that she was to give each of us a soupspoonful of it right away. My aunt filled a spoon, but when she was just about to give it to me, she became anxious about the strange color and strong odor, and then she really took fright and waited until my father got home. It was potassium cyanide, sent by a different druggist for disinfecting my father's instruments. One spoonful of that liquid would have meant an instantaneous, horrible death. My father never quite got over the distress he felt when he realized what might have happened. I think his solicitude became even more emphatic; he who did not take very good care of himself, and was even hard on himself, probably exaggerated our bumps and bruises a bit, to such a degree that we were made to show him every scratch, even the slightest. He never let go of a certain anxiety. He would just happen to telephone from the hospital to see if the "little ones" were all right. In the winters, when there was a lot of snow on the roofs, he sometimes would not even let us go to school, for fear of avalanches.

Sometimes we took walks with him; I enjoyed them only later, when real conversations became possible. While we walked across the meadows, he would make us jump over the low boundary walls. I was a coward and afraid to jump; that annoyed him somewhat. Once I stubbornly refused to jump, and my father immediately took the way back. He thought that would punish me, but, in my heart of hearts, I was very pleased, because I knew that walk, and it had quite a few walls to jump; I was delighted to have avoided them.

There were other things, too, that my father made me do. I could not get over my dislike of the film on milk; I was forbidden to skim it off, so I would drink my milk by turning my cup very slowly around between my hands, in an effort to make the film stick to the cup; that succeeded rather satisfactorily. One morning, there was so much film on the breakfast milk of all sizes and kinds, from the thinnest to the most abominably thick, that there was nothing to be done; it was impossible to let the milk seep through my clenched teeth; it was even impossible to make the film stick to the cup. My father saw what was going on; I was not managing to drink my milk. Finally it was time to go to school. When I came home at noon, the same cup of milk, still almost full, was waiting for me; it stayed in my hands without getting much emptier until time for class. For tea and for supper, there was nothing else. I was so unhappy I did not even feel hungry; finally, before she put me to bed, the maid finished the whole cup, or what was left of it—and there was scarcely less than a cup—in one gulp. Unfortunately, I don't think all that served any great purpose; I have never learned to jump over a wall, and even now I have to make a real effort to drink any milk at all, because I am still always afraid of the film. Nevertheless, I know my father was right.

Sometimes my father would sit us down on either side of him on the sofa in his consulting room and show us pictures in a big illustrated dictionary. He explained many things to us; Hélène was very fond of geography, as my father was also, so he often used to explain the atlas maps to us or show us series of pictures of mountains or towns. Geography was and is my weak suit; I have no sense of direction; that irked my father a little but greatly amused my sister. When we took our walks, I never knew how to locate places or how to point out what road to take, even if we had already been over that road before; perhaps I was too inattentive and too riveted to immediate details. I would pick flowers or watch the ants, and I never ceased to enjoy watching the reflections of the sun in the puddles.

It was only later that my father truly became my friend; then, I felt he was very close when things were not going well, when difficulties piled up, but, except for those moments, I think he was somewhat unknown to me and that he really intimidated me.

THE WALDAU

The Waldau was a very large mental hospital, of which my uncle was the director. His living quarters were in the main building, which included immense wings reserved for the patients. The Waldau was a place that was both splendid and abominable. It became a true, very beloved home for me when I had lost my own; but in my childhood, its existence held something of a nightmare. My uncle Willy, my father's brother, lived there with his sister, my aunt Jeanne. My aunt Jeanne loved my sister Hélène above everything; she was her treasure, and, to be honest, Hélène took advantage of the situation a bit. She chose the games and made me play them, at least the indoor games; outside, a paradise opened before us and, with it, a series of delights.

The dining room had three doors, each of which was double, that is, enclosed a dark space of about a half-meter in depth. Hélène, and we with her, called them "darkrooms". She organized a game of "school", where she was the teacher, and I was, according to her, a dull-witted pupil who therefore deserved to be punished. So, she would shut me in between those doors, in the darkroom of her choice, and I would have to stay there quietly until she came to let me out. In the years when the terror of the "skeins" was at its height, my sojourns in darkness were really too frequent. Sometimes Aunt Jeanne would be rather surprised, but Hélène would explain to her how difficult I was to teach and that by being severe with me she was actually helping my mother. I think that with an ounce of energy I could have talked my way out of it and changed the situation; but I hated making excuses for myself, and, in the depths of my heart, I honestly did not mind the darkness. It was even perhaps more attractive than the prospect of doing idiotic sums or rereading some story or other for the hundredth time. In summer, we had to pick an infinite number of red currants off their stalks for desserts or jam. I did not like doing that, not so much because of the monotony of the work as because of the sticky hands, of which I had a horror. I thought I'd never seen baskets so enormous as the ones they brought in full of red currants; Hélène had very good excuses to get herself out of the chore. No, it was no fun indoors at the Waldau; but how delightful it was outdoors!

My uncle's garden was a few steps away from the house. There was a little cottage where we installed our entire household of dolls at the beginning of vacation. And best of all, under the hazel trees, there was a shady spot where we began to dig a hole, a really gigantic hole that was to take us down into the fiery regions in the center of the earth and out the other side, the side where people walk upside down. How much ground we dug up, and how many disappointments, how many times renewed, when the gardener, despite our entreaties, filled up the hole between vacations!

We had to start all over again, and work faster this time than before, in order finally to accomplish this very worthwhile undertaking. Sometimes we would stop digging to climb the hazel trees. It was hard to sit down in them, but sometimes we succeeded, and what a triumph it was then to manage to read a few minutes at such a height. Aunt Jeanne did not appreciate the hazel trees as much as we, for our skirts and underclothes suffered numerous tears.

There was a very profound harmony between my uncle and me; it was a kind of tacit understanding; we were in some way accomplices. In the mornings he would have breakfast by himself in his office, at exactly 6:00 A.M. without fail. I often joined him; he tried to fill in the gaps in my knowledge of geography, to teach me about the Alps that could be seen from his window, or to make trips from one town to another on the map. It was hopeless; I was perfectly dense. Suddenly, he would say, "You'll help me? Do you want to?" Of course I wanted to; and he asked me just to go play with my doll beside a lady who was feeling very sad because she could not have her own little girl; or else he would ask me to play dominoes with an old woman who would get angry all alone and grumble in a loud voice; or to play croquet with some young ladies who were getting bored always having to play among themselves, without ever having a different partner. I would go. Often everything seemed simple and natural to me. No special problems arose, but sometimes I had almost the impression that I was the grownup in the midst of a crowd of rather difficult children. The situation was painful with some of the patients; I felt surrounded by suffering and would have liked to understand a little better and to help; there were tears and visible sadness, and I had trouble afterward going back to my own life with my family. It was almost as if we were forbidden to become any further involved in the patients' lives, it seemed to me that we did not know enough about what they were going through, or, when we did know, we had an almost excessive possibility of forgetting.

Sometimes, too, they would allow me, or even ask me, to visit the disturbed patients. This was just about my favorite duty. I would sit down next to the one who seemed most agitated, and little by little I would succeed in taking her hand, stroke it a bit, like that of a friend, and she would calm down and, in the end, even go to sleep.

Certain patients were permitted to attend Sunday services in the institution's little church. Some of them always began to cry or talk. This was obviously strange, and I sensed that it was only their illness that made them act that way; and yet, there was a kind of vital participation there. I believed, in a confused manner, that it might be possible to make use of this distress that they were voicing in such a vivid way, in order to explain something more to them, in order to help them. I did not have the courage to speak of it to my uncle, whom I knew not to be religious, and yet the problem presented itself: Wasn't God using this very real mental disturbance to ask a question, and couldn't we help to formulate an answer?

When midsummer came, we helped with haymaking. That is, we mostly just hid behind the haystacks and drank the lemonade that the patients who worked out of doors received as they wished and on which we feasted. Our assistance could not possibly have been at all substantial, but we had a grand time riding back to the barn in the big wagons piled very high with hay, on which we stayed perched only with some difficulty.

There was much distress at the Waldau, and even where we would not have expected it. In the middle of the main building, there was a tower with a large clock that rose about ten meters above it. Part of the fun we had on our vacations was to climb there once each visit, with my aunt, and to be in the midst of the pulleys and wheels of all sorts when the clock struck noon, when the hammer strokes of the hours reverberated the most and caused the ladder on which we had made our ascent to vibrate. When I was about twelve or thirteen years old, one of the doctors died, and I found out then something that they had at first tried to keep from us: he had hanged himself in the tower, in the midst of the bells, and his son, who was exactly my own age, had found him the next day. I remember the intense emotion that overwhelmed me that evening and plunged me into a depression that was revived each time I heard the clock strike; I almost felt that it would never again be possible to be happy, knowing such a horrible secret.

We heard of suicides every once in a while at the Waldau; it was always very painful, but they were somehow part of the illness, and none of them affected me the way that doctor's suicide had.

When we returned home after vacation, we always thought we had grown a lot, because our furniture was not as tall as our uncle's and it always felt at first as if our own table-tops were pressing on our knees. This sensation disappeared only after several days, about as long as it took for the good resolutions that I never failed to make while I was at the Waldau to fade away. I wanted to work very hard so as to become a doctor sooner. Another resolution is harder to formulate exactly. I had a deeply rooted conviction that the patients at the Waldau especially needed personal, in a way, moral help, help that would draw its strength, too, from the character of the doctor, and I thought that perhaps it was above all a matter of learning how to become better; I desired it without being able to determine very well how one should begin; I saw, as it were, the goals, which were not, however, being developed. I think that if I could talk now to the little girl I was then, I would try to show her, too, something about the power of renunciation, and I would try to detach her a bit from her idea of morality in order to entrust her more fully to God.

When the weather was very hot, my aunt would sometimes take Hélène and me to the woods; then, we would *"gratigner"*. *"Gratigner"*, in our language, meant digging tiny houses in the ground, close to the trees, where it is divided by the roots and lends itself to all kinds of partitions. These little houses were to become a dwelling for mice. We made furniture with little pieces of wood and prepared delicious meals with the scraps left from our tea. How we would have loved one day to come upon a mouse feasting on chocolate while comfortably seated on one of the chairs prepared for it! While we were working on our building, Aunt Jeanne would tell us stories. She did not have an inexhaustible repertoire, but she was such a fine storyteller that we never tired of hearing the same one several times over. Besides, I think my aunt was infinitely happier in the woods than she was at home. Her voice changed, and she seemed to have plenty of time; we never left the woods in a hurry but quite peacefully at the end of a story, and I never had even the slightest suspicion that the stories were being drawn out or cut short to suit my aunt or the work that awaited her at home. As we went back, my aunt would become a little tense and, as it were, distracted again; besides, she would never have told us any stories in the house itself, and I doubt that it would have entered our minds, either, to ask her to do so. She complicated her work so much, moreover, and managed to complicate that of others as well, that there was room around her for nothing but housework. I cannot succeed in understanding how it took us whole hours to clear the lunch table, but that was the way it was. There was no way to fight this waste of time, however hard we might have tried.

At the Waldau there was also the gardener with his hot-houses and flowerbeds full of flowers. We could go and cut as many as we wanted. This always made us very happy, and when we went back to La Chaux-de-Fonds, it was always with huge bouquets and bags full of goodies that the house-keeper of the Waldau gave us: by the time the flowers had wilted, the goodies were all gone too.

THE LAST TWO YEARS
OF PRIMARY SCHOOL

In the third and fourth years of primary school, the class was composed entirely of girls. At the beginning this seemed bizarre to me, especially since they went to great lengths to explain to us why this separation was imperative: we were supposed to be becoming real young ladies, and the boister-ous presence of boys would, apparently, have impeded this harmonious development. Suddenly I realized that several of the girls were starting to act conceited, putting on little airs and taking mirrors out of their pockets and calling each other "my dear". I really couldn't stand it. A kind of void of close friendships followed for me; now I looked for soli-tude at school too. I continued nonetheless to play with the

Adrienne standing in front of her father

As a young girl

others at recess, but I no longer had that admiration for my fellow students; it seemed to me that a misunderstanding lay deep between us. The curriculum was too easy for me. Somehow I started getting bored.

In the next-to-the-last year, the teacher, Mademoiselle Zehntner, was always dressed in black with a very high collar and long sleeves. She was rather horse-faced with long, slightly separated teeth. She was infinitely kind. I liked her very much, especially the sound of her rather lilting voice. At recess, she occasionally had me stay with her and would tell me that I should become a teacher later: I could take over her job, and I would be able to give livelier lessons. I said No; I would be a doctor. She cried out with shock: Medicine was no profession for a woman, but the work of a teacher, what a vocation that was, if one knew how to understand it well! I stood firm, but I liked to talk about the future with my teacher.

At home, there was a secret in the air. Mama and Hélène talked about it, but always so that they could explain that they were not going to tell me, because of some stupid thing or other that I had just done. Honestly, I did not care in the least about knowing the secret. It merely humiliated me that they so often dangled it under my nose, just so they could say to me: "Look, it's true, you don't know the secret yet, I was going to tell you but I was forgetting that only yesterday you. . . ." Then they would enumerate everything I had done wrong, things that I had truly forgotten for the time. The secret was galling; I had no idea that it was to become one of the greatest joys of my life. One day, as she was knitting a baby's vest, Mama told me that a little brother or sister would be coming in the spring. It was only that evening, after I had gone to bed, that I really understood that there were going to be four of us children. That night,

I did not stop praying, I was so happy that I prayed without words, in complete happiness; my words would not have been adequate to thank God properly. And yet, there was a tinge of sadness in me too; the next morning I asked Papa, "Couldn't God have given this baby to me, instead?" Papa laughed and said, "You would make a funny little mother."

There were children who lived in neighboring houses along our street who played, on the sidewalk, every evening until darkness fell, at games we never could play because they needed an asphalt surface and our little garden was full of pebbles. These children would draw squares with chalk and would hop from one foot to the next, pushing a pebble that was to make a special path, marked with magic numbers. Watching them through the window, there was no way to understand it; but it seemed to me that I would have loved that very game more than any other, and I hated the diabolo that you had to throw up in the air and then catch again on a string, all by yourself in the courtyard, while the neighborhood children all played together. One day, I had a fine idea. I called to the children through our hedge and invited them to come join me, and even sat them down on my parents' chairs, and we played, but we played our games and not theirs, and then my conscience was not quite at peace. Mama said, "That was all right this time, but don't do it again." And I wanted so much to do it again! A short while later, a girl, one of those who had come into the garden, suddenly placed a little cat in my arms. It was black with a white tummy. Papa let me keep it until the baby was born; I didn't like cats very much, but this one was really cute; it had fun with everything and let itself be wrapped up and put to bed in a doll bed. Willy had a lot of fun with it, and Mama said it was keeping him from learning his poems. Then one day the cat disappeared, and I never knew why. Willy had to go away for a long course of treatments; when he came back, the new little brother was already several weeks old, and all Willy could find to say when he saw the baby for the first time was: "I'd have liked the cat better." The family was indignant, but I think I understood, and I took pains to be nicer to Willy.

When we hadn't finished everything on our plates or when we left a bit of bread lying around, Mama would say to us: "As long as you have not tasted the bread of the poor, you won't know what it is." I did not absolutely understand what this saying meant. To me, it had something about it that simultaneously drew me and scared me, a hidden meaning. I sometimes thought about it but without any success at unraveling it. And at that very time in my life, a girl at school said to me: "You know the Catholics eat the Lord, in little pieces? At every Mass, they hand him out like bread." I don't know why I didn't dare show my fright to that girl, but I was horrified. Something inside me hurt, really hurt. I thought to myself that the bread of the poor was not far from all that; I didn't understand any of it, and such a kind of bread seemed to me something altogether too mysterious. It certainly tasted just like ordinary bread, of course, and, yet, why did it have so many serious problems? The Lord and the poor, that I saw rather well, yes, but what did bread have to do with it? And Mathilde, who was genuinely poor (she even wore the socks we knit in our handwork class for the poor of our town)—she was a pale, lanky girl with almost colorless hair, and she had red blotches all over her face. She wore a gray smock that covered her entirely and didn't have any embroidery on it whatsoever, and she had a mother who did other people's washing in their homes and had never been married. Well, Mathilde had a big piece of white bread, almost without any crust, in her hand, and she said to me, "This is blessed bread, I'm giving you a piece of it." "What's it for?" "To eat, naturally." And I asked her: "Where does it come from, this bread? And who blessed it?" And she answered, "It's bread just like we buy every day, and the priest blessed it, so don't worry, take some." She gave me a big piece, and I ate it slowly, it took all my saliva, it was utterly tasteless, nothing like ours. And suddenly I ventured, "Mathilde, is this bread the Lord from the Mass?" "No, dummy, it's our own bread." Then another girl, Berthe, came up to us (we were in the gym) and she started to call at the top of her voice, "*Catholique, à la bourrique* [Catholic, go to the devil]!" Others came up and cried out, too. As for me, I was miserable. I slowly finished my bread. I would have liked to save a little of it, but, above all, I wanted to cry, and then even more I wanted to know what all these breads meant and why it was that the Lord and the poor had that incomprehensible bread that we who weren't poor and weren't Catholics did not. At home, I boldly reported: "I ate some of Mathilde's bread, a big piece." I think I was going to go on, so I could finally find out, but Mama got angry in the middle of my sentence: "You don't have enough to eat at home, you have to take bread away from that poor little one?" "But Mama, you yourself said nobody would ever understand if he didn't eat the bread of the poor." Mama was not at all satisfied, but Papa said to her, "Come on, let the child be; you can surely see she's suffering." And yet, I didn't talk to Papa about it, and, for long years, the whole mystery of bread kept on bothering me whenever I thought about it.

On the eve of my tenth birthday, I understood all of a sudden what it means to get older: it simply means that every year, unavoidably, you carry one more year on your

My Early Years

back, without being able to do anything about it, until all those accumulated years make a life. And then death would come. You can't escape it. Up till now it had taken only one number to indicate my age; now it would take two, all the way to the end, never three. Almost nobody lived to be a hundred. So, life was short. It was short, and it slipped away from us since there was no way to hold onto it. Our maid knew heaps of things. She was called Marthe, and Hélène and I used to say, just between ourselves and in a whisper, "*Marthe-prunier* [Marthe-plum-tree]", because she used to shake us like plum trees when we weren't good and when she was sure nobody could see her. I had gone and asked her if God could, if he really wanted to, keep age from advancing. At first she didn't understand. When she finally did understand, she told me that God could do everything. I knew perfectly well he could do everything, but I would have liked to know if he could do that too. Finally Marthe didn't answer me anymore. I consoled myself by writing a poem in which *vieillesse* [old age] rhymed with *tristesse* [sadness]. I always read my poems to Willy, who listened to them seriously. Except for that, he was rather bad with poetry, since he had a terrible time learning poems by heart. When it was just a matter of listening to a poem without any danger of having to memorize it, he had nothing against it.

For that birthday, I received a very small violin. Some years previously, a violinist had given a few concerts at La Chaux-de-Fonds: her name was Vivien Chartres, and she was still practically a child herself and had come to play with us several times. On the night of her principal concert, we brought flowers to her onstage, and dresses had been made for us to match hers. We had to go through numerous rehearsals to learn how to accept graciously the kiss she would give us in front of a large audience. I no longer remember very well how it all went, but that first concert made a very big impression on me, and I dreamed of learning to play the violin. My parents said that with my back trouble that would never come to pass, and besides, I had too little talent. But at last I received the hoped-for violin. It was a toy violin: impossible to tune or even to play a scale on it right; after that, the matter was no longer open for discussion.

We were making presents by hand for Christmas, and I don't think we would ever have finished them in time without the help of our governess. The ones we made at Grandmother's house were always ready long before Christmas, because she prepared them for us well in advance and tried to make them fun for us, and she always succeeded in doing that. On December 24, a tree was set up in the playroom, and there was no one present but our parents and us, the children. Mama got the tree ready after dinner, and my father would take us for a walk until it got dark. Everything was sheer anticipation; we were as delighted as could be and tried to make our father guess what we had made for him, but we would have been heartbroken if he had happened to guess right. Fortunately, in spite of all the obvious blunders we committed, he never seemed to guess but rather came forth with the most outlandish suppositions, which amused us greatly. When we got home, we would wait in the dining room, all neat and our hair brushed, until Mama rang a little white metal bell, which she did after she had lit all the candles. Then our wait was over, we admired the tree and looked at the tables ready with presents. Each one had his own table covered with a white cloth on which were arranged the things Mama and Papa or distant relatives were giving us. Two days later, the second Christmas Day took place, when my grandparents and our various uncles and aunts took part. Then, the tables would be redone, and their gifts would be added. These two celebrations at our house had no religious character about them, and I could not understand why, at Sunday school, we celebrated Christmas as the birth of the Infant Jesus, while, at home, it was solely a question of a lighted tree and numerous presents. One time, I took a small New Testament and read, very softly to myself, the Christmas Gospel while the candles were burning. But Mama did not care at all for this way I had of calling attention to myself. Yet, my parents were religious and went to church from time to time.

Thus, Christmas always left me, in spite of all the joy I experienced seeing so many of my wishes fulfilled, with a vague feeling of emptiness and bitterness. Something was missing for me. I had tried to fill that emptiness by reading the Christmas story, but I could not say whether that had, at the time, really been enough for me, because even at that point in my life I sensed something in the nature of an unanswered question welling up within me, and I was often, but not in a continuous way, disturbed by it.

And always, in the final moments of anticipation before Christmas, it used to seem to me that this time everything would work out. Usually we did not go out in the evenings, but a few days before Christmas, when all the stores were lit up, we were allowed each year to walk for a while along the interminable rue Léopold-Robert to admire the shop windows. What impressed me even more than the displays filled with gifts and surprises were the people; they formed a bustling crowd, and, despite the cold and the snow, they looked contented, even happy. I tried to share in their happiness, to submerge my obscure uneasiness in their joy, to let it turn into true hope. All these people I didn't know were close to me, I was sure that they possessed an unknown truth that would burst out suddenly, simple and unalterable. I even thought that they were a part of this truth, that it existed as much within them as outside of them. I suppose it is from these evenings before Christmas that I get my love for anonymous crowds; I feel good in the midst of them, I breathe freely there. But known faces disturb me when I see them in crowds, they disappoint me when I know that they are living outside the truth, or, even more that, while possessing the truth, they do not make it their whole life.

Mama was becoming bigger and bigger, she no longer went out unless she was wearing a large cloak of black velvet that she called her maternity cloak. And in a wardrobe, tiny diapers and baby's vests piled up, while Mademoiselle Adèle, our governess, put the finishing touches on an all-white bassinet. Then Mademoiselle Adèle and Willy left for Basel. One day Mama said, "It tires me too much to go up to Grandmother's, I'm too heavy." The next morning, when we were getting ready to leave for school, Papa came to tell us not to come home at noon but to go directly to our grandparents'. We went to kiss Mama, who was still in bed, and she said to us: "Today's the day."

At school, as soon as the roll had been called, I raised my hand to announce: "M'selle, Mama is expecting the baby today." The teacher said: "That's fine, sit down and come and see me at recess." When I went to find her, she explained to me that people don't talk about those things until they have already taken place; one did not announce the birth of a baby beforehand, one rejoiced once the baby was there. Decidedly, I had no idea what she was talking about, since Mama herself had told us. Until then, I had always had the impression that there was a kind of unity to the things that happened; what concerned me, me or my family, also concerned the school, as well as vice-versa. And when Henri Schmid broke his hand or Carlo Paccanari had his appendicitis operation, and when I, all excited, had reported this at home, I really felt that the emotion on Mama's part was very small compared with the gravity of the events.

It took a good half-hour to go from the school to les Tilleuls, my grandparents' home. That day, Hélène and I, who never went together without some special reason, became inseparable, and we were not even tempted to play the forbidden game that, despite the danger it involved, was the most tempting of games: the game of blind-man. It entailed walking together down the street with our eyes tightly shut. Before risking it, you would look over the route to be covered and decide on the place where you could open your eyes once again; the danger was not that of getting run over but of getting your ears boxed. One time when we had crossed the rue Léopold-Robert in that manner, with our eyes shut tight, the tram had had to stop because of us, and the conductor had gotten down. He didn't box our ears, because we were the doctor's daughters, but he gave us a big shaking, which was just as disagreeable as having one's ears boxed, and he threatened to tell our father, which was much more disagreeable still. From then on, we had given up playing blind-man on streets where the tram went, and I no longer remember what it was that prompted us, much later, to abandon this absurd game once and for all.

On arriving at my grandparents', we learned that nothing had happened at home yet, but, since that day was my grandfather's birthday, there was a dinner in celebration, and we were even allowed to eat mustard.

When we returned at four o'clock that afternoon, Grandmama had disappeared—she was at our house. Grandpapa did not have much to say. We did our homework, lit the gas lamp without asking the maid to help us as if it had been the most natural thing in the world, and then we went to have supper with Grandpapa in the big dining room that was always dark because there was a big veranda in front. Since Grandmama was not there and Grandpapa did not seem to notice anything, we poured coffee into our milk; I didn't find it very good, since I wasn't used to it, but it was really the fact of demonstrating the height of our independence that intoxicated us a bit. When there was no more milk to mix with the coffee, we drank the coffee straight from big cups made of blue-and-white pottery. I loved those cups so much; they had in particular the great merit of not having handles like the ones we had at home. That coffee was dreadful; I had no desire to finish it but not enough nerve to leave it. All of a sudden the telephone rang, Grandpapa rushed to it and came back very quickly to say: "You have a little brother." Then he went to the cellar to get a bottle of vintage red wine, and he, too, disappeared to go to my parents' house. Hélène and I were overjoyed and decided to have a big party and invite the maid. To begin with, we went to empty our coffee cups into the sink. The maid brought in a big chocolate egg, which she divided between us without wanting a single bite for herself; now this egg, which she'd received from the house, was all salty. I think it had been packed with some of the salt destined for the Easter eggs; we didn't have the courage to admit this unfortunate state of affairs to her, so we ate tiny bites of this unenjoyable chocolate with some difficulty.

Then we decided to continue the festivities in bed, that is, to get into bed and tell stories to each other until our grandparents returned. It made us feel terribly grown up to have such a little brother; we suddenly considered ourselves young ladies.

When Grandmama came into our room before 9:00 P.M., thrilled with the prospect of telling us all about the baby, she found us sound asleep and could not, despite her great desire, find the courage to wake us.

The next morning we took our dolls in our arms and went into our grandparents' room. My grandfather was just opening the door at the very instant when I came up with my doll, and the latch on the door smashed her porcelain head. I couldn't help crying, because I loved my doll very much, so it was through tears that I listened to my grandmother explain how darling and chubby and pink the baby was, and what a fine head of hair he had. Then Grandmama said she was going to make a gift for us: she would buy some pretty material to make us each a Sunday dress. This time I began to cry even more: No, No, I didn't want a dress, especially not a Sunday dress, I'd rather have books, or colored pencils, or, oh, yes, building blocks; anything but a dress. Some years before, when I was still smaller than Hélène—I had since then grown taller than she—I had generally worn her old dresses from the previous year, and that had been perfectly all right with me. Grandmama was not very happy about this, so she had, in the greatest secrecy, a cream-colored silk dress with an immense lace collar and a wide leather belt made for me; the dress was adorned with very tiny pleats and embroidered in matching tones, a real marvel of a dress, with little short sleeves. Grandmother and the dressmaker who did the fittings were ecstatic about it, and I sang at the top of my lungs: "I have a dress fit for a princess! I have a dress fit for a princess!" Well, I never wore that dress, even once; when I returned home, with my dress in a suitcase, Mama decided I could wear it when my behavior improved. The following summer, it was never warm enough; and two years later, either the dress had become ridiculously small or

I had become so ridiculously tall that all the dressmakers in
the world could not have managed to make it wearable. So
I hadn't the least desire to receive a dress from Grandmama:
I was too convinced that it would turn out bad once again,
and I preferred to avoid that disappointment.

Finally, instead of dresses, Grandmama gave us each a silver watch with a long silver chain. For a long time, we wore
our watches in tiny watch-pockets sewn onto the left sides
of our woolen blouses and then later on leather wristbands.

Grandmother announced that when school was out we
could go to see the baby. At school, the very first thing, I
raised my hand again and announced with a kind of triumph:
"M'selle, we have a little brother." The teacher congratulated me, and the lessons began as usual. At first I did not
understand why they did not have some sort of celebration,
such as reading something out loud or a walk; but nothing
really extraordinary took place. At noon, I bounded home
and arrived, breathless, at Mama's side. She gave me a very
poor welcome, repeating to me the exasperating words I
had heard all during my childhood: "If I had put you with a
wet-nurse, I would think they had exchanged you, but since
I didn't put you with a wet-nurse, I'm going to have to get
used to believing that you are my daughter, and I understand
nothing about it. Why, then, must you be so senseless?" All
that happened because Mama thought I would be coming
home from school at eleven o'clock, but I kept from giving
an explanation because all through my early childhood, I
don't know why, I had formed the habit of never answering
back, and, instead of defending myself, I made little consoling speeches to myself, all alone and very softly of course. In
the end, I was still permitted to go and see the baby; he was
sleeping in his white bassinet, with his two tiny fists closed
tight on either side of his head. Really he was quite darling,

and I went back to Grandmama's with a heart full of joy, asked her for some white wool, and started to knit some stockings for him. A few days later, when I went back to see the baby again, his nanny had just given him a bath. He was completely naked, and she explained to me that she had already potty-trained him, and how she always potty-trained all the babies she looked after from the very first day. At that very moment, and as if to protest, my little brother soaked the length of Nanny's white apron; I was delighted with his sense of timing. From then on, I knew I would get along especially well with the baby.

From Grandmama's house, we went to spend our spring vacation at the Waldau. We felt a little sorry for our uncle and aunt, who hadn't yet seen our little brother. We couldn't stop talking about how marvelous he was. Then life resumed its usual course at home. Willy returned from Basel, curious to see the baby. Hélène and I surrounded the cradle to see what he would say. He walked up slowly, looked, and said: "I'd really have liked a cat much better." It somehow took our breath away.

I had changed schools and teachers; the new teacher was named Mademoiselle Bandelier, and she was very small and lively. She showed a great preference for me right away; I hated that. The other teachers had all liked me very much, and I had liked them too, but they had never been unfair. One day, when she had gone out of the classroom for a moment, there was some noise; when she returned, she was angry that we had not been quiet, she scolded and slapped a girl who not only was innocent but was also the least gifted and probably the poorest of anyone in the class. With one leap, I got up and gave a good slap to the teacher. That naturally gave rise to an enormous fuss, but my father was not at all upset. He explained to me that I had been very wrong, even though I was absolutely right. That wasn't the only time, moreover, that something like that happened to me. About three years later, in the grammar school, the geography teacher was hitting a student in the face with a ruler. Then, too, I ran at the teacher, grabbed him by the neck, turned him around to face the class, saying to my fellow students: "Do you want to see a coward? Here's one!" I wouldn't have remembered this incident if one of my classmates hadn't recently reminded me of it. I hope I wasn't violent toward my teachers on other occasions, but it is true that injustice was capable of making me commit any act. Besides, I felt obligated to lodge a complaint with the teachers when a fellow student had been treated worse than he deserved, and at the time I was obsessed with not giving in and with inciting the whole class to revolt. I taught them to pay no attention to the bad grades that did not fail to rain down on us when we showed too pronounced a team spirit, and I would make up "speeches to parents" for them to be sure to recite when handing over their report cards. At our house, moreover, that always went very simply in such cases; I don't know who had warned my father the first time; when I presented the report of my misbehavior or some unflattering remark, he asked, "Because of another student?" "Yes." "No good will come of it; that's O.K."

The fuss with Mademoiselle Bandelier troubled me for some time; I tried on several occasions to resolve the matter, but it was impossible. It seemed to me indispensable that she should acknowledge she was in the wrong and apologize to the student unjustly slapped; there was no way to make her understand that. Finally I had to give up, all the more because my classmates figured that for that poor girl, one slap more or less. . . .

That summer we took the baby to the Waldau for the first

time. He was out in front of the house nearly the whole day in his pram, and I had fun looking out of the window at the people who went to admire him as they passed by, for it's very rare that women don't stop to look at a baby in a pram; if they gave him only an absentminded glance, I was not at all pleased. In the evenings he was always given a chamomile bath, which he greatly enjoyed, and he always tried to catch at least a little mouthful of it; he was a happy baby who very seldom cried and smiled at everyone.

When we left the Waldau, we were always laden with un-believable packages, because the housekeeper would give us lots of biscuits and even some cheese; old ladies who were part of the administrative secretarial staff or compan-ions to patients would give us chocolate, and Hélène and I would have stored up preposterous treasures, pretty stones, branches, boats laboriously carved from bark, nests of moss, tea patiently dried, forgotten in a sudden shower, and then dried all over again, little boxes of different sizes that had formerly contained drug samples and now contained a but-terfly's wing or odd fruit pits or a string of glass pearls, too ugly to be worn at home but which we had no fear of putting on at the Waldau. All that comprised our vacation souvenirs and disappeared quickly, we knew not how, as soon as we were home.

That summer, on returning from the Waldau, I sought out my father in his consulting room and asked him to register me at the *gymnasium* in the spring: since I wanted to be a doctor, we ought to start before it was too late. I no longer remember my father's reply; I know he was se-rious; he promised me he would think it over. That was not enough for me. Suddenly, he understood what this dis-cussion meant to me: I was undertaking a solemn commit-ment. A decisive transformation was taking place within me at that very moment. I saw clearly that the perennial "when I grow up" had lost its meaning. My life was beginning now, it had been begun for a long time already, it was real and personal. There wasn't any barrier somewhere that separated tomorrow from today or yesterday; everything was today; my youth was much more than a time of preparation; it was life itself; my childhood was entering consciously into my adulthood, disposing of it with an absolute right, and that right was a duty. All these reflections were swirling around within me, filling me with anxiety and joy. The playroom was empty when I returned. For the last time, I took the drawer out of the green table, turned it upside-down and set off in my boat on a voyage of thanksgiving.

It very quickly became evident that my mother did not want my plan to be realized. She had no wish to see me in a *gymnasium* designed for boys that admitted, somewhat as a favor, a small number of girls. The idea of my studying medicine seemed premature and slightly fantastic to her. She said to me: "As homely as you are, no doubt you'll never get married, and you'll probably have to support yourself; you could become a teacher, and that would enable you to stay two more years in primary school and then you could go to the girls' secondary school. That would be much more useful for you than to begin studies you perhaps will never finish and during which you will learn nothing but bad manners." From this lecture, which was often repeated, with a thousand variations, the idea of being a teacher particularly held my attention. I would not have had anything against that, and many other professions besides teaching seemed fine and desirable to me, but my own path was marked out. I would be a doctor, and I was happy; the choice had already been made, a long time ago.

My father did not take the matter lightly. He made a trip to

Basel to speak to Mademoiselle Gutlé. Mademoiselle Gutlé was a French teacher who ran a girls' school. He respected her and admired the soundness of her judgment. Happily, she thought one should not thwart a clear vocation without very good reason: she advised giving me a try.

At home and at school, life went on as usual; I still had to spend long periods lying down. I had a great deal of free time, because the homework from school was too easy for me and I generally did it right there at school. I read a lot, and I worked for the poor; but I often lacked the materials. One day, when my aunt and uncle and their two little girls were at our house and my mother happened not to be, I proposed to them the idea of founding a society called "The Three MACs", which contained the initials of our five first names. My uncle was to put up a subscription; my aunt would buy wool or cloth with the money and would promise to give me a lot of remnants. As for my little cousins, they were to give up their treats, which my aunt would set aside to round out the packages for the poor. "The Three MACs" survived for a long time, and I don't know how many shirts and skirts I sewed and trimmed, or how many socks I knitted. Three years later, when I was friends with Madeleine (from whom I learned a lot of things about how to empathize with the poor), the society became known as "The Four MACs".

Willy said, "Didi has become a Mason; she has a secret society." No argument could persuade him to join our society himself. He had so many pencils of all kinds that he could have given us one of his old ones when he got a new one. But he would have no part of it. Despite the presence of Uncle Constant—a presence more effective than real— he considered us to be a women's club and that a man of his age—he was eight—had no business in it.

That winter was a long one. There wasn't much snow, but it stayed on the ground and turned black. I now had permission sometimes to take walks by myself, and I used the opportunity to wander around the poor neighborhoods; they offended sensitivities a little, but I dreamed of my profession. I would be a doctor for the poor. The black snow and the gray winter sky cast a rather melancholy shadow over my plans. Sometimes I would pray a bit as I walked, but at the end of an "Our Father" I didn't know what more to say; then I would take a verse from the Bible along with me, sort of as a companion, I would repeat it softly, pausing at every word. One day, I was alarmed, as it were; it had become obvious to me that I did not understand. It was almost as if I were pronouncing words in a language I did not speak. One day, I saw a man all by himself in front of a closed door, crying out: The name of God, name of God, name of God! I went up to him very gently, took his hand, and said, "You mustn't upset God like that." He smelled of wine or something stronger. He looked at me and said, "Why, you're the doctor's little girl! Go home and tell your papa he ought not to let you go around where the drunks are." Finally I left, and I felt sad; I'd have to become a doctor for drunks. There would never be an end to that. But maybe, some day, it would start.

That Christmas, Grandmama died. On her last visit to us, I had heard the baby babbling "Mama". I tried to get him to say it again for Grandmama, who told me: "I'll give you a franc when I hear him say it." But she never came to visit us again, and she never heard the baby speak.

In February 1914, a female medical student came to have dinner at our house one day. My father began to recall memories of his youth that we'd never heard him speak about before. The first thing that astonished me was to see him treat as a colleague this young, blonde, elegant, rather self-assured girl, who discussed medicine as an object that belonged to her, something over which she had control. What astounded me even more was to see my father talking to her about the evolution of science. Up until then, I had thought that there were completed, accomplished sciences, whose primary and eventually multiple truths were irrefutable; I thought medicine was one of them, that the numerous advances were added in a way as external ornaments, designed to make its immediate and unchanging beauty more obvious. And suddenly it became clear that medicine was a living science. This revelation gripped me and shook me to the core. I avoided moving, almost kept from breathing, for fear of interrupting the conversation, of learning no more about it. But just when I was being absolutely quiet and had stopped eating, with emotion—certainly the first time I'd ever done that—Mama suddenly noticed it and made some remark that Papa interrupted by asking if perhaps I wanted to ask the student about anything. No, I did not want to ask her anything at all, but in my heart, I resolved never to forget what I had just perceived and to remember always that medicine was a living science, which already at that time, although still vaguely, meant for me: in God, living in God; because I could not conceive of any possible life outside of him. I never saw the student again, but her husband, a well-known surgeon, died in the middle of an operation, before they had been married a year. Some day, though, I would like to tell her what her visit meant to me.

THE OPERATION AT BASEL

There had always been some discussion about my having an operation soon for the appendicitis that had already played a few tricks on me and had obliged my father several times to hire a car to take me home when we were on trips. The prospect of this operation did not worry my parents in the least. It was a little like an item so unknown that one could do nothing about it; at the most, a purple and white dressing gown and a new, black and white checked dress reminded that the appointed time was approaching. The operation was to take place at Basel, and since the people in Basel were very formal, I was, rather belatedly, made to be in mourning, in the form of this dress, for my grandmother. The preparations were made, and the day of departure, which was to be a Monday, was definitively set.

The final Sunday at home was memorable. That afternoon my parents went to the first air display that ever took place at La Chaux-de-Fonds: the plane was to take off from a meadow in Eplatures and land there again. I wanted terribly to go, and I insisted that they take me. I had seen an airplane only once, very briefly, as it flew between two clouds, and I would have loved to see one better, at length. The conquest of the heavens seemed to me to have something unreal about it; couldn't one, suddenly, be in the same place as God? My thoughts, certainly, were confused, but I sensed an extraordinary mystery there. There was nothing I could do; I had to stay at home. My parents came back very soon, all upset; the plane had hardly reached any altitude when it had dropped down again, crushed; the pilot was dead. My mother said several times: "It looked like a dead leaf that turns round and round as it falls." We had a thousand questions to ask, we felt upset about this misfortune, as if it had somehow touched us. Suddenly, my father said to me with some emotion, "Come and take a walk with me; put on your things." I did not understand a thing about this kind of honor. Neither did Hélène. When I took walks with my father, I often held onto his hand. It seemed to me that there was no more perfect happiness than to walk along beside Papa, with my hand in his; that was my consolation for going on walks, since at that time I still was not too fond of walks; besides, I got tired too fast. We went along by the railroad station; at first, Papa did not speak. I shared in his silence; the effect was new, rather serious. I felt grown up. Shortly I would be much bigger still, entrusted with new responsibility, the responsibility in a way for my own life. Papa said to me: "Do you see, an hour ago, the pilot was still alive; he had decided to climb up into the air, using a good plane, with which he was familiar. He knew very well that accidents are possible, but he was counting on his luck, he was feeling sure of himself, he was so strong, so healthy that he wasn't thinking about death. Death always seems unthinkable when one is in good health oneself. And yet, it marks a limit one can very quickly reach, almost even without realizing it; it can even be an instrument God is using." At this moment, I ventured a question: "Do you think maybe the aviator was going up into the sky to look for God?" Papa did not understand right away, and when he understood that I thought that God and heaven were a kind of material unity, somehow accessible by airplane, he began to explain some things about the sky to me, in little short sentences, in his deep, almost hoarse voice.

Then he went back to his original intention. He compared the projected operation to an airplane flight: no immediate necessity, and yet a desirable operation, that perhaps would prevent some grave complication but carried with it a few hazards in itself. It was possible that it could involve a fatal accident. An operation, even a planned one, even if performed with all possible precautions, was still a risk; there was considerable room for progress in medicine, like other areas, and in surgery as well; but there was always an elusive, unforeseen remnant. He had been thinking about this operation for a long time, which had been strongly recommended by the surgeon; he had made up his mind to go ahead with it, he had taken responsibility for it, and now, after having seen the airplane go down, he no longer wanted to assume that without warning me. I needed to reflect with him, to give him an answer of my own; but he expected, of course, that that answer would be a reasonable one. All of a sudden, it seemed to me that I no longer had anything to envy the medical student; with me, too, my father was speaking as if I were a grown person. Inwardly, I drew myself up to the full height of my eleven years to reply to my father: "If you and Professor de Quervain agree, then that's sufficient." But Papa insisted, he wanted me to know something about death, about the danger surrounding every anesthesia, every laparotomy. Suddenly he said: "You could die, we would no longer have but one little girl." I burst out, "But Papa, I would love to die!" He gave me a strange look and asked, "Are you really unhappy?" I was speechless: But no, of course I was happy, with all my heart I was happy, but obviously I would be much happier still in heaven, and I was really very eager to die, and also just a tiny bit desirous of living. All that was not exactly clear to my father, and maybe no more than for me. The operation was settled; I took no little pride in having had a part in the decision. Still, Papa said gravely: "If one day you

were unhappy, you'd tell me right away, wouldn't you?" I
promised that I would, and we continued our walk around
the station, and Papa told me a little about what life would
be like at the *gymnasium*; I would be entering there as soon
as I returned to La Chaux-de-Fonds.

   That evening, at home, I firmly resolved not to go to
sleep for a long time, so that I could reflect on all these new
problems. What concerned me most was this sort of boundary surrounding life on all sides; I felt it was impossible to
move forward in life without coming into contact with this
envelope one could encounter everywhere—the envelope
called death. There was something else too: Papa had shown
me that we are granted one kind of possibility to order our
lives. There were intense, almost resonant moments, when
one could say Yes or No. All at once I understood: the limit
was reserved only for earthly life; in heaven one would no
longer collide anywhere, everything would be beyond the
limits. This was the prospect of true happiness. In the courtyard the voices of the neighbor children could be heard; they
were playing tag; every other night, I envied them a bit. But
not tonight, and, in spite of my resolution to stay awake,
I fell into a trustful sleep, with my fists curled on either
side of my head (they always used to make mild fun of my
having kept this sleeping position, like a big baby).

   The next morning Mama, Willy, and I left for Basel. Willy
was going to have his leg operated on, and they had reserved
a room for the two of us together in the hospital. Arriving
at the hospital was a big event for me. Willy, unfortunately,
was used to it because he had already had frequent operations; he treated all my astonishment with great irony. At
teatime, they brought each of us a pot of hot milk and a pot
of coffee. Now, at home coffee was forbidden; but Papa had
said that at the hospital we would have to obey the nurse—

and the nurse had given no orders. The coffee was terribly tempting. A real matter of conscience. After having thought it over carefully, I went to ask the nurse what we ought to do, but, for fear she might discover an error, I ventured to ask: "Are we supposed to drink all the coffee, or can we leave a little of it?" Willy was dumbfounded at such boldness. The nurse said, "Drink what you want and leave the rest."

These first hours in the hospital were very rich in impressions. Some of our parents' friends came to see us, and almost all of them asked us if we weren't afraid; the fine confidence of our first "No"s gradually disappeared. Being older than Willy, I didn't have the nerve to show my anxiety, which had become truly real; that whole hospital smelled so bad, and Tine, our friend, had come to tell us that the most terrible thing was really the anesthesia. After supper, Heini came, the real, flesh-and-blood Heini, who had been Willy's doctor for so many years and who was for Hélène and me a legendary figure which we played every evening, since the game of our endless chats was called playing "Heini and Valy". Willy was already asleep, and I had a long conversation with Heini. At first I was rather frightened, and all my usual boldness now unaccountably resembled timidity. Heini explained to me that, after all, one could only be afraid of something one would do oneself, where one was in danger of failing at one's task; but an operation was quite different. And again, as on the previous evening with my father, I thought I understood perfectly what was being asked of me: nothing but trust for a thing judged necessary. I think the experience of these two conversations had an enriching effect on the whole of my life forever afterward. I fell asleep happy; then in order to be a doctor, I really needed to learn just a little about what it is to suffer.

When we woke up, my father was already there; he was
visibly uneasy. He couldn't stand still, and, at the last minute,
he who ordinarily was the epitome of calm and assurance said
to me: "You know, if you don't want to, just say so." But
I wanted to, I really wanted to. I have a delightful memory
of the operating room: the nurses were so kind, and it was
extremely hot; but Tine was right, the ether was very disagreeable. That evening, when the professor came in on his
rounds, I sat straight up in my bed, so fast that no one could
stop me, to show him how well I was doing. I was roundly
scolded. Then came the days of convalescence; there were
chaise longues in the garden, under the trees, and I spent
long hours there, enjoying spring days such as I had never
known, days full of sweetness, without any heaviness, a real
revelation. I thought over many things that have been close
to my heart up to the present but which lacked clarity: sick-
ness, death, and above all healing and hope; this was the first
time I had felt a clear sense of hope. When they took me
back up to our room, I tried to make Willy understand, but
he was so passionately fond of a new game of cut-outs that
he didn't want to talk about anything else, except maybe
the nurse, one Sister Violette, who was young and pretty
and for whom Willy had been seized by a love as sudden
as it was violent. I helped him praise her virtues and found
some that Willy had not yet discovered. She called us her
model children. But obviously, we had been good for too
long, and that had to come to a bad end.

Until three every afternoon, we had to take a nap, or
at least stay totally quiet. During that time, one afternoon,
someone knocked. We were still so strongly caught up in
obedience that we whispered very softly to find out if it
would be all right to answer. The door then opened very
slowly, first revealing a half-moon of black, a belly, and upon

the belly a hand holding a small book, also black. The whole
was then completed and became a pastor. He began to talk
volubly, to explain who he was; he had a voice like a whistle
that passed through his teeth and spewed forth jets of saliva;
you felt splashed all over. Maybe it was the feeling of re-
vulsion I experienced that made me say, as if it were an undeniable fait accompli, "*I'm* not a Protestant, you needn't
trouble yourself about me, and besides, this is the time I
am supposed to be sleeping a little." With a dignified air,
I turned over in my bed, with my face to the wall. Willy
was thunderstruck, and, when the pastor approached him,
he said simply, but nearly screaming, "Goodbye, Sir." We
were afterward seized with a fit of uproarious joy; we were
proud of having gotten rid of an unwelcome gentleman all
by ourselves. We grabbed the metal lids from off those con-
tainers that are among the indispensable equipment of a sick-
room. I handed mine to Willy, and he began to beat one
against the other like cymbals, in a wild rhythm, while we
sang at the top of our voices, or rather bellowed with all
our might—the better, perhaps, to stifle the little uneasy
voice of our conscience—"Good-bye, Monsieur Dumol-
let!" That didn't go on for long. Sister Violette came to put
an end to all this uproar. We apologized very quickly, for
we understood very well that in a hospital. . . . But the incident had its consequences. Somebody—and I don't believe
it was Sister Violette—reported the thing to my mother,
who took it very, very badly. This pastor was the pastor
of the French parish, a gentleman as respected as he was
respectable; he had gone to the trouble of inconveniencing
himself for us. Mama was speechless with indignation; and
then, to say I wasn't a Protestant, but finally, what was this
pastor to think: What was I, then?—I believe my mother
wrote a letter of apology or paid a visit, I no longer know,

but I do remember that no one came to see us after that without speaking of our "concert".

One Sunday morning, my father came to get me. Willy and Mama were still staying in Basel. My father took me for a walk. We rode the ferry—I'd never seen anything like it—we crossed the Rhine and walked the length of the promenade along the bank of the Petit-Bâle. For the first time, I saw the cathedral; we took the ferry that led to it, we stopped a moment on the Pfalz terrace, and finished by sitting on a bench in the cathedral square. My first trip to Basel was coming to an end, and it was the last time I was there with my father. First of all, he talked to me about the successful operation and about how thankful we should be to the surgeon and to God. That day, he told me that he had never attempted an operation, even the simplest, that could not go wrong, without praying beforehand. At that moment, I said to him, "I'll do the same thing, Papa," and then very softly—I don't know whether he heard me— I added, "in memory of you, Papa." Then Papa told me that I wouldn't be starting the *gymnasium* the next day as I'd thought but that I would need to stay two more weeks at the Waldau to finish getting well; he would take me there that afternoon, when he went to take Hélène and the baby back to La Chaux-de-Fonds. So I would be all by myself at the Waldau. I wasn't entirely happy at this prospect; my aunt Jeanne, whom I loved so much, scared me a little and had a mania with which my need for solitude was poorly adapted; she was always finding a succession of occupations that progressively generated others, with the result that there was never a way to sketch or play in peace. She constantly interrupted everything, to such a point that, much later, when I wanted to work during my vacations, I always had to do my work between 4:00 and 8:00 A.M., before she got up, since during the day I managed to set aside only a rare quarter of an hour.

We first went back to the hospital to say goodbye to Mama and Willy. Mama was still rather put out because of the fuss with the pastor. This was, I believe, the first time she said to Papa in front of me, with a genuine dissatisfaction, "This child will end up being a Catholic, you'll see", and then, with a sort of logic that irritated me, "She truly does enough stupid things to need to go to confession." All that seemed incomprehensible to me, I retained the words without grasping their meaning. The only thing that seemed incontestably obvious to me was that there was truly an urgent necessity for me to do fewer stupid things, and I'd have to start by not asking any more questions, so as not to stir up my mother's anger. Seated comfortably in the train with my doll in my arms, I asked Papa: "Can a person become a Catholic?" "Yes," replied Papa, "one can." "What's going to confession?" "Telling your sins." "Yes, I know that, but still, why do I need to go to confession?" He didn't know, and I didn't either. But from that moment on, it stayed with me that there were people who *did need* to go to confession. In that respect, was Catholicism responding to a need?

It was only twenty-six years later that I became a Catholic, and now, when I see all these small steps in my childhood, tailored to the size of my childhood, as if offered to my child's feet, I do not understand why I didn't walk, right then, confidently and joyfully, on the path that was being prepared.

THE *PROGYMNASIUM* [1]

Two weeks later, my doll and I went back to La Chaux-
de-Fonds, all by ourselves, on a Sunday toward the end of
the afternoon. Papa and Hélène were at the station. Hélène
had been a student at the girls' secondary school for two
weeks; the girls' secondary school shared the same building
with the *gymnasium*. She already knew where my classroom
was. There were fifty-one boys and, counting me, six girls.
The teachers called everyone the formal "*vous*", even girls
my age; for those of Hélène's own age, that would be quite
understandable, but for those of mine, Hélène found that
quite ridiculous. The boys I was to be with looked mis-
chievous; oh! she was entirely happy to be going to school
with girls; she also had three female teachers, while I would
have only male teachers. Everything Hélène told me there
made a rather deep impression on me. Thus, when Papa
asked me, the next morning, if I were not too big a girl to
have him accompany me to school, I instantly asked him
please to be so kind as to come with me, and I really felt relieved that he was willing to do it. We started off a little late,
because Papa wanted to find the teacher in the classroom.
The door was in a rather dark corridor, on the ground floor,
all the way at the back, on the left. Papa knocked, and Monsieur Rossel came out to speak with us for a short while in
the corridor. He was blond, he seemed very nice, and when
he and I had taken leave of my father and entered the classroom, I was perfectly at ease, but I knew absolutely no one.

---

[1] In Switzerland, where the way schools are set up depends on the canton to some extent, the *gymnasium* (equivalent to the French *lycée*) generally
comprises a six-year course of studies. In some localities, the first cycle of
three years is called the "*progymnasium*"—ED.

That morning, I went from discovery to discovery, I mean, from delight to delight. It seemed to me that I was starting a whole new life; nothing happened to remind me of my past existence; among the throng of pupils crowded into the big room, there was not a single face I knew, not one friend from preschool or primary school. Hélène had been perfectly correct, the teachers called the students "*vous*", the boys by their surnames and the girls by their first names. There was a different teacher for each subject. I remember that that morning I had my first Latin lesson and my first German lesson; the other students already had fifteen days of lessons behind them. At the first recess, I asked a girl to teach me quickly what they had done during those two weeks. A boy, whose name was Charles Wolf, came up and said to me: "You won't learn anything from the girls; if you wish, I'll show you", and he showed me so well that at the end of the first week, when we had written assignments in German and Latin, I got the highest mark in both subjects. I felt no small pride in this, but actually less for myself than for my father, who experienced true joy when I brought home good reports. That first morning I met nearly everyone in the class; the six girls were seated in front, in the first row, but at the end of the week, when the class was arranged according to academic standing, they were scattered all around, and I never again had a girl sitting next to me in the *gymnasium*.

I considered everything to be fabulously interesting. I had a real joy, almost a fever for learning. I also began to read a lot, and again it was Charles who helped me in my choice of reading. He read widely and passed on to me what he thought would be good for me to read; there were also some books that he liked but stopped me from reading by saying: "For a girl, you are still too young; that might do you some harm, or else you wouldn't even understand it."

A little later, he did me a service I shall never forget; he did it for me as a true friend, without attaching any importance to it, and he never reminded me of it. We had to write, in a special notebook every week, a certain number of words that we had come across in the course of our personal reading that we did not know, and we had to copy out their definitions from the Larousse dictionary and learn them by heart. In some of our French lessons, we had to hand in these notebooks to our teacher and recite for him the words that he asked us about. At the top of one particular page, on the left, I had written the word *concevoir* and beside it, its prescribed definition. Charles was supervising my notebook. When he saw the word, he said kindly, but in a voice that seemed to brook no argument, "You're going to tear this page out and recopy it, leaving out the word *concevoir.*" I was a bit obstinate and said to him, "No, I can't see why." "Precisely," said Wolf, "I thought you wouldn't understand, but all the same, you have to do it. The teacher could ask you annoying questions, and the whole class would laugh. You must avoid that." "But," I pursued, "I know that Mary conceived a son, and I don't see anything to laugh about in that." Charles said simply, without a trace of impatience, "You have to do what I'm telling you. I'm going to take your notebook so that you won't have it, in case the teacher asks you for it. I'll give it back to you, and you can recopy the whole thing at home." I wasn't called on in French class, and I recopied the page that afternoon. Charles and I never mentioned the incident again. I spent all the recesses with the boys, but I went home alone or with some girls, because Mama didn't like me to be with boys, but I found their company infinitely preferable, although that did not prevent me from acting silly with the other girls.

Suzanne lived on our street, practically across from us, and she was the one with whom I once caused great distress to my sister Hélène. Although Suzanne was almost our next-door neighbor, Hélène and I had never seen her. We had never been allowed to play with the other children on our street; a real barrier erected by our governess and my mother's instructions separated us from them. But walking home from school was something else entirely; this was not only allowed but even desirable. Suzanne related a thousand stories to me, including stories about us: we were thought to be haughty, my mother was very wealthy; my father was good to the poor but terribly proud; my father was religious, but my mother wasn't. All these stories interested me a little at first but very soon became boring; but Suzanne's superiority in *knowing* such things was obvious to me. I would have liked to impress her, too, a bit, but how? I had just learned what a *cousine germaine* [first cousin] was; up until then I had only known the much less attractive word *cousine*. One day, at the corner of rue Léopold-Robert, in front of the post office, Suzanne and I ran into Hélène. In introducing her to Suzanne, I said nonchalantly, "This is Hélène, my *cousine germaine*." Hélène said nothing, gave me an indignant look that presaged a terrible outburst, and ran home. I left Suzanne rather abruptly and went home feeling very uneasy. Hélène was in tears, saying that I had forfeited the right to be her sister; Mama was very indignant and found that the *gymnasium*'s influence had definitely not been long in coming.

Shortly after that, Suzanne said to me: "I know a man who tips his hat when he says Hello to me." At first I did not understand at all what that meant, because I had never noticed any change; I had not noticed that men perhaps only nodded when they greeted a child but tipped their hats to greet young ladies. When I had really grasped the difference, I explained to Suzanne that gentlemen had been tipping their hats to me for ages; she voiced serious doubts that I undertook to dismiss very quickly by saying in a really loud voice "Good day, Sir" not only to gentlemen I knew but especially to the many more numerous gentlemen I did not know; I accompanied my greeting with an inclination of my head that I judged to be solemn and serious, and hats rose into the air as if by magic. Suzanne and I found this game quite amusing, we forgot our initial rivalry, and we did our best not to leave a single hat on its head. All that came to an abrupt end, because my sister Hélène caught us at our new occupation, and the very day when I counted the most hats was also the day I found my mother waiting for me at home with a stiff lecture; she demonstrated the baseness of my intentions so profoundly that never afterward did I try to obtain greetings with a tip of the hat to which I had no right, except for one single time, twenty years later, when, while riding in London in a splendid, rented open barouche, I started bestowing modest but warm greetings on people to see what would happen, and also to cheer up and shock a bit two very serious lady-friends with whom I was visiting the city.

Suzanne, moreover, the one who lived on our street, left school at the end of a few weeks; Latin was not her forte. So for a while I made my way home alone and almost running, for I was in a hurry to get home and attend to my hobbies, that is to say, above all, reading and sketching. I had a true passion for reading, but I can hardly remember on what I fed it. However, I do remember spending some time choosing books from the school library; it was composed of large adjoining rooms, and a librarian would take the lists we gave him and bring the books. That gave me the impression of a very living machine; I would choose titles from the catalogue on the basis of books I had already read or on the abundant advice of my friends; but one of those, Charles-Henri, used to choose his books by leafing through them and would walk through the whole room and take a book from one shelf or another, weigh it in a way in his hands, look as if he were sniffing it, and decide either to take it or to put it back with a disappointed air. I witnessed this scene several times, and yet it was always new to me and left me with the impression of an intense life, one that could be lived only in the environment of books, a life that drew its *raison d'être* from them and thereby even its continuation. It was probably seeing Charles-Henri in the midst of books that led me to make my reflections on life itself; up until then, I had lived in a way without knowing that I was really living.

Sometimes I spent recess with Charles Wolf and Charles-Henri. Charles-Henri would explain the way writers saw things. That, too, was quite new to me. Up until then I had thought that a thing either was or was not, but I had not realized that there might be different ways of considering it on the human plane; I thought that everything uncertain came to us from the divine plane. When I thought about something and did not succeed in considering it from all angles, or did not understand it, I never wasted much time on it, for I thought that God knew it and that, if we took the trouble to get to know him better, he, for his part, would teach us thereby to know what did not seem very clear to us and that the understanding he would grant us would have but one meaning. A few conversations with Charles-Henri sufficed to overturn this concept.

There was yet another thing concerning life that had been with me perhaps since my earliest childhood. In general my life had been spent either at our home at La Chaux-de-Fonds or at the Waldau at my uncle's. Now, since I was only one person and had only one life, in which, in their turn, my parents or my aunt and uncle took part, I had come to imagine that reality was somehow located there where I was and that, there where I was not, only a life in slow motion existed, a pause in life, an ephemeral kind of life. It seemed hardly believable to me that my father might really live in a place where I was not, although I knew that I could live without him; so I thought about a certain delay or suspension in my father's life while I was at the Waldau. This idea was old, it had been a very long time since I had given it any further thought, but I had not been cured of it. Listening to Charles-Henri, I saw that lives were isolated, like the ways of looking at things, and could touch each other or complement or contradict each other as they pleased. This new world of ideas enchanted me; the number of conquests to make seemed incredible and most desirable. I was going to be Charles' and Charles-Henri's cooperative student: they were very good friends, both of them keen on ideas and discussion, but Charles-Henri had a very clear need to make disciples, and he read so much and knew so well how to explain things that I had, under his direction, departed for unknown lands. I admired everything as a whole, both my friends and their ideas; but at the end of a very few days, a doubt, a true uneasiness, occurred to me: What was God doing in all that? I asked Charles-Henri, who explained very quickly and very nicely that God, on the one hand, devoured strength, while, on the other hand, he replaced, for fools, the powers of reason they lacked. At first I was almost speechless, but almost immediately I made my decision and declared that I would be on the side of the fools. Charles-Henri was very nice and told me that he'd let me have my God without counting me among fools for it. Besides, there was this to consider: every week in class, we were ranked, and we were the three best, but in this order: Charles-Henri was always third, while Charles and I alternated rather regularly as first and second, and Charles-Henri explained to me that my academic standing could serve me as proof that I was no fool. Certainly this was very consoling, but right away anxiety took hold of me, one more profound than the first. Charles-Henri left me my God because of my good grades, or more precisely my good grades prevented him from thinking me a fool. This was horribly troubling. I felt my child's world shaken with great tremors and a new responsibility take hold of me, just as chaos was drawing nigh. While we were in Latin class, Monsieur Rossel was explaining the basic differences between the dative and the ablative; I was feeling the differences shifting and growing worse between Charles-Henri's world and my own. I was letting the dative become a changeable, far-off notion. And, suddenly, I felt responsible: I had to learn to defend God, and right at that same moment this seemed very clear to me: one had to begin at first with the dative and the ablative, we were all still only children, and we had to begin by discerning our responsibilities as children. Those responsibilities were real, and school could teach us those that were immediate. I sensed that I was limiting something within myself by allowing school to play such a preponderant role, but I knew that this solution was somehow necessary, that it was not definitive, and that this waiting did not mean wasted time. I felt myself distancing myself a little from Charles and Charles-Henri, of whom I was very fond; I was lowering myself in their eyes, but it was necessary; and then, our course of studies at school, our reading, gave us enough subjects for common reflection and discussion.

There were three subjects that I very especially liked: Latin, French, and mathematics. I remember that translating my first few sentences from Latin gave me profound joy. It seemed to me that I had received a key that opened a new world and at the same time abolished the incredible space that had separated us from the Romans until then.

A WALKING TOUR IN THE ALPS

When the first summer vacation came, I was very unhappy about it; I didn't like this interruption. School had let out one Friday at four in the afternoon, we had said long good-byes to one another, my friends and I, and we had decided to write to each other. I got home rather later than I should have, but what a surprise I had at finding a state of total confusion at home. My father had decided to leave with Hélène and me at the end of the afternoon to take a walking tour in the mountains. These decisions always had a certain look of abruptness since they could be made only at the last minute, when it was ascertained that there was no patient who needed my father's presence. Since he did not like to change his decisions, my father had gotten into the habit of making them only at the last moment, or rather of not revealing them until the moment he was certain of them. So, off we went; I am not sure who got everything ready; I, like my sister, put on a navy-blue pleated skirt and a grayish-blue flannel shirt, a hideous little blue straw hat that was too tight on my head, and hiking shoes that had belonged to my sister, and then a backpack about which I remember only that it made me rather proud, since it bore a slight resemblance to my father's.

That evening we went as far as Gunten. I have completely forgotten the journey, but I do remember as the first great impression that it was very difficult to walk in hobnailed hiking boots on the smooth stone floor in the entrance hall; I'd have had much better balance on roller skates. It was already fairly dark when we arrived, and, in spite of that, they served us a full supper, in a huge dining room full of little empty tables; these little tables made an impression on me: one felt that they were part of a hotel life in which we were now taking a very tiny part, though we remained isolated, outside it. We were served hors d'oeuvres, this was the first time I had seen anything like it, and, with each little dish, I would politely ask the waitress and my father if it were all right to take some, and I made little piles of the different salads and fish on my plate. I don't remember if it was any good or not, only that it was very astonishing. There was another waitress who brought the next course. My father served himself without saying anything, I watched him and waited, and still he said nothing; suddenly, I cried out, "But Papa, we must tell her that we've already had supper"; then my father explained that the whole thing was all one supper, and that the hors d'oeuvres had been only one course. My bewilderment knew no end, but as for the rest of the meal, it was impossible for me to go on, the hors d'oeuvres had been quite enough.

After the meal, we went for a short while into a parlor and saw the guests of the Hôtel du Lac, those mysterious guests whose traces we had discerned on the little tables. They all seemed to know one another, and, perhaps for the first time, I had the impression of being a foreigner. Up to this point, I had seen foreigners, who had that quality about them, who were not a part of my own world, which was very real, and were probably part of their own world, which for me was unreal. Now everything was transposed; it was I who had not yet gained admission; but surely I would gain it, and this certainty filled me with joy.

My father led us to our room and showed us his adjoining one. My father disappeared, I poured out a flood of words onto Hélène; it seemed to me that I was finally going to find what I had been seeking for so long and that together we would enter into this world we had only just glimpsed and which was not yet the world. But Hélène said all that was boys' ideas, and I sensed the rivalry between the girls' secondary school, represented by my sister, and the *gymnasium*, which I represented. We ended by going to bed, and Hélène opened something that I hadn't noticed until then, or had thought was just a window, and which was a door opening onto a balcony. From my bed, I saw a string of lights that looked like shining pearls all of the same size, strung at regular intervals. My happiness kept me awake, and very softly, quite late, I got up, went out onto the balcony where there was a big armchair, and sat down there. There, I began to reflect on the past few months, and I was filled with joy; and the happier I felt, the more the joy continued to increase in me. The lake, sleepy and completely motionless, with here and there a little fisherman's light, seemed to be of a strangely new beauty. And this necklace of lights at the bottom, which went quite far up and then abruptly stopped someplace for no apparent reason, seemed to me to contrast with the tranquility of the lake. Some stars in the sky were mirrored in the lake. For a long time, I looked at all this that was so new to me, that was outside me and seemed to be

offered to me. I felt myself linked to the hotel and to its unknown life by the chair where I sat. A certain constancy had
vanished from my life; I perceived its disappearance without
regret, it was replaced by a joy so dazzling that in spite of
everything it did not fail to worry me a little: Would there
be room for anything else beside it? At that exact moment
I knew in a very sure way that God would be in my life,
forever more, that my joy was in him, and that there would
be no joy were he not. I knelt on the stone balcony and
thanked God for this tranquil lake, for these lights on the
mountain, for this deep joy. A little later I sat down again
in the armchair; my thoughts calmed down, my happiness
became peaceful. When the night faded into the uniform
gray of approaching dawn, I began to feel definitely cold in
just my nightgown, groped my way back to bed, and fell
asleep at last.

The following days we took some long walks; I didn't
care for so much walking, I got tired fast. And then, Papa
and Hélène could recognize all the mountains, knew the
names of the flowers and villages, while I knew absolutely
nothing and could not even recognize today's steep mountain as the Stockhorn, which yesterday had seemed round
to me. On the first day we got as far as the Grimsel hostel.
Papa, finding me too tired, had me ride in the mail coach
up to the Handegg falls; I was enthusiastic about this slow
ride in a horse-drawn coach. At the summit, I sat down on
a snowbank a few meters from the hostel to wait for my
father and my sister, and as I waited, it seemed to me that
the world of the Alps was also a new world, unknown, immense; it looked very lovely to me and, like the world of
the lake and the night, belonged to God.

When we entered the hostel, there was once again the
battle for equilibrium produced by the cleats of my boots

on the smooth flagstones; we ate at a big *table d'hôte*, and the guests did not form their own private world but rather small, very different groups. This was almost reassuring, like a kind of accommodation or compromise; it was almost as if one could arrive without having really left, without having a destination. Right after supper we went to bed, and again, despite increasing fatigue, I remained awake for a long time. Since that summer at Bellevue I had known nothing more of the night, because they always put us to bed before seven and since, except for the moment reserved for playing Heini with Hélène, I went to sleep immediately. Between the twilight, with the children playing in the street or in the courtyard, and the dawn, my life was empty, there was only sleep, of which I never knew anything. But now, it was night, a very cold night, with stars high in the black cold, snow that was always given life a little by the moon, and a silence quite unlike the silence in Gunten, a snowy, far-off silence. While we were walking during the day, I felt the fatigue of the walk and of those heavy shoes, and also the lack of sleep from the previous night. My thoughts had been dormant, or perhaps simply abridged: they had not gone beyond the end of my feet or the side of the road. Now they had a new burst of life, as if the silence of the night were favorable to them; they jumped about madly, carrying me away in their course; it was somewhat as if I were letting myself be drawn along while following only very imperfectly; the distance between them and me increased from moment to moment, I tried to recapture them, but I knew it was futile. Suddenly I said to myself that God surely would be easier to understand in this night, this wilderness of snow. Everyday temptations, and by that I meant distractions above all, things that got in the way of solitude, would be considerably lessened and prayer could become entirely different. I certainly had no concept of continuity in prayer, but I thought about a greater joy in it; a joy more of comprehension than of pleasure. Since my conversation with Charles-Henri, I had felt it was not enough to say "I believe in God"; one had really to believe, to defend one's faith, to love. In the snows of Grimsel that seemed easy to me; but I knew that this ease had a very different quality during my life at school; I very quickly forgot to think of God and his will. I resolved to keep "the silence and God" within myself as a unity, something I had now understood. And again, joy kept me awake for a long time; no sound could be heard, it seemed to me that I had never before taken part in so absolute a silence. Finally, though, it got the better of me and sent me off to sleep.

My father woke us at dawn the next day; and in the cold and fog we started on our way very early. First we went down to Gletsch; slowly the mist dissipated, the snow disappeared, and, when we arrived at Gletsch, a summer morning had broken, radiant with sunshine. To my great amazement my father offered us for the second time a full-course breakfast; this was indeed the only time in my life I've eaten breakfast twice in the same morning. That day our hike was a very long one, because we were going over the Furka to Hospenthal; I was tired and dejected, the day was very different from the night. Hélène and Papa were alert; only as evening began to fall did they also feel tired. In front of the hotel where we stayed that night, a hotel in the center of the village, there was a bench where we spent a long moment before supper, watching people go by and witnessing a small part of the life of the villagers. They went to the fountain, carried baskets, and formed little groups to exchange news. Suddenly my father began to look concerned about what they were saying and finally went to join them: when he came back, he seemed worried, but it did not last. However,

I asked him what was wrong. He said, "They are talking about the war." The war? To me, wars were only part of the history books; I did not at all see what this July in 1914 could have to do with my schoolbooks. That evening, there was no night, the forty kilometers we had covered got the better of me.

The next morning we went up the Gotthard; I remember only a long, painful climb and a cabin where we drank goat's milk; my father found it delicious. As for me, I detested it; since my father took such genuine delight in giving us some at every opportunity, I could never tell him how I had to overcome myself in order to swallow this lukewarm, cloying, strong-smelling stuff. At noon we had a picnic, and then my father questioned me at length about school. I told him about it, with the very clear impression that I was being understood. It seemed to me that my father, in his youth, had been both Charles-Henri and me in turn; he knew our problems, he had lived them, but only later. Until then, he had not yet grasped to what degree we had already been deeply shaken.

Up until that time, the rapport between my father and me had been more or less tacit. I well knew that in him I had an understanding friend; he had a way all his own of standing up for me at home: it consisted primarily in letting me do as I pleased, in clearing away obstacles rather than in encouraging me. He never imposed his point of view on me, he asked me my own and voiced his objections when he did not agree; but all that passed for conversation between the two of us always had the nature of something improvised and never a defined character. It resembled a series of beginnings, mysteriously linked together but showing no clear outlines; and yet, they did not simply follow upon each other; a unique tendency could be recognized, but also a real fear of weighing down something that might not yet have the strength to bear it. I think I have met few people with as pronounced a respect for the individual personality as my father had.

The downhill side of the Gotthard that took us to Andermatt was the happiest part of the hike for me. Having slept was obviously good for walking, but also I felt united to my father in a new way, somewhat as if we had discovered a common past that went infinitely farther back than my eleven-and-one-half years.

Again, that evening, there were the cleats of my shoes on the infinitely smooth flagstones in the hotel where we stayed the night. The guests were all tourists in odd-looking getups; they formed among themselves something that somewhat resembled the groups of villagers of the day before; but they gesticulated more, they exchanged newspapers and appeared to be excited. Very soon a telegram was delivered to my father; the baby was very ill, and my mother was worried about the threat of war. At that moment, my father explained something to us that appeared to me to be curious: the twofold bad news affected my mother more than it would have if it had really been separated; that is, my mother was much more afraid of war because the baby was sick, and the baby's illness terrified her particularly because she associated it with the threat of war. I had some difficulty grasping the mechanism of this addition that changed into multiplication. Only then did I ask my father if war could really happen again, which he immediately affirmed. The next morning my father told us as we were leaving that the baby's condition was better, but that he had promised my mother that we would go back that very evening; we would just walk for a few hours early in the morning, we would see the "Devil's Bridge" that we already knew very well from a picture on a playing-card at home. I was somewhat disappointed with the "Devil's Bridge", for it did not seem to me to be at all deserving of this terrifying name. Toward the end of the morning we took the boat at Flüelen and went on as far as Lucerne; I found that the lake looked too much like a geography map, it was too complicated: there was a little competition of who knew the most geographical and historical details, my sister or my father. In contrast, Lucerne delighted me; first my father bought each of us a real two-bladed penknife with the lion of Lucerne on it; then we went to view the actual stone lion as well as the bridge with the pictures. And a large sun shone over the whole city; it looked new and sparkling. Then my father put us on the train for Bern, while he took another; the journey from Lucerne to Bern seemed interminable to me, and the whole landscape looked infinitely flat after all the mountains that had surrounded us. That evening at the Waldau they told us the baby was all well, and no one spoke of the war but rather of the national exposition.

THE BEGINNING OF THE WAR

The first time we went to see the exposition, it was with my father who had come from La Chaux-de-Fonds to see it and took us along. The big impression it made on me was produced by a hall reserved for heliotherapy, where photographs of tuberculous lesions and children with scrofula were lined up chronologically. The lesions disappeared as if by magic in the sunlight, and the sickly children grew chubby and overflowing with health. There were curved, emaciated backs, you could count every vertebra as if on a skeleton; they straightened out, and the anatomy of the vertebrae disappeared beneath the sinews of strengthened musculature; horribly thin arms that had been covered with fistulae became plump arms on which you could hardly discern the scars. There were photographs that showed a snow-covered landscape—Leysin in winter—and even of the doctor who had accomplished these miracles with the help of the sun, whose secret he had uncovered: Doctor Rollier. When my father saw that I could barely tear myself away from all these pictures of healing and the easily understood graphs that accompanied them, he said to me: "That's fine. You can stay here and take your first lesson in medicine." When he came back to get me, he had visited some other pavilions with Hélène, and he offered us a cheese ramekin or some cider; it was hard to choose, so one of us got the drink and the other one got the ramekin, and we shared.

Cousin Marianne was there for several days with her elderly father, my uncle Gustave, and her two sons, who were about Hélène's and my age. It was hard for me to believe that Cousin Marianne was their mother, because she treated them rather like our governess treated us, that is, she asked them very specific questions about the use of their time, as if she were conducting an inspection. One day she took us all to the exposition; on arriving at the Rollier pavilion, she was shocked that I found it interesting, forbade me to stop, and in the evening intervened with my aunt about having the indecency of all that nudity explained to me. I understood nothing of that, but I had already had a good enough look at the pictures to understand them thoroughly, and the impression of the power of medicine had been so deeply engraved that giving up the photographs had become a matter of absolute indifference. Little did I know that my next contact with Leysin would last two years and would bring me to experience myself both the sun and Doctor Rollier and his renowned beds.

We returned to the exposition once more, with our governess. Generous afternoon snacks, the merry-go-round, and Russian swing each provided a part of our joy. When we returned to the Waldau, war was declared. The next morning I accompanied Uncle Gustave to the station; he was going back to Givrins. I can still see the intense anger that shook him all of a sudden; he said to me, almost more with his body trembling with emotion than with his voice, which he was working hard to control but which escaped as if in little bursts that broke off again so as to continue all the louder: "They are all Boches, all those Bernese, all those people who speak German; I've got to hurry back home, where they speak a free language, where people understand each other. Oh, you don't have to tell them: they are all Boches!" And that word "Boches" nearly strangled him, he could barely manage to spit it out and would have had even less success in stifling it. Once he was in the train, he said once again, through the open window, "You don't have to tell them, but don't forget it." As the train pulled away, he kept making signs with his hand and his hat, as if his hand and his hat were repeating in a clearly perceptible if mute language: "The Boches! The Boches! The Boches!" I returned alone in the carriage that had been waiting for the train's departure: the driver ran an errand on the way. All along the road I repeated very softly: The Boches. I knew that the Boches were really my enemies, but I hadn't succeeded in imagining that my aunt and uncle were a part of these enemies. There was a multitude of mysteries there. The driver showed the profit from his errand: two big cases of peaches that couldn't be sent to their destination, Germany, because the border was closed. It was really difficult to picture how a border could be shut, seeing that a border was more or less a line drawn in the air or marked out by a river. Aunt Jeanne said: "You can eat as many peaches as you want, they're incredibly cheap." Up till now, peaches had been kept exclusively for the dessert of the adults, who peeled them, sliced them, put sugar on them, and finally ate them with great ceremony while we swallowed our whortle-berries or raspberries, with permission that only held good at the Waldau to line them up first according to size, to divide them into classes. And now, the first effect of the war was that we could eat peaches, even between meals. It didn't make sense, and it bore no comparison to what the history books had not only led us to believe but also to learn. And behind all that lay this mystery of Uncle Gustave's departure, which one wasn't supposed to forget.

The first Sunday of the war my parents came together to the Waldau, but only to spend the day. My mother explained that perhaps at the end of the vacation we might not go back to La Chaux-de-Fonds, because—we had to be sure to see things in their overall importance—if Switzerland abandoned its neutrality, La Chaux-de-Fonds would be much more vulnerable than Bern, being very much at the perimeter, near the border. Then Mama said each must do his duty during the war and that, if we wished, we could ask Aunt Jeanne to buy some yarn for us, and Mama would pay her for it. Great! I knitted ever so much during those few weeks at the Waldau; I hardly took walks anymore without knitting in my hands; I knitted so much that when I returned to school—how I would have hated not being able to return to school with my friends—I turned over to my mother a bill on Aunt Jeanne's behalf for more than a hundred francs for yarn. That gave her quite a shock and earned me a stiff lecture; I believe that, on an average, I knitted a sock and a mitten per day.

There were soldiers quartered in the stable at the Waldau, and the lieutenant who commanded them, Lieutenant Guye de Neuchâtel, invited us to share in the soldiers' *spatz*;[1] we went many times, Hélène and I, and Willy in his little cart. One day we went to the Allmend to see the swearing in and the general; whenever you went into town you had to cross the Allmend anyway; it was often used as a drill-field for the soldiers, especially the cavalry, and I liked hearing the very different rhythms of the trot and the gallop. I also had a real weakness for military music: it almost always made a sort of heroic impression on me and urged me to desire earnestly to give my life for something good.

I think it was during that summer that we once had permission to go on the Gurten; this walk represented an event for us, and the plans for it had been put off several times. Then one day the governess, Hélène, and I set out. Right at the beginning of the Allmend, we met Mademoiselle Koenig, my uncle's secretary, who was on her way back to the Waldau. Hélène said to her: "Mademoiselle, we're going quickly to the Gurten." The word "quickly" left me almost speechless. I felt that it both absolutely denied the importance of our hike and at the same time was full of extreme dignity. Hélène was thereby elevated in my eyes: what an incredible stroke of inspiration she had had; she had minimized our pleasure, she had aligned herself with the grownups! In my impulse of admiration, I immediately told her what an impression she had made on me. But Hélène did not find the word "quickly" the least bit inappropriate, while I found that it

---

[1] The "*spatz*" is the Swiss soldier's noon meal. It includes a piece of meat (= *Spatz*)—ED.

stripped our trip in advance of everything that might have been special and unique; the trip, by that one, single word seemed bereft of all the thought and preparations we had devoted to it and also of the memories it would have left us. In fact, that word "quickly" absorbed my whole memory of it.

When we returned to school, the first morning was full of the unexpected. Several of our teachers had been called up, and a period of rapid changes commenced for us; for Latin, we had a large number of more or less capable substitutes. The student Bickel, who was later to become a celebrated internist in Geneva, took his job so seriously that we felt almost obliged to resist him whenever we could. One day he told us that, instead of making so much noise at recess, we would do infinitely better to review our lessons. As luck would have it, for the next lesson we had to read a selection whose first words were: "*Asinus leonis pelle indutus* [an ass clothed in a lion's pelt]". With me standing in the middle of about a dozen of the boys, flanked by Charles and Charles-Henri, we went over the lesson in loud voices in the schoolyard, squeezed close together in a line. Bickel was on duty. We contrived to get to the word "*asinus*" each time he passed by us, and, by common agreement, we would all yell "*asinus*" and then go on in a more discreet fashion and then resume with all our strength. Candidate Bickel did not extend his experiments on us unwilling guinea-pigs for very long. For a short while we had the rabbi as our Latin teacher; he was very nearsighted, and we, except for the numerous Jews[2] in our class, used to make more noise than we ordinarily did. As for me, I felt rather sorry for him, since he

[2] The original has "*dont les Juifs*"; the last sentence in the paragraph suggests it should read "*sauf les Juifs*" [except for the Jews]—ED.

was too myopic to hold his own with such a large crowd of young savages as we were. I really would have liked to be Jewish so as to have refrained as well, alas!

In spite of it all, we made progress; and for some subjects our teachers didn't change at all.

We had religion class once a week. These lessons had a peculiar character about them, and I think they were what increased my uneasiness about religion. It is not easy for me to be absolutely precise about my situation at that particular time from a confessional point of view; I believe I already had a kind of absolute certainty that I was on the wrong track. I prayed a quick "Our Father" every day, before I got up, and once again in the evening; then I was silent. I thought a great deal about God and his truth; I was fully convinced that he guided our lives, and equally convinced that he expected something from us, but I didn't know what that something might be; in any case, I knew it was something "other". Pastor Moll was the one who gave us the religion lessons, whose subject, throughout the entire first year, was the Reformation, or, rather, the Reformers. He would present a biographical sketch, situate the man in his epoch, and elicit the consequences; he didn't indulge in anti-Catholic polemics, or at least very little. I remember nothing from the lessons before summer vacation. One of the first lessons after we returned had to do with Luther's relationship with his father; there was a letter in it where the father was explaining to his son the difference between "however" and "nevertheless"; from that we learned with what care Luther had been brought up; they let nothing escape him, and they prepared him to acquire all the logic he would later need to formulate his Theses. At that point, I was whispering something to the student sitting next to me; Monsieur Moll, who was short, meek, potbellied, and wore ill-fitting false teeth, asked me what was going on. I said aloud what I had been whispering: "If the Reformation amounts to the difference between a 'however' and a 'nevertheless', I can't see much use in it." Monsieur Moll did not scold me, but he didn't give me any special explanation either. However, at the end of the lesson, which always took place between eleven in the morning and noon, I accompanied him home. I don't know whether it was his idea or my own. He asked me to put my questions to him directly and in private, because otherwise people might think I was moving away from religion. From that day on, I accompanied him every week. He was always very nice, but his answers never satisfied me. We rarely talked about the Reformation, almost always about the Gospel; I always claimed that the verses meant something else and especially something more than what he explained to me. Often he interrupted me, saying: "That's Catholic: Where did you get that? Who's putting these ideas into your head?" Then I defended myself: I hadn't been talking to anybody about my concerns, and I didn't know any Catholics. Besides, I don't think I had any special attraction at all at that time to Catholicism, with which I wasn't familiar. But I had been reading the Bible a lot, I loved God and I wanted to serve him, and I thought the Gospel was a true path; it seemed to me that all our pastors made it too narrow. The road on which I accompanied Monsieur Moll to his house was not very long, hardly ten minutes' walk; afterward I took to my heels so they wouldn't notice I was late. One day, however, as the soup was being served, Mama asked, in front of the whole family: "Why do you always walk Monsieur Moll home? What can you possibly talk about?" Before I had recovered from my horror—for it was horror, I was very attached to my secret—Papa said: "Just things, I suppose." And nobody ever spoke to me about it again. I have always been grateful to my father for this answer, by which he got me out of this difficulty and allowed me not to talk about something so close to my heart. I had to be able to keep silent about my uncertainty, my deeply felt poverty, and all those futile words would probably have stifled it. It was necessary that it remain alive.

On Sundays I always still went to Sunday school at the chapel, but I also went to catechism class at the Protestant church; catechism was arranged something like Sunday school; monitors drilled small groups in the lesson for the day, but all of it was, or at least was supposed to be, adapted to our age groups. I vastly preferred it to the religion classes. Between the two sessions there was still time to go to church, but Mama hated for me to go, for fear of overdoing things. When my father went to church, a rather rare occurrence, he took Hélène and me with him, because he loved his daughters very much. Besides, we too enjoyed very much going out with him, and in that time of war, we were especially proud that all the soldiers we met had to salute him. As for me, I was literally enchanted by it, for it seemed to me to recognize a homage that was personally due him. I loved for people to respect him, and I loved even more for people to love him, and when I met country people on the stairs on their way into or out of his consulting room and they asked me if I were the doctor's little girl, I was delighted then to hear them recount how much they loved him and all the good he had done them. Sometimes the country people would give me twenty centimes, and one time even a franc. I upset my mother by taking everything. To teach me to forego this habit of accepting, Mama never let me keep any of what I received, but still I never succeeded in saying No.

I think it was around this time that my father decided to give us pocket money. He let us choose between fifteen centimes a week and sixty centimes a month; right away, I decided on fifteen centimes a week. "Why?" asked my father. "Because most months have four and a half weeks." Whereupon my father offered sixty-five centimes a month, which was then what I chose. We had to keep strict accounts, and we received our allowance only when we presented our report; but it was understood, nevertheless, that we were free to spend our money as we pleased, and my father never remarked on the usefulness or the uselessness of our expenditures. Alas, this was the only period in my life when I had any order in my accounts and really kept them. The books in the Nelson Collection cost ninety centimes; so I could buy two of them every three months;[3] this I did quite regularly for a fairly long time.

Hélène had lent me her writing table, and I had become so used to this loan that I would have been more than a little indignant at having to give it back. It was a problem only at times of great disputes, which had become very rare, for I did everything in my power to avoid them, I suppose especially because I felt very vulnerable; I lived so peacefully among my friends at school that I had no desire to leave that atmosphere. And, on the other hand, the religion lessons and God required peaceful reflection. I felt I was not to withdraw from it, and that is why, at the back of a drawer in the writing table, I hid a thick notebook bound in black oilcloth—I had without a scruple snatched it from its scholarly destination—which had become my journal. Every day I wrote long pages in it, trying primarily to sort out what God wanted from what those around me wanted.

---

[3] The manuscript has "every three weeks", obviously an error—ED.

I think it would be just as difficult for me today as it was then to take stock of my situation; I had the clear feeling that something was wrong, but nothing happened to show me where that "wrong" lay. For a long time I wrote down everything I heard about God, and I tried to sketch a sort of picture of God, with commentary; then I made a comparison but arrived at nothing. Then I chose another approach: I wrote down what there was to be done, set it alongside what I was actually doing, and tried to find a kind of balance between the two. After that I wrote down what my mother said about God and what she did. And I asked them questions, both my mother and God, and I worked diligently to find answers. All that turned out very badly, because one day I forgot to put the notebook away; it was the second notebook, it was almost filled; my mother found it, read it, looked for the other one, read it too, and bitterly reproached me: my ingratitude was wicked, she had never seen anything of the sort. Since I myself had the very clear impression that none of this would lead to anything, and that I did not possess the key to the mystery, I sadly hid my notebooks away in another drawer, and a few days afterward I burned them in the big black furnace in the kitchen. I later regretted it, because, even so, writing had helped me, if not to find, at least to have the feeling that I was seeking, that I was trying not to turn my back on the problems that presented themselves.

The war continued; we hardly noticed the seriousness of it; we did not always read the newspapers, and at school we spent our recess discussing ideas. I was very far from following the boys in their reasoning; they were much stronger in that than I; and even if by chance I tried to make an effort and took up some little book of philosophy, I put it down again very quickly. I had a practical mind; I needed something to lean on that could be converted into reality. But I was so happy at school that I did not trouble myself at all over this lack of a speculative mind. At home, I was less happy than before the business about the journal, I experienced a sort of uneasiness, constraint. Before, I had merely had the impression that I did not understand very well—but I was inwardly certain that that would sort itself out in the end—and now I felt misunderstood, which made a big difference and, it seemed to me, was never to be sorted out. There were very few girls at the *gymnasium*; one day Esther, who was in the last class, came to find me and to tell me that a group of Christian girls at the *gymnasium* was being formed in which girls from the secondary school were also admitted. They had thought that, since I was the youngest, I would give the first talk. The subject was up to me. I accepted; obviously I was very proud to have been chosen but also deeply puzzled. I racked my brains over it for several days. I had already fallen into that horrible habit, which I've never overcome, of not making up my mind to work until the last moment, when there was really no way to do anything else. We always had four to six weeks to complete compositions; I never wrote them until the last day, or the last few days if they needed to be somewhat longer, despite the pleasure I usually found in receiving a new subject. Obviously I gave it quite a bit of thought during the time I waited, but it was a long way from thinking it over to writing it out, and the "hatching" period was always painful. For the talk, I found it impossible to stop at one subject. Finally, the night before I was slated to give the talk, I decided on a title. Since I was not really timid, I was going to go all the way. The subject was: silence and God. I do not remember what it was like, but I was twelve years old that day, and, in a certain way, the world was open to silence. After the talk—about a dozen girls attended—a lengthy discussion ensued. Girls' discussions were quite different from boys'; they voiced loads of doubts but did not know how to explain them; they said No, they didn't know why, or else Yes, and that seemed extraordinarily strange. Then they asked me to give a series of talks, I think three or four. One was called "The Spirit of God"; I've forgotten the titles of the others. Each time, there were more girls. Mama wasn't pleased and said: "They're adulating you." I had to get the dictionary to see what adulate meant. Once my talks were over, I never went back to the group; I don't think they met very often after that. Besides, inasmuch as I felt I belonged to my class of boys, so much the less did I feel anything much in common with the girls at the *gymnasium*.

This conflict with Mama had been getting worse in recent years. But only recently it had really worried me, if only by fits and starts. I would forget about it for entire days, and, on the days when it did bother me, it was not without letup. I would have loved to make it go away. When there was some big, new fuss, Mama would have me come to the blue room that was her little private sitting room. We never went in there unless summoned. The carpet was blue and the furniture was upholstered in a velvet of the same blue; the furniture was light, flecked maple. On the round table there was a candy dish full of pralines. The room would have seemed delightful to me if it had not been associated, as far as I was concerned, with all or almost all of my memories of sharp scoldings. Sometimes, at the end of a particularly serious reprimand, Mama would say that scolding me wasn't enough since that was not enough to change my character; I had to start a new life. Mama would then forget my past; as for me, I would have to make a special effort to show that

I had really changed. I was to read less, I was to play more with my brothers and sister, I was not to dawdle on the way home from school anymore, I was not to tear my stockings or my smocks, I was not to join the boys at recess (that I never promised), and, most important, I was to be less deceitful. One day, with great courage, I asked my mother in what ways I had been deceitful. Mama said: "One never knows of whom you are thinking, and you have far too little to say; it's ghastly, one could spend hours with you without your opening your mouth." I remember that on two occasions, in the course of such conversations, Mama asked me point-blank what I was thinking about, and both times it turned out very badly. The first time, I said: "About God." Mama declared that that was absurd; it was preposterous. The other time, I answered, "About you, Mama." With Mama insisting and me not wanting to be deceitful and making a desperate effort to be precise and truthful, I explained my entire thought: I thought that Mama was depriving herself of the chance to be herself, because she was always afraid of "what other people would say"; this was always her supreme argument: What would Uncle, or Monsieur So-and-So, or Madame What's-Her-Name say if they found out? I was sure that she ought to be saying: What does God say and not what would such and such a person say. Mama said that someone was putting me up to this (but who, then?) and that I would never change my life this way. As for me, I much preferred stiff scoldings to these conversations aimed at a new life that I knew would not be achieved. And then, after giving me a good reprimand, Mama was relieved, while after these conversations full of proposals, she would wait for something that didn't happen, and the disappointment would irritate her. I knew that Mama really suffered from all of that, I felt it without

managing to do anything to bring about a change. Once
when I was alone with Papa, I asked him, just like a big
girl, what he thought about it. He said only, "It's not your
fault": thereupon, in one second, I became once again a little girl who was not at all unhappy.

At school, I liked all subjects, all except one: cinema.
There was a compulsory presentation every Wednesday, I
think from ten to twelve; I didn't like that. There was always an instructional part and an entertainment part; the
latter generally seemed stupid, and, in the former, I was
bored watching herds of cattle in the fields being metamor-
phosed until they became corned beef that excited parents
ate with their offspring while giving the poor child explanations about canned meat and table manners. These explanations came out of their mouths in little streams of letters,
and for the little stream to be clearly visible, they had to
speak in profile; it looked humorless and unnatural. Once
it was corned beef, once it was tuna fish, once by chance
it was soap that foamed, and, in the bath, the little black
children (to whom they had probably neglected to give the
right directions), took on a lighter shade until they changed
from dirty urchins to children exhibiting, to my mind, an
exaggerated cleanliness.

There was something that happened one Sunday that perhaps contributed toward giving me forever a certain dislike
of the cinema. Willy and I were playing by ourselves in the
playroom. It was pouring rain, and we were quite happy to
amuse ourselves quietly, when suddenly my father came and
told us that panoramas had evolved into movies. Sometimes
my father had taken us to see panoramas; you went into a
big room, you sat on a high stool and looked through a little
glassy hole to see a landscape in Africa or Palestine; when
you had looked at it all you wanted to, you moved on to

the next high stool—there were about ten of them. I had never found that especially entertaining. Now, then, it was the cinema; they showed entire stories there, and my father invited us to go with him. So we went there with him, it was very close to our house. When we got there, two guys were fighting in the baggage-car of a train that was crossing a landscape with unheard-of speed, and when one of the combatants was down, the other put him into a barrel, nailed on the lid, and sat down on top of it with a perfectly innocent appearance. A moment later—I don't remember if it was in the same story—a gentleman was talking on the telephone in his office when a man came and chloroformed him by holding a pad over his face. At that very moment, my father told us to shut our eyes and keep them shut; this I did. Willy confessed to me later that he had only blinked his eyes, because he was determined not to miss anything of this exciting spectacle. When the first intermission came, we left with our father, in front of people astonished to see us leaving. When we got home, my father told us that someone had invited him to this performance saying that it was also for children; he was indignant and made a big fuss about it, fearing that the cinema might become a bad influence. After that, it was four or five years before I saw another movie; my father's indignation had been so great that I couldn't forget it.

On top of that, I didn't like the theater much either, and I'd only been there once or twice. The first time, invited by Monsieur Charcot who had just returned from the Pole and who was giving a lecture at the theater with lantern-slides, I thought that was what the theater was. I was thrilled with the penguins, but I scarcely understood the rest. I had too little imagination to give the words their proper meanings; I was quite willing to believe that icebergs were dangerous, because Monsieur Charcot, who must really know, said so, but I did not succeed in giving the least degree of reality to the aspect of this danger.

THE SECOND YEAR
OF THE *PROGYMNASIUM*

The second year of the *progymnasium* began in 1915 and differed only in very few things from the first. We translated "De bello Gallico" [Caesar's Gallic Wars] and the "De viris illustribus urbis Romæ" [Illustrious Romans]: neither of them was terribly thrilling; but one day we translated a very short chapter from one epistle of Saint Paul, and it really seemed to me that again a world, whose door was Latin, was opening.

We had changed pastors in the religion classes; it was now Monsieur Junod who gave them to us. I do not remember the subject matter; perhaps there wasn't even any specific subject, unless it was something like the Christian virtues, because I remember that we always left these lessons with a burning desire, no doubt sincere at that moment, to want to be better people. I made some serious decisions; this time, really, everything would change; but from the decision to its practical realization was too large a step; I was hardly taking it, since the next lesson led to the same irrevocable resolution to change everything that could be changed.

Monsieur Junod was a good friend; I also walked with him part of the way home from school, but never all the way to his house, since he lived rather far away. He had seven children, three of whom were sons; two of them were twins and were in our same class, and the third was one grade behind us, but he had religion class at the same time we did. It was from him that I received my first love letter. He had it passed to me—and it contained a serious proposal of marriage—during one of his father's lessons. I nearly choked with indignation when I read it—not because of the marriage proposal; why not, after all?—but because he had written it during religion class, which was for me the finest hour in the school; and yet, I read the note during that same lesson, and my respect for that lesson did not make me put off this untimely reading until later.

Monsieur Junod's children were well known for their obvious lack of good behavior; often, on an afternoon off, I would meet one of them who would say to me: "Don't tell anyone you saw me, because Papa went out and locked me up before he left; I escaped out the window; now it's only a question of getting back before Papa or Mama notices it."

Monsieur Junod, one day, had me come to his house; I don't remember why anymore. Right away I went to the kitchen, where Madame Junod, whom I was seeing for the first time, was ironing her husband's white crocheted cotton ties and a pile of handkerchiefs. I had never seen so many handkerchiefs. With dignity, she showed me how full of holes they were; they were really in tatters; several weren't even square anymore because a good portion of them was missing. I dared to ask her if she didn't want to mend them; she explained that, since she was without a maid and had such a large family, it wasn't possible for her both to iron them and to mend them. That seemed quite obvious to me; however, upon reflection, I asked her if she couldn't just mend them at one wash and then iron them at the next.

No, that couldn't be done either; and she said the only thing she could do was to buy more, but that was too expensive for so many children. I furtively slipped my handkerchief in among the others, I don't even know if it was clean, but I thought that Madame Junod would be really happy suddenly to iron a whole handkerchief, a handkerchief that would, as if by chance, have resisted destruction.

Then I went to see Monsieur Junod, in a little office with a large desk and many photographs from the missions: one of his brothers was a missionary in Africa. How tempting that looked! I asked Monsieur Junod if it wouldn't be much better if pastors didn't get married. He told me, rather seriously, that in his own case it would have been better, because he had too many worries with his big, unruly family, but that other pastors who had no or few children were quite happy once married. I insisted, "But priests don't get married." He answered, "No, but they commit sins." I didn't understand that at all. In the first place, I said, "We are all sinners." He: "Of course, but priests sin with women, and that's very bad." I gave up trying to understand, but really I did not believe that priestly celibacy was equivalent to a sin, whatever it might be. Deep down, and in spite of Monsieur Junod, from then on I remained persuaded that priestly celibacy was absolutely justified. The torn handkerchiefs of the Junod children remained, somehow, as an undeniable proof of that.

From that day on, the Junod children were particularly dear to me. I still knew only the sons, and I also wanted to see the daughters; but that was to come about only later. Samuel, one of my schoolmates, had a real talent for drawing; he did portraits of children and cats that were very funny. After my visit with his father, I looked at his work with a rather heavy conscience: Wasn't it a bit like murder to have had the idea that it would have been preferable if he had not been born?

At this time, in the first class of the *progymnasium* there was a girl named Lilly Fetterlé; she was very sentimental, blonde, and quite dainty. I don't know exactly why her parents had decided it would be good to have her taught Latin, because she certainly wasn't gifted along that line. She stayed at this school only a few months; she was truly afraid of boys, finding them all coarse and disagreeable. It is true that the boys in her class seemed to me quite different from the ones in mine. But this Lilly had a real knack for inventing secret writing, in code or otherwise, and it became a veritable passion. At almost every recess we traded encrypted notes that of course contained no real secrets, but it was really exciting to decipher them. I'm afraid—and I see scarcely any other possibility—that we wrote and read our lucubrations during classes. That lasted only a few weeks, because one fine morning Lilly had left school. I saw her again sometimes at her mother's, who, later on, gave me embroidery lessons.

All except one of the girls who had been in my class could not keep up with the curriculum, and now that the class had also been purged of a good number of boys, we had become what is known as a good group, and I think we really worked well together: in any case, we all loved both school and recess.

During summer vacations at the Waldau, we all helped a great deal with the haymaking, which consisted, for Hélène and me, mostly of climbing each evening onto the wagons piled high with hay and riding back to the barn on them. Now there were more patients than formerly who helped in the fields, because due to the rationing brought on by the war, they had stopped serving café-au-lait at teatime to patients who did no work, and many patients, even private ones, preferred to work and have coffee rather than see an interminable afternoon ahead of them that would no longer be cut short by a tea that was, if not copious, at least distracting.

When the harvest was in, there was always a harvest celebration at the Waldau. It brought together all the available personnel and all the patients who were capable of being withdrawn from strict supervision. Still, on this occasion, there were always a few who took advantage of the darkness and the relaxed supervision to escape. Generally, at the end of a few days, everyone was back in place again, some having returned of their own accord, not having been able to enjoy their freedom as much as they had thought, others having been brought back by their families or by not very fierce policemen. I was extremely fond of the harvest festival. In a large garden lit by Japanese lanterns there would be a supper invariably composed of sausage and potato salad. Then they danced in a big hall and in the garden, with anyone at all, as if staff, patients, and visitors were all one big family; generally the orchestra consisted of a few accordions. To me, it was very pretty, and it always had quite a few surprises. The festival closed with big fireworks in the garden.

All the celebrations at the Waldau had a character that was very warm as well as naturally rather special. At home, on the contrary, it was a little as if you left feeling disappointed. Anticipation was always the greatest joy; sometimes it really seemed to me that that was my own fault; other times I felt that, on the contrary, no effort on my part could have brought me to understand what remained hidden and what was, in the final analysis, the very mystery of the celebration itself. I would, however, console myself: perhaps even exaggerate to myself a joy, so as to have something in hand after all. That year the baby kept reaching his tiny fingers close to the candles on the Christmas tree; he did it with a greedy little look and, at the last moment, pulled his finger back with a little pout.

It was that winter, I think, that the Salvation Army organized a big religious mission at La Chaux-de-Fonds. Its director, Colonel Peyron, was being treated by my father and was staying at the clinic; he left it only in the evenings to go to what were called the "revival meetings". Out of politeness my parents attended the first meeting, which took place in a very small room. There were only a few people present; in the first prayer, the Colonel asked God to grant that for the last meeting, one week later, the big State church might be too small to hold those who would wish to attend. His prayer was answered. My parents also attended again, but my father was very embarrassed because, in the middle of his sermon, the Colonel explained that it was thanks to my father's skill that he had managed to make this mission, and in his final prayer he asked God in the crowded church to bless Doctor von Speyr and his family. In the middle of that week, the Colonel came to have supper at our house. After the meal, when he was alone with my parents in the blue room, he knelt down on the floor—my parents had to do the same too—and offered a long prayer that ended just in time to allow them all to get up before the chambermaid came in with the coffee. My mother, who could hear her steps approaching down the long corridor, was trembling for fear she would arrive before the ceremony had ended. Besides, my mother was rather worked up by the two meetings she had attended and moved by the confessions she had heard. One or two Salvationists had spoken of their lives of sin that had been succeeded by a definitive conversion, and then they had invited those attending to come and sit on the penitents' bench and publicly and in detail confess their sins, so that they, too, might be converted.

My parents' accounts of these meetings did not leave me indifferent. I asked to go to one of the afternoon meetings; I was very sure I would never get permission to go to one of the evening ones, so I didn't even try. Since my earliest childhood, as far as I can remember, I never begged for anything desirable when I thought I might be refused; this kind of lack of obstinacy, whether reasonable or a sign of weakness, has been with me all my life. I still give up all too quickly whatever desire I may have to "have my own way". This time, at least, permission was granted for me to attend the afternoon meeting. My mother, however, placed one condition on it; she required my solemn promise that I would not go to sit on the penitents' bench; I promised I wouldn't. The part of town where the meeting was to take place was a rather bad neighborhood, I didn't know it well; for fear of arriving too late, I left so early that for a long time I wandered in the nearby streets where it almost seemed to me the people looked like they were from some other country. Finally, I went into the designated house; the hallways smelled musty; it was cold. In the small room a black cast-iron stove was making a lot of noise but seemed to be using up all its energy that way and didn't have any strength to heat the room. There were few people there, one or two really seedy-looking men, a few women without any hats on, no children—I was the only one. In the front, a smiling young Salvationist was urging people to take their places, but we were all already sitting down; she must have thought we looked a bit scared, for she was visibly trying to reassure us, to put us at our ease. I was not nervous but somehow a little disconcerted; I knew that I was really expecting something, but I also knew, already, that I would be disappointed. Two or three more Salvationists came in and began to sing hymns, standing and facing us; I knew the hymns; they were the same ones we sang in Sunday school, but between the verses a chorus had been inserted, the same refrain for all the different songs: "Glory to God, to God, Glory to God." Then they made a welcoming speech; our presence here meant that we had taken the first step; the remaining steps would be easy, because we were now from henceforth servants of God just like the Salvationists themselves, and perhaps one or another of us would receive a genuine call too. Then they explained to us how wicked we were, that is to say, rather, how wicked we had been, because the very fact that we were sitting there showed the beginning of the new life that would leave all sin behind; and then—at last!—we were invited to sit on the penitents' bench; one of the Salvationists would do so first, to speak to us about his past life and to show us how it had to be done; then it would be our turn. I had a certain anxiety about what would happen, but what I heard next left me rather indifferent; suddenly, I knew very clearly that that was not the way to confess one's sins. I would have been quite incapable of saying what was wrong or what would have to be changed in order to make it right, but I felt both offended and attracted; not for a second was I tempted to sit on the celebrated bench; for once it was not difficult to keep my promise. I remember the drunkard who kept repeating, "Oh, what I've drunk, what I've drunk!" There was a triumph in his voice, and the triumph did not seem to me at all related to his conversion but rather had to do with his capacity to drink. Between the confessions, and there were three or four of them, there were prayers of thanksgiving for those who had finally had the courage to break with their past lives, hymns and exhortations that were as pressing as they were enticing to please come at last to confess their sin, not to miss such a golden opportunity.

I am not too sure how or why, when the ceremony was over, I found myself with the drunkard in the kitchen, drinking sugary tea and eating bread and jam; there were two very nice Salvation Army women there. I felt rather at ease; I knew I was in the wrong place, and yet I felt neither strange nor uncomfortable. Suddenly the drunk began to speak, and went on and on saying at some length: "What I could use now is a pair of shoes." The Salvationists were out of shoes at the moment but had heavenly promises that were worth some good shoes. I don't know anymore how it all ended, I didn't mention the tea in the kitchen at home, or the very clear suspicion left me by the drunk, who, on the stairway right before we left, said to me: "If it'd had some schnapps in it, that tea would really have been good."

When I told about my Salvation Army experience at school, my classmates decided to go there in a group, but I didn't go back with them, and to this day that was the only meeting I've ever attended, but it started prolonged discussions at school; finally Charles Wolf summed up the consensus of the class: It is a way of teaching morality, no worse than any other way, and it even has the advantage of teaching us, us too, how behavior needs to be improved; and, for the Salvationists themselves, it teaches them to love. Learning to love, Yes, there was a real problem.

But that did not keep us from enjoying school during the last weeks, as the school year came to a close. Only the singing lessons were terribly boring. The teacher, Monsieur Zellweger, had once toured Switzerland on foot; he loved to tell about his adventure: it had taken him exactly one month to walk from La Chaux-de-Fonds to La Chaux-de-Fonds. We would get him to tell us about it for hours on end, and he would forget about the scales and everything else. The story began this way: he started off one morning, and he had hardly gone two kilometers when he met a friend at Eplatures; the friend asked him, "Where are you going?" "To 'La Tschaux'!" "To 'La Tschaux'? But, you fool, you're heading away from there." "I tell you, I'm going to 'La Tschaux', you can believe it or not, but that's where I'm going." "Listen, Zellweger, you're drunk, I'm going to take you back home." "I'm going to 'La Tschaux', I don't want to be taken home, I'm not drunk, and I'll find my way all by myself; *Salut!*" Often when Monsieur Zellweger was telling us about various geographical details, we would call out: "Sir, tell us again the part about the beginning." Kindly, he would stop what he was saying and start again or at least repeat the beginning, and thus, we did not have to sing the infinitely varied scales that would have made us forever capable of competing with any celebrity whatever.

As for the German lessons, they were to be as unfruitful as those of Monsieur Zellweger. The teacher, Monsieur Wülser, a rather coarse man from Aargau but who showed a fatherly tenderness for the students he liked, had to give in to our reasoning: we would not on any account learn Boche, but since German was part of the curriculum, well, we would go through the curriculum, we would attend the classes, but we would not learn. One day, big excitement. Monsieur Wülser was in the hospital, they had taken out his appendix. When he came back to school, down deep he was quite happy to see his undisciplined gang again—we imagined, perhaps correctly, that our class was his favorite. He talked at length about the joys and horrors of the hospital, but he had such a terrible Aargau accent that it made the most agonizing moments laughable. At recess he called to me and told me he was going to show me something. From his pocket he took a little glass bottle—I can see it yet, it had a long neck, about ten centimeters tall—in which his appendix floated in alcohol; it was at the same time fascinating and repulsive. He explained to me that, as long as he lived, he would always carry his appendix around in his pocket and would show it as a curiosity to those who wanted to see it, because it was educational; but more than that for him, it remained the testimony of an important experience. As for me, he had shown it to me because I wanted to be a doctor.

About this time, Mama gave me a long speech: alas, I didn't suspect a thing! Hélène, too, would also have liked to become a doctor, but since obviously we both could not study the same thing, Hélène, with her noble character, had given up the idea in my favor. That wasn't fair. It would be better for me to give it up as well. I tried vaguely to say: but Hélène isn't a good student, and since she can't continue in the girls' secondary school, she would be even less able to hold her own at the *gymnasium*. My mother said several other things to me that didn't make any special impression. Then it was a question of the primary school certificate, which I could do this very spring at the end of the second year of the *progymnasium*. Since my father had not said a single word to me about all this, I wasn't at all concerned; not for a minute did it enter my head that this referred to something that affected me directly.

A little while afterward, the teacher in our class announced that students desirous of taking their certificates of primary studies should announce themselves. None of my classmates raised a hand, but since my mother had wanted me to, I did; the teacher was surprised, and I confessed that I was just as surprised as he was; he called my attention to the fact that the certificate had no value in comparison to that of the *maturité*.[1] Suddenly, he said to me: "You're not going to leave us, though?" At that very moment, a terrible uneasiness seized me, and my "Why, no, Why no" took on, even as I said it, a sense of certitude to the contrary: they were going to make me leave the *progymnasium*, but I wouldn't let myself do it, oh no, they'd see, I would earn such a good certificate that there wouldn't be any question of all that.

On the appointed day, I found myself at the primary school. The only person I knew there was my old school-mate Henry Schmidt, the one who had received a doll as a gift on my account.[2] The examination seemed infinitely easy to me, I came out first, with grades of six in everything. Then came the *progymnasium* exams. Charles Wolf was first, I was second. This occasioned another conversation with my mother: these examinations were obvious proof that I was not especially gifted for anything; no subject had produced unexpected results—I ventured: "But Mama, after all, it's absolutely impossible to do better than six!" Mama did not trouble herself over something so minor: if you compared the fact that I had come out first in the certificate and second at the *progymnasium*, you could see very well that since I had missed being first among the boys by half a point— at the primary school the student body had been 25 percent girls, while all the girls at the *progymnasium* had disappeared in those first two years—it would be better to give up these boys' studies and go on to the girls' secondary school. I did not know how to defend myself. My father was not very happy that Mama had talked to me before he had. He told me he was still worried about my health, that Mama was

[1] The "*maturité*" in Switzerland corresponds to the French *Baccalauréat*—Ed.

[2] In the chapter entitled "Bellevue", a different gift is referred to—Ed.

complaining that I was becoming more of a tomboy all the time, and that maybe it would be better, on a trial basis, to go to the secondary school: he promised he wouldn't leave me there if I was unhappy there, but he advised me, without making it an absolute requirement, to obey. So, I said goodbye to my friends at the *gymnasium* and to our teachers; I acted as if I were going of my own free will, but I felt really unhappy; since I felt sure that in spite of everything my father understood me, I swallowed everything I might have let show on the outside.

MADELEINE

In the spring of 1916, I entered the girls' secondary school with very mixed emotions and a great sense of uneasiness. The Mistress was to be Mademoiselle Loze, the former teacher at my sister's private school. The first thing that caught my eye when I entered the classroom was a school-bench covered with very neatly aligned pencils and notebooks, in front of which stood Madeleine, attired in a dark blue skirt and a shirtwaist of a slightly lighter blue with white cuffs. Madeleine! Really, it was the last straw; I was heartbroken. Madeleine Gallet was a rather distant cousin, who was infinitely well-behaved and perfectly well brought up and who had always seemed to me rather exasperating. When we were small, our mothers or other relatives had sometimes invited us together; since I did not know how to play the well-behaved games of little girls very well and did not find it all amusing to become for one second only the mother of dolls I wasn't familiar with, these invitations always left me with a dismal memory, and, with time, I had succeeded in avoiding them rather well. To me, Madeleine represented those afternoons spent in strange playrooms, with grownups asking me questions I didn't know how to answer and those new and not very amusing games with which they occupied us, without leaving us time for a single thought of our own. And now Madeleine here! I had only just recognized her, and probably would have resolved to avoid her definitively, when Mademoiselle Loze gushed: How lovely for two cousins so unlike each other to be together at school! What good work we were going to do! We must sit together, side by side; that would delight our mothers. Really, it was too much.

After a few days my father called me into his consulting room and talked to me as if I were a big girl. I explained to him how miserably bored I was. At the *progymnasium* we had already done much more French and mathematics; and then, too, the girls themselves were dull; they talked only about clothes; they argued about who was such and such a teacher's pet; they grumbled; they had no feeling for life; they didn't even know that you could really love God more than a friend. My father told me that he had gone that very morning to see the director of the school, who had advised him to leave me at the school for one year on a trial basis, without making any determination about the future. I could learn what the girls were learning and strengthen my health. He, Papa, knew very well that this was hard, but he thought it was reasonable; and then, too, he wondered if I might not have some influence over the girls and maybe teach them a little about what was dear to my heart. Have an influence over the girls? To me, that seemed very astonishing, more than astonishing; it was perfectly impossible. Papa said, "It's not impossible, try, but be reasonable. And then," he went on, "maybe you could take up piano again." But that was exactly what I had no desire at all to do. Over the past few years, I had had lessons during certain periods, but I had always had to stop them on account of my back, and always, it seemed to me, just when my fingers were beginning to obey me, just when I was beginning to know how to express what I wanted to say. I had no desire whatsoever to start again, only to be interrupted another time. But, I would stay at the school.

At the end of the first week, Madeleine Gallet said to me during recess: "We have to convert Mademoiselle Junod." This was the pastor's daughter I liked so much, but she scarcely did her father great honor. I was dumbfounded that it was actually my slow, level-headed cousin who had had this idea, but, all the same, I found the suggestion absolutely brilliant. And this conversion, that we were a long way indeed from obtaining, was the beginning of my great friendship with my cousin, who had a tremendous influence on me, especially during this year we spent at school together. In a certain way, and thanks to her, this year was to mark a turning point in my life.

The word "convert" made a great impression on me and led me to change many things in myself. Up till then, I had been very much concerned with God and truth; I sought, I prayed, but I did not feel responsible for other people. I had liked my teachers and my schoolmates at the *gymnasium* very much, but it would never have entered my head to convert them, to lead them to change their opinions, to bring them truly closer to God. I did, of course, pray for them, but, in a way, unintentionally. When our ideas seemed to me to diverge too widely, I withdrew very quickly. I must confess, too, that I was fully convinced of a thousand things that had to do with God, but I was just as much convinced that I was still very far away from a great truth that would perhaps, one day, burst open the envelope of uncertainty that surrounded me.

Madeleine Gallet—from now on I shall just call her Madeleine—became a close, intimate friend, someone to whom you could say anything and who could also say anything herself. She was a slow student who had trouble keeping up. She always looked as if she were pondering some secret known only to herself and never let what she was concerned about show on the outside, except in our conversations, where she revealed herself entirely, in rather timid, completely colorless sentences, in which no one word was emphasized more than another and yet which revealed great secrets, an intense interior life and a tremendous desire to mold her whole existence and environment to the great love for God that filled her. Sometimes I would get carried away; I would explain to her things that seemed new to me, and then she would say, in her very sweet, slightly hesitant voice: "And practically?" Then I would stand there with my mouth open, for in practical terms, nothing came to mind. Sometimes I would suggest: "Wait until we know the truth, and then we will be able to find practical solutions." She would answer, "No, they must go hand in hand."

I had been doing a little work for the poor for a long time. One day Madeleine received a sum of twenty-five francs from her grandmother to wallpaper her room which needed it very badly. Madeleine resolved to sacrifice her twenty-five francs for the poor: she entrusted the money to me, and together we went out to buy unimaginable (it seemed to me) quantities of blue and white flannel to make into shirts and trousers. I cut them all out and marked off meters and meters of scallops by drawing around a centime; we embroidered them in blue, and, to us, they looked gorgeous.

On Saturdays, Madeleine received fifty centimes for her ten o'clock snack; school was out at that time, and we would go together to the market to buy *sèches*[1] and—at least during a certain season—cherries. We ate them right there, just as they were, while we looked around the market, which we enjoyed a lot. We never stopped talking about God and the poor and about everything that has to do with God and the poor. One day, as we were in the act of munching some plump red and white cherries, it suddenly occurred to us: what we were doing there was not at all good. We were talking about the poor, but we were forgetting all about them. We weren't hungry, yet we were eating; we were wasting money that could be put to good use. It came to us so suddenly we were dumbfounded. We sought out some poor children—they weren't difficult to find—to give them our *sèches*, which we'd already taken a bite out of, along with the rest of our cherries. And from that Saturday onward, the *sèches* and cherries were replaced by a corresponding measure of flannel, but we still continued our excursions to the market.

Madeleine's parents spent their summers at a farmhouse surrounded by a large park, full of beautiful trees, with lovely well-kept paths, where we would walk for whole hours on our afternoons off, telling each other about what filled our hearts. One day Madeleine said: "I've resolved for both of us that we will no longer read books that are on the Index, or cheap novels either." As always, I agreed, since the proposal came from Madeleine, but I did not know what

[1] "*Sèches*": a kind of dry pastry, without cream filling; these are still sold in La Chaux-de-Fonds—Ed.

the Index was, not to mention what cheap novels were. She explained about both to me. I had only one objection: How would one know ahead of time, without having read them, what books we would be forbidden to read in the future? Madeleine reassured me: as for the Index, she could very well make inquiries, and as for cheap novels, it might be that our opinions would differ, but in any case, we wouldn't waste any more time reading books we knew were not useful. If that happened, we would stop right then, and we would warn each other. She even made a list of authors who were out of the question, and I think we kept our commitment conscientiously, except in cases where school itself obliged us to make exceptions, for as long as I lived in La Chaux-de-Fonds.

We were always together on our afternoons off, she and I. But for recess, we had made a rule for ourselves of always having another companion with us; we had not fixed any program for our conversations or any rule of conduct. One day, Jeanne Humbert, Madeleine, and I spent a very happy ten o'clock recess together—it was the longest recess, lasting a quarter of an hour. Jeanne was in the class above ours, she was delightful, full of life and joy, but she had a great deal of difficulty believing in God. She went to Sunday school, or rather to the catechism class, with us, and often she used to scandalize the monitor with her preposterous observations. I don't remember anymore what we were talking about at this recess; I remember only that we laughed a lot, and probably I in particular. We had that afternoon off, and Madeleine and I went for a walk in the park. She looked preoccupied. When something wasn't right, she often started her sentences with "Dear . . .", a word she also used in her letters. Suddenly, she said to me, "Dear, that mustn't happen again." And while I stood there thunderstruck, she explained that I had no right to be wasting my recesses laughing; of course, I could laugh a little bit, when it was necessary, but laughing was not an occupation for me; those who shared our recesses expected something of us, especially of me, since I was more quick-witted, and I was shirking my responsibilities by losing time in laughing. Jeanne was disappointed, and God certainly saddened. I hadn't realized it. That sort of responsibility was unknown to me.

On the whole, Madeleine was right; I was guilty, I felt it very keenly, but this was getting complicated: one could be guilty without realizing it, do wrong without bad intentions, and even distance oneself from God in one lost recess. My contrition did not have time to go much deeper, for Madeleine continued, with her same, small, slow voice that seemed to weigh her words without giving them any weight, for all the weight was in her: "It's better you know all that before you enter the convent, then you'll already have a bit of the road behind you." This time I was absolutely at the end of my comprehension; and since I could make no sense of what Mad was saying, I thought at first she was crazy. I knew, from the Waldau, that there were a lot of insane people who could be quite reasonable on certain points; that didn't disturb me much. Almost my first thought was: If Mad is crazy, she could come to the Waldau with me, since vacation is so close, and it would really be very nice. But Madeleine told me, when I asked her, that the idea of the convent came, not from her, but really from me. I denied it desperately at first. She explained that I was always talking about how necessary it was to pray more, that one needed to retire into complete solitude in order not to be distracted from God, that one should bring together groups of friends who would also learn to know the Lord in silence; all that already existed, and it was the life of the convent. I said to Mad, "But convents are Catholic, and do you think that agrees with our ideas?" My friend thought that, as far as Catholicism was concerned, it would work itself out; as for the rest, she knew—and she asserted it without getting at all excited—that the convent was precisely that. But, I suppose that at that moment the idea of conversion didn't cross either of our minds; on the contrary, I believe we both knew that we had to abide in a new way by the dispositions of God.

The next morning, we spoke of the convent in a very vague way to Jeanne Humbert, simply to see what she knew about them. She leaped at the thought: for her, the convent would be her salvation; she was too pretty and too flighty a character to stay in the world; it would end badly (and actually, she did subsequently lead a rather restless life, although she kept her dazzling beauty); she would be very willing to enter, but at least one of us would have to go with her, for alone, she would not have the courage to stay. Since the convent was not really an option for us, we didn't speak about it in any depth after that, but the idea of it continued often to touch our conversations.

Madeleine and I called each other Mad and Ad. That gave us pleasure because no one else called us by those nicknames, so it seemed to heighten our intimacy. It was the first time I had really had a friend, and I found it delightful. Since Madeleine had very good manners, Mama hoped they would rub off on mine.

At school everything went rather well; I don't think I ever took home any homework, because I was fairly well up on what was going on. Mademoiselle Loze left me alone. She was always saying: "Above all, you have to build up your strength." She gave us French lessons, of which I don't have the slightest memory; lessons in home economics, which

I found delightful, because I was amused at the idea that sweeping could be an exact science and mending, an art. And lessons in morality. Since I had a penchant (alas, one I've never lost) for moralizing, I took real pleasure in it and discussed the most useless problems as far as the eye can see; the other girls read serial novels under their desks or dozed while I dissected some moral problem or other with the teacher; I have, moreover, completely forgotten what we talked about, but I know it interested me passionately. Mad felt that I exaggerated a little, and she was right.

Mademoiselle Loze had to attend as a chaperone the lessons the men teachers gave us; that seemed very funny to me. One day, I asked Mademoiselle Loze what reason there might be for it; she said, "Be happy that you don't understand."

At that time, my mother lent me the notebook she had written during her religious instruction. One sentence struck me particularly, and I still know it by heart: Mary conceived her Son without the aid of any man. My fourteen years were ignorant of what that meant; I don't know why, perhaps because the notebook came from her, I asked Mama to explain it. She became very upset and repeated many times, with growing anger, "I forbid you to think about that. I forbid you to think about that." Those were her only words, and, as for myself, that was the last time I ever asked her to explain anything. It stayed with me, however, that it was better not to touch on that subject, and I did not ask Madeleine what she thought of the man's role, which certainly must be significant, in conception, since a lack of it was mentioned in Mary's case.

During the summer vacation, we wrote to each other often, but we did not know how to put our ideas down on paper. At the Waldau, I resumed doing what I had always done. The year before, my uncle had told me that Madame Motta was there, very ill after having had ten children; my job was to act as a replacement for one of them; so I went every day in the morning and in the afternoon, and I liked being near her very much. I talked to her about school, about Madeleine, about anything that came into my head, but not about God, because she was a Catholic, and since she was very tired, I was afraid, I think, that she would get things confused, or maybe I was also afraid I might add to the distress she suffered. Sometimes I went into town with Monsieur Motta; he treated me like a grown person and thanked me for what I was doing for his wife; he told me stories about the *gymnasium* he had attended. This time, when he asked me how my Latin was going, it hurt quite a bit to admit to him that I had changed schools.

When we went back to school, Mad and I were ecstatic to see each other again. On Sunday, we went to catechism together. I went to meet her at her house. Her room was reached by means of a little iron spiral staircase, of curious construction, which connected the corridor on the floor where her parents' room was to hers on the floor above. That winter, she had a dress of deep green velvet, with sleeves of a matching green georgette; her coat and hat matched too; I was all admiration. As for me, I always wore a sailor dress, that is, a pleated skirt and a middy blouse on top with a big collar and sailor cuffs. It had become a uniform; my mother found that that was best suited to my ungrateful age, and I didn't care. Besides, I had only one idea: not to be noticed. Mama kept saying, if not every day, at least quite often, that I was terribly ugly, so naturally I preferred it if nobody looked at me.

I went with Mama to Basel for a few days to have some complicated dental work done. We stayed at the Hôtel de la Croix Bleue. The dentist had his office on the market square, and from the big chair one could see, reflected in reverse in a mirror, the merchants' multicolored umbrellas; it was very pretty. How I wished the women in the market-place in La Chaux-de-Fonds had umbrellas like that! One day, we had dinner with Madame de Quervain, my god-mother; Mama was already there when I arrived, having just come from the dentist. My godmother was just saying "You know, this child has extraordinary charm", and in her high voice she repeated, "Extraordinary!" I was speechless. She was talking about me, there was no possible doubt. But I didn't have time to enjoy this triumph, because after dinner Mama explained to me that my godmother, in her great kindness, had said that to her to console her a little, since she knew how distressing it was to have such a child; she still always wondered if I hadn't been exchanged for someone else's child as a baby, because I was really too different from the rest of the family. That didn't keep Mama from saying repeatedly, some years later: "To think that your godmother found you so charming before; what do you suppose she'd say now?"

Madeleine, then, always looked particularly pretty on Sundays in her beautiful clothes. Her family, besides, spoiled her quite a bit; she was the only girl among three boys. After catechism, we had a hard time parting from each other, be-cause there were always so many things to say. Mad's father had a surprising idea, for a man: he invited me to have dinner at his mother's every other Sunday. His mother was one of my great-great-aunts, my grandmother's aunt. She was a very old lady with a very cracked voice; at dinner, Madeleine's father carried on a sort of literary and political conversation; he treated his mother with the greatest respect, and what he had to say was very interesting. But he did not believe in

God, which scandalized his very pious mother. Mad said: "What do you want, he's a man, he has other qualities, and besides, he'll come back" (twenty years later, Madeleine's sudden death restored his faith). Until teatime, while her father and her grandmother were resting, I stayed alone with Madeleine; then the rest of her family came; among others, her cousin Charles, who played the piano marvelously; he let me turn pages for him and even, from time to time, had me play something and improvised an accompaniment so that we could play duets. He was in class preparing for his *maturité*. Two years later, he died of influenza at Colombier where he was finishing recruit school; and several years after that, his best friend told me that Charles had told him he loved me, but that he wanted to wait until I was eighteen before telling me. Really, I wouldn't have doubted it, because he used to tease me a lot; but he played the piano really well, and his improvisations were a delight to me.

For the religion classes, our pastor was now Monsieur von Hoff; his theme was Saint Paul and his travels; I liked that much less than the Bible studies; there was too much history and geography for my taste. All the same, I would rather have liked to have the strength of a Saint Paul. Our conversations were filled with him. One day, I said to Madeleine: "Saint Paul was not in the least Protestant." Madeleine agreed: "Besides," she said with justice, "in those days, Protestantism hadn't been invented yet." So there it was. Protestantism was an invention. I was quite taken with this new formula, but it didn't get me any farther in my search for the truth, a search that was continuing painfully along its very slow path. Shortly afterward, as a result of some error or other, Mademoiselle Loze had to redo her "inventory" of the class. The Protestants had to raise their hands to be counted, then the Catholics, then the Jews, then the atheists. I never raised my hand, but really I wasn't intending any evil. Mademoiselle Loze added up the raised hands in vain, but the accounts would not balance. There was always one hand missing for the class to be complete. Suddenly, I cried out: "It *can't* balance, because it's missing my hand, I didn't raise it"; slightly annoyed, Mademoiselle Loze said: "That makes one more Protestant, then." I objected: "I'm not a Protestant." "What does that mean?" "I have the same religion as Saint Paul, and Saint Paul was not a Protestant." "What kind of invention is that?" "It's not an invention, it's the truth." "No more discussion: your parents are Protestants, so you are a Protestant." As always, I shut my mouth too soon, and to my great mortification the accounts balanced because one more Protestant was marked down in the addition.

At the next recess, Madeleine was the only one who brought up the incident. "Dear," she said, "where are we going?" "I don't know," I answered, "but one can't always be silent." She agreed, and then everything was all right. Although my friends from the *gymnasium* were in the same school, I met them only rarely, and I don't know exactly how it came about—maybe it was Mademoiselle Loze's influence—I spent only very brief ends of recess with them; Madeleine's affection compensated quite a bit for theirs, but I missed them just the same.

That Christmas of 1916, I don't quite remember why, I received four francs. When we went back to school at New Year's, I explained to Mad: "I can't give these four francs for the poor; I need a candle and a Greek grammar." Cohn, one of my former classmates, had had to stop taking Greek. I asked him to sell me his grammar for three francs (they cost four francs at the bookstore); he wanted three francs sixty. He got them, and I had some left over to buy a candle; with the stubs of the ones from the Christmas tree it would last a while. Without telling anyone, only Madeleine was in on it, I got into the habit of getting up every night about 1:00 A.M. I would steal into the playroom and study a little Greek grammar, do a written translation, and say over the Latin. I arranged the books in my big briefcase among the other schoolbooks so Mama wouldn't get hold of them; after the business with my journal, I was wary. Generally I would work about two hours, one hour for each subject, and naturally I had a good deal of trouble getting up the next morning. My candles were used up rather quickly, but Mad brought some from home. One morning Papa said, "It always smells like a candle in the playroom." I didn't say anything, but I could feel myself turning red. Hélène, who slept in the same room with me, had never awakened. A short while after that, I was just in the process of translating an exercise and shivering slightly in my nightgown, when the glass door that separated the dining room from the playroom opened softly and my father, who had been called to the hospital, came into the room. He didn't need to ask many questions: once he had understood, he had me quickly recite a few verbs and decline a few nouns and said: "Yes, that's good work. Who's checking your work?" "My friends at the *gymnasium*, I see them every day at first recess." "And are they glad you're coming back?" I didn't know how to take this; Papa asked no more questions, his decision was suddenly made: I would return to the *gymnasium*! "And Mama?" "She certainly won't want you to keep on getting up in the night like this. Now you go to bed, and, in the future, you are absolutely forbidden to get up at night; you'll work in the daytime." The next day my father sent me to the Greek teacher, who gave me six private lessons and pronounced me now qualified to rejoin my regular class in the spring. As he told me that, he handed me a bill for twenty-four francs, which I never forgot; it looked like an enormous sum and I panicked; could my father really pay such an amount? I handed the bill to him, and, without a word, he gave me the money right away. Then I ventured, "Papa, I'm sorry to have cost you so much money." Papa started to laugh so merrily that I boldly joined in. Twenty-four francs to catch up on a year of Greek, that was nothing. I was happy; Mama didn't seem displeased, and Mad exulted: "You're going to be able to read the New Testament!"

The last few weeks at the girls' school, I took one more cooking course. One time when Mama was away, I offered to make Papa some supper all alone. He accepted with pleasure. I made *spätzli*.[2] They were very beautiful, and I was quite proud of my achievement. When we began to eat them, I had forgotten the salt; they were still bad no matter how much salt I added; but Papa, who really liked *spätzli*, said it didn't matter and took three more helpings.

THE FOURTH YEAR OF *GYMNASIUM*
Spring 1917

An enormous uproar welcomed me back to my old class. I was now the only girl, and since there were twenty boys we never failed to say that we were twenty-one. The uproar consisted of a welcoming speech by a classmate, a speech punctuated by the horrible sound of rulers striking the desks

[2] A kind of noodles—ED.

in a wild rhythm. At the first recess, we formed a procession in single file across the courtyard, and, when we met up with my old class of girls, the procession surrounded them with gestures of victory: the boys yelled, and I foolishly yelled with them "Allah is Great, but Adrienne, but Adrienne, but Adrienne is with us!"

I had to begin to work seriously, for the year spent with the girls had taught me no mathematics, no Greek, no Latin, no literature. I had indeed theoretically caught up on Greek in a way; however, I had missed the drills, and for the first time I knew at close hand what hard work means: but the boys really helped me.

We had a curious collection of teachers. For Greek, Dettling, a young fellow from Basel who spoke French with difficulty but gave excellent lessons; he was there only as a substitute for a few months, which we all regretted. At the beginning, he was kind enough to have me stay each time for a few minutes more, to give me and have me recite some additional exercise. In this way, the visible gaps rapidly disappeared. Another student, Fankhauser, who came from the Saint-Imier valley, was also behind. He had started Greek with a pastor who had not made him learn to write any signs or accents in his Greek, so he more or less had to learn it all over again.

We had French and Latin with Monsieur Rossel, whom we called Tiger Cat. I think I had the best lessons in my life from him; we all felt incredibly privileged, and we worked like mad. We worked especially hard on analysis, and he knew how to make this analysis so lively and so subtle that we were sad when the bell rang.

For German, it was Wülser: he wasn't interested in what we did, and often, at the beginning of the lesson, he would say to me: "Go away, little lady, and take Charles Wolf with you." He didn't have to say it twice, and we would go for a walk: in the winter, during this time, we prepared many a slide over the snow that the whole class would then use during recess. I think that while we took these walks the principal subject of our conversations was French and Latin analysis.

At home I had heard it whispered that Charles Wolf's mother had written a book entitled *Maternity*. I asked Charles what was in it. He told me, "You shall read it later; don't let anyone else lend it to you." More than a year afterward, he brought it to me one day, with a rather solemn look: "You're old enough now." I don't think I understood much of it, and in any case I don't remember anything about it.

We read a lot at school, I believe especially the classics. We also wrote fairly good compositions on rather abstract subjects.

For history, we had Monsieur Fahrni as our teacher. He was a small man with a white goatee and a florid complexion: he had a reputation for drinking a great deal. His lessons were really boring; he would make us memorize a page or two and then would make us recite them word for word; if we had learned our lessons well, he would let us read *Don Quixote* aloud; he had a passion for *Don Quixote*, and we ourselves enjoyed it very much; during the reading, we were well-behaved; during the rest of the lesson, we were rather undisciplined. But one day he took his sweet revenge: he played the flute; we had gone on a hike with him. It was evening; we were all dragging our feet a little; there was no end to the long road. He began to play with spirit: that revived us; we walked with more good humor; suddenly he burst out laughing; for more than half an hour he had been making us trot to the tune of "Deutschland über alles" without a single one of us recognizing the melody.

In religion, we again had my dear Pastor Junod, but I no longer liked the religion lessons; I even feared them, because in spite of everything I was disappointed each time. I no longer know what his theme was; I don't think it was anything special, but rather he had selected "evangelical truths". One day, I couldn't stand it any longer: after the lesson, I walked him home and explained to him that all these truths were as though abbreviated, as though taken out of context, disconnected; that made me unhappy. He was very nice, but he understood nothing about it. Since Hélène was just making her six-weeks with him, he invited me to come on Sunday afternoons. These six-weeks constituted the religious instruction preceding confirmation. During this time, you didn't go to school, but mornings and evenings you had religion lessons, and on Sundays the whole group of catechumens went for a walk with the pastor and finally held a sort of meeting where you could ask questions. So I went. Hélène was not delighted; I was too young. I found that the meeting answered nothing; questions were rare. I was embarrassed to say to Monsieur Junod that it hadn't moved me forward at all. He said to me: "You will see the influence that the six-weeks will have on your sister, and then you will understand that religion is not made up just of problems, but that it often changes the believer without his realizing it." I saw nothing. Hélène was not changing. She was, indeed, very nice at that time, but really no more or less than that.

Meanwhile, one Sunday, Monsieur Luginbühl told us that one must not put one's faith on one side and one's life on the other. One had to have the courage to act. One could not build on ruins: it was necessary to make space for a new life. One had to ask pardon of all those one had offended. This time, there it was: I had understood. On my return, I said to

Mad: "We must begin, Mad; there's nothing between you and me, is there?" "No," she said, "nothing." "Mad, are you really going to ask forgiveness of everybody?" "Yes." "Isn't that very Salvationist?" "I don't know, but you see, it is perhaps a path."

And I started. The hardest were Mama and Hélène. Papa said there was nothing; our governess, who was a Moravian and very scrupulous, reflected for a long time before consenting to forgive completely. The next day, it continued at school. I had a lot of trouble, which seemed to me as necessary as it was ridiculous. Caldé was the third or fourth one, and he said: "These things are for the confessional; you shouldn't do it this way." This was the first time I'd heard anyone speak of confession;[1] he didn't say much more to me, but how I envied him for being a Catholic and for knowing how it ought to be done! From then on I ceased asking forgiveness of everyone around me but tried to take pains not to do so much that needed pardon. That day or the next morning I met Pastor Luginbühl on the steps of the school, and quickly I slipped over to him: "I tried to ask pardon, but that isn't the right way to do it." He sort of thanked me for having tried, but he didn't tell me anything about the right way.

Shortly after that we were to take a day-long hike with the school. With my backpack well provided, I wanted to go to sleep in my little room. No way. It was, I think, the first sleepless night I'd spent at La Chaux-de-Fonds. Since I'd been back at the *gymnasium*, I'd had a small room of my own that looked out onto the street; it had a small bookcase with my books, a work table, a rather large one so there would be room for the drawing board I needed for mathematics,

---

[1] Compare with 95 and 135—ED.

and in a corner, my dear doll, in her white bassinet; I didn't really play with dolls anymore, but I loved her still, and I would have been sad not to have had her near me. When Madeleine came over in the afternoons, we were served our tea in my room; I had completely forsaken the playroom and much enjoyed a world of my own. Papa would come there to say hello and to take a look at whatever I was working on; often, too, we would read together from Monsieur Oltramare's Latin anthology. In the evenings I still ate with my brothers and my sister at six, but afterward I had the right to have my light on only until nine. It was Papa who had made this decision.

Well, that night, there was no way to sleep. I sat in the window and from time to time saw someone passing in the street. I wasn't at all familiar with this kind of night-life— my life at Gunten had not had any other people in it—and that made a big impression on me. Initially I thought that those people, since they had had to go out at such a late hour, must have been forced to do so by problems, so I began to pray for them. Suddenly a kind of revelation came to me: there existed some sort of union of prayer between people; these people were no longer strangers to me, they were linked to me like my friends, but since I didn't know them, I could talk to them only through God. I was thrilled; as this was my first prayer vigil, I was hungry, and I began to eat up the provisions in my backpack. I don't remember when I finally went to bed. The next day I had to leave very early; I was terribly sleepy, but with some bread that the cook gave me, I quickly replaced the provisions I had eaten. I would have vastly preferred not to go on the hike so that I could have gone to tell Madeleine about my new discovery, but there was no way to get out of it.

Moreover, Madeleine was no longer at school; she had

not received good enough grades in the spring and was now in Mademoiselle Loze's private school, where my sister was also. We naturally saw each other a little less often than when we had been in the same class together, but we continued to share everything with each other.

When I told her about that night, she was very sad that her own room did not look out onto the street. I consoled her by telling her that it wasn't really necessary to see the night people in order to pray for them. Besides, there were also all the day people, all those one rubs shoulders with without knowing them.

Mad had found, somewhere, a collection of pious English novels, and one, in particular, made a big impression on us both: *The Wide, Wide World*—in spite of the tinge of boredom brought on by the family prayers on Sundays. These novels perhaps taught us to understand personal problems better, but they revealed nothing on the subject of the real essence of truth.

One summer afternoon I was running down the stairs; I wanted to go to our tiny little garden to do my homework; I had the big Greek and Latin dictionaries in my arms. I nearly knocked down a gentleman who was coming up; in my shock, I dropped the dictionaries; he helped me to pick them up and explained to me that he was my distant cousin, Pastor Perregaux, and that he was coming to pay a call on my mother. My mother was not there just then; so if I would like it, he would visit with me. He had only been in town for two days; he had been named fourth pastor of the independent free church to which my parents belonged. I very proudly led my new cousin into the parlor. Oh, how I regretted that day that our parlor was so horribly ugly! The only useful piece of furniture in it was the piano; the pieces of Louis XVI furniture—I don't know if they were real—

looked like fragile knickknacks and were upholstered in rose and gold. There were no flowers, but two huge, very splendid Chinese vases of great value, which one feared to break merely by looking at them, various bronze birds, a large pastel depicting my mother beneath an immense plumed hat, and a red leather box containing an open fan. This cousin was a delightful person, quite unusual, and we immediately became great friends, but that day I absolutely avoided speaking to him about God or about prayer. And I know that very softly I told myself that I was wrong, that perhaps it wasn't so bad for Protestant pastors to get married. He was a fine musician, which didn't prevent me from quite shamelessly playing something on the piano for him just as my mother came back, he having paid his tribute a few moments earlier. Some time later, he confided to me that he would marry only when a certain little girl he knew grew up to be a big girl. Only three years later, he asked me to marry him. For a few days, when I was fourteen, I could really see myself as a pastor's wife: it seemed to me that it would be good to gain the right to go do washing for poor women. I really believe that this was what I found most tempting about that occupation; but as a temptation, it was tempting. I will tell later on about his offer of marriage and all the dreadful anguish I went through as a result of it. But I have always liked our cousin Louis Perregaux very much, and he has remained unmarried.

Every year there was a sale at our church. That autumn, I went to it for the first time with Theddy, who was four and a half. We met Pastor von Hoff there, who had baptized Theddy and to whom Theddy said in his small, very wise voice: "Sir, aren't you the one who splashed me?" The little fellow had the habit, which he kept, of saying everything he thought, without the least hesitation. Further, he was full of

Adrienne with Theddy

flashes of inspiration; when he had been bad, he would beg: "Get me a new engine, mine is too broken; when I have a new engine, I'll be good." The whole family loved him dearly, and he was quite adept at taking advantage of our fondness to get all his little wishes. Even Willy, who, when Theddy was born, said he'd have preferred a cat, spoiled him.

That year I was allowed to go to the theater once or twice. I saw *Tartuffe*, which impressed me very much, and *Le Bourgeois gentilhomme*. Then, once or twice, I attended lectures with Aunt Marie. I really loved Aunt Marie; she was my grandfather's sister; she was very devout and was on I don't know how many church committees. Before going out with her I had on the whole never seen her except in the family. Now I was alone with her before and after the lecture. I would very much have liked to know if her piety signified that she knew the truth; but it was impossible to ask her questions, because every time you asked her one, you could be sure that in a few days Mama would question you about the meaning of your question. So, I tried to make her talk without actually seeming to take much interest myself. "Making someone talk" was a school trick, the means by which we succeeded in preventing the teacher from making us do written assignments. It succeeded with Aunt Marie; once she got started, she never stopped. Alas, she didn't look as if she knew a truth existed, her activity was enough to fill her days and nights; she asked herself no questions, there were none; but she gave me the life-long impression that activity could completely stifle a life of prayer and become an absolute restriction on thought. Since I was full of self-confidence, I told her so, and at first she appeared astonished and then buried me under an avalanche of explanations: I was much too little to understand, and besides there was nothing there *to* understand; everything was clear; the Bible was clear, the sermons were clear, and activity in service of the independent church was also clear (just like women's suffrage, which was so dear to her heart).

Naturally I discussed these things with Madeleine. She decided: "We don't go well with grownups."

During the summer vacation, I had learned to ride a bicycle at the Waldau, and I had derived a great deal of pleasure from it. I took a number of rides through the Bernese countryside and in that way achieved a little of the solitude that I generally lacked during vacations. For my fifteenth birthday, I wanted a bicycle; I wanted it passionately, as I'd never wanted any other gift. When my parents asked me what I wanted, I had said: a bicycle, and I had given the same answer to my uncle, when he had asked me that question. Besides, fifteen was a venerable age, and it was a custom in our family to have a more marked celebration of birthdays at each five-year interval. A few days before my birthday, I was seized with anxiety: What if I received two bicycles, and how disappointed those who gave me the gift would be to find themselves outdone. I really wanted to avert the catastrophe. On the other hand, if I had two bicycles, I would exchange one of them for a man's bicycle and give it away to a real poor man. On consulting Madeleine, she was in agreement, and, with her pretty little smile, she told me: "Don't do anything; you probably won't get a bicycle at all." But I didn't want to consider that possibility; I so hoped to get a bicycle.

On my birthday, we had a school hike. Early in the morning, I went to meet Mathilde Kocher; she was a girl in the class above mine; she was coming with us. When I got there, I met an unknown German-Swiss woman who was having breakfast with her: my future sister-in-law, Frieda Kaegi, whom I would not meet again until seventeen years later. All day long Mathilde, Charles, Charles-Henri, and I talked about serving and loving and God; Charles and Charles-Henri seemed to have the same plan as we, except that God was replaced by a complicated philosophy, in other respects not very disturbing. The weather was magnificent; we stayed in the immediate vicinity of La Chaux-de-Fonds. It was the day of Emil's first marriage.[2]

By that evening, I had nearly forgotten my idea of the bicycle. When I got home, Mama said: "Come to your room; your party is ready." "And Papa?" I asked. Mama had almost forgotten Papa; he was still at the hospital. So we waited for him. I was rather impatient: two bicycles? Or one? When Papa arrived we went all together to my room: they had had a little writing table repaired, one that had been my mother's when she was a girl, and a work table. And no bicycle at all, truly none. I didn't dare say that the writing table suited me less than the old table; there wasn't enough room on it for me to work with the big dictionaries and still less room for the drawing board. But there was *Around the World in Eighty Days*, by Jules Verne, a gift from Papa, a very pretty embroidered handkerchief from Mad, and beautiful red roses from Aunt Marguerite.

When I went to bed, I made, I think, my first examination of conscience. I was clinging too tightly to the things of this world since I had been upset not to have a bicycle; then too, I still didn't have a very good idea of what I was to do with my life: I wanted to be a doctor, of course, but what then? Should one become a doctor without knowing the truth about God? Suddenly, I got up, knelt down beside

[2] Emil Dürr was to be Adrienne's future husband—ED.

my bed—something, I think, that I had never yet done, and I prayed a long, long time, without words.

After that, I was grateful that I had not received a bicycle; I had received something else. Mad teased me for ages about the bicycle. For her birthday, at the beginning of November, she received a biography of Florence Nightingale; we read it and reread it, and when Mad had a daughter, she named her Florence.

THE VISION OF MARY

In that same month, November 1917, very early one morning, when it was barely light, I woke up because of a golden light that filled the whole wall above my bed, and I saw something like a picture of the Holy Virgin, surrounded by several other personages (who were somewhat in the background, while she was right in the foreground) and several angels, some of whom were as big as she, while others were like little children. It was like a tableau, and yet the Holy Virgin was alive, in heaven, and the angels were changing position. I believe this lasted for a very long time. I looked, as if praying without words, and I was struck with amazement; I had never seen anything so beautiful. At the beginning, all of the light was like very vibrant gold; it faded little by little, and, as it faded, the face and the hands of the Holy Virgin became more alive and clearer. I was not frightened in the least but filled with a new joy that was both intense and very sweet. Not for one instant did I have the impression of anything unreal, and it never entered my mind that I might have been the victim of any error.

If I remember correctly, I said only one thing about it to Madeleine, relating the fact as something completely natural. Mad said only: "I would really have liked to have seen her too." We never spoke of it again. The memory of this apparition remained very clear within me; for a long time it accompanied me like a wonderful secret; I possessed, as it were, a place of refuge. Later, I would have liked to have spoken about it to someone: once or twice I was tempted to go see a priest and to speak about it to him; but I didn't know any. I never thought of talking about it to a Protestant pastor, although I do not believe that I in any way knew, at that time, that I was going to have to become a Catholic. From then on, I had a sort of faraway tenderness for the Holy Virgin. I knew that one had to love her, but that in itself never really bothered me. However, after my Catholic instructions began in earnest, I told the priest who was instructing me about it, knowing clearly that I had to do so.

When the Holy Virgin disappeared, I knelt down beside my bed, as I had made it a habit of doing since my birthday, and I think I prayed until it was time to go to school.

THE DEATH OF MY FATHER

Christmas that year had a very special character. We celebrated it, as usual, on the twenty-fourth. Papa was a little tired. I felt sad at all the celebrations; it always seemed to me as if the true realization were missing. Some days previously, I had written an urgent letter to my uncle and my aunt at the Waldau, asking them to come and spend this day with us. They had not come for Christmas since 1908. Usually, that was not very easy for my uncle to arrange, since he himself organized every celebration in his immense institution; but against all expectations, they came. My aunt said that they had come because I had insisted so emphatically. They were a bit worried to see my father so tired, but he told them that the joy of having his brother and his sister with him at Christmas truly relieved his fatigue, and he promised that we all would go together to spend a few days with them at New Year's, which we did in fact do. It was Papa's last Christmas.

I had received a book that I had wanted to read for a long time: *Doctor Germaine*, by Noëlle Roger. At night, when I was in my room, I began to devour it. It was the story of a woman doctor torn between her infinitely loved profession and the demands of her life as a married woman. In the end, she gave up her profession in order to devote herself entirely to her family. There was no mention of God in this book. And yet, it was enthralling; it seemed to me that it outlined the problems of my own life. But I could not picture to myself a day when I would open the door of a waiting-room and see women really asking for help that I would have to know how to give them. I read this book— certainly mediocre in itself—several times in succession, always finding new aspects in it. It surprised me that precisely a woman doctor managed without God, and that added to my perplexity.

On Christmas Day, I was to have been present for the first time at the catechism class' Christmas celebration, and I was very happy about it. I thought that perhaps Christmas really celebrated in a church would be a true celebration, full of a Christian meaning that would finally measure up to my expectations. I don't remember very well who it was who had asked me, several days beforehand, to help to decorate the two immense trees in the independent church. I joyfully did that, along with an elderly teacher whom I had not met before but who told me that for thirty years she had always been the one to attach the balls and place the candles. The most thrilling moment was when I had to climb up into the pulpit to attach a large banner: ''Peace to men of good will.'' It was made of red velvet, and it was very dirty. The letters on it were embroidered in white pearls that had in truth turned gray. But from a distance it looked all right. Once in the pulpit, I intentionally exchanged a few remarks with the teacher who stayed down below, just see what it felt like to be a pastor and to preach. One instant I asked myself: Would it not be better to become a pastor than a doctor? But back without delay came the implacable answer, the same one that so often had come into my mind: How can you be a pastor, if you do not possess the truth?

On Christmas Day, I had a very swollen jaw: the mumps. My father had a hard time making me understand that I could not go out. I wanted to exercise a bit of self-control. It was not a matter of self-control: mumps were catching. This obligatory sacrifice cost me a lot. No Christmas at the church, and so no fulfillment of my expectations.

I had a fever, so they kept me in bed for several days. Then we went to the Waldau. The whole family stayed there, except for my father and me; we left again immediately the next day. Then we had several good days alone together at home. I accompanied my father to the clinic and to the hospital. At the hospital, he even let me stay with him during his rounds in the children's wards; I appreciated that very much. Sometimes he even gave me a short medical explanation, and once I was present at the extraction of a foreign body using a large electric magnet. Afterward, on the way home, we spoke a little about God, and my father told me that he had never yet operated on a patient without praying beforehand;[1] I felt almost dizzy when my father told me that, and yet I didn't dare speak to him about the "truth", about that sort of conviction I had that God was different from what we thought, infinitely greater and more powerful, and that he also accompanied us much more closely. That evening, I don't really know why, I could not do my homework in my room, and I installed myself in my father's office, at his writing table. There was a whole row of pencils and many rubber stamps on the table: looking at them, all the while repeating Greek verbs, I suddenly knew: soon this table would no longer belong to my father, because he would be dead. The responsibility that would fall to me would be heavier than I could bear. I was very frightened, but I was afraid to tell my father, lest I frighten him too. However, the next morning, I think, my father told me that he intended to leave La Chaux-de-Fonds and go either to Basel, where they might perhaps be planning to offer him a professorship, or else to Aarau. I could then not keep from asking him: "Papa, do you think that would be worth the trouble?" And when he asked, "What do you mean, trouble?", I avoided a more precise answer, saying vaguely: "Life is so short." Then Papa replied: "Yes, it is short, and I will soon be fifty. I'd like to go back to Basel and live among my friends; I don't have any true friends here." When he said that to me, I felt sad for him, because I myself had many true friends, but of course they were too young for him. For a second I almost felt consoled at the prospect that he might die soon: one would be fine in heaven.

---

[1] See above, 94—ED.

On one of the days that followed, I fell ill. When I went out for the first time, it was a morning in late January, when the foehn was blowing. I was all the way at the end of the rue Léopold-Robert, by the big fountain, with the interminable street straight ahead of me. There were little piles of dirty snow on the edges of the sidewalks, and the street and the sidewalks were as if illuminated by a host of puddles glistening in the sunlight; the sun itself hung ponderously in a sky heavy with big gray clouds between which the blue seemed excessively deep. The houses looked darker than usual, and many windows cast reflections into the anxious atmosphere of this winter, which for an instant had turned into spring. Suddenly I understood. Inside this whole long row of houses, there were a very great number of people, each with all the cares and joys of his own life; and for all these people there was but one God, just one for all of them, with one single truth, and he was offering his truth to all those who prayed. I shall never forget the instant when I felt that; it was at the same time a very sudden sadness that I did not know this truth and a great promise: the day would come when I would know it. I walked along the rue Léopold-Robert, all the way to where the houses end, then I retraced my steps and started again. As I walked, I did not cease to pray for all those who lived in all those houses; I asked God insistently to make them know his one, unique truth. When I returned, I was quite exhausted. My parents wanted me to go back to bed, but I asked them to allow me to return to school. I could almost no longer bear the idea of the greatness of God; I had a consuming desire for more concrete, more immediate duties, perhaps even more suited to my age. I was happy to obtain their permission.

Since the autumn Hélène and I had been going to dancing class on Saturday afternoons. They taught us not only how to dance but also how to use a fan, how to curtsy, how to walk with ease. I really hated that; I was terribly lacking in natural aptitude, and it seemed stupid to me to make lengthy promenades across the room with just some boy from school, to whom I'd never for the world have given my arm on the schoolyard. It had its fun side, too, though: I liked dancing very much, especially the waltz and the fast dances. The languorous tangos exasperated me.

There was a spectator at the last dancing lesson: an elderly lady who walked painfully, leaning on a cane. She was dressed in gray silk; she had very pronounced features and would have been frankly ugly had she not had very lively, almost black eyes. Some of the mothers were also present. At one point, they came and told me that the elderly lady wished to speak to me; I went, a little surprised. She said lots of charming things to me; it was Isabella Kaiser. Naturally, I had never heard anything about her, but I understood she was famous. I had the nerve to ask her to write something in my album. She promised to do so but said to me: "You may bring it to me this evening, and you will come to my room tomorrow and pick it up yourself. You shall have tea with me." What an adventure!

That evening I went to her lecture with Aunt Marie. I was terribly excited about what the next day held in store. In her lecture, Isabella Kaiser recounted that she had been born in La Chaux-de-Fonds, that she had returned almost as a stranger, but that this very afternoon she had met a young girl who had given her homeland back to her. Then she read some poetry and a short story. Aunt Marie said: "I wonder who the little girl is?" I didn't say anything. The next day I searched my drawers in vain; I had, in fact, destroyed everything. This did not keep me from telling Isabella Kaiser, somewhat as if I had been a young colleague: "You know, I've written a great many poems in the past, but I don't write them anymore, because I'm too old." Nonetheless, she encouraged me to start again and to write stories, anything that came into my head. And again I proved not to be equal to the situation; I explained to her: "All I could write would be a story about the truth of God, but, you understand, I'm really too young for that." She advised patience. It seemed to me that I loved her like an old friend. I never saw her again.

I think it was the next day that Mademoiselle Pfenninger, a teacher at the school who was in the process of converting to Catholicism, told me at recess that she would like to talk to me. I hardly knew her, except from afar; I had never had any classes with her. She asked me to keep a journal and to give it to her to read. I abruptly refused: a journal is written only for oneself. "No," said Berthe Pfenninger, "one could also write it for someone one likes; and, too, you could write this journal as if it were a story; I assure you it would be fine. I would give it all back to you when you were older, and then that would give us the opportunity to talk about many things." I understood that Isabella Kaiser had spoken to her; and yet I refused. She would not accept this refusal as definitive. I promised to think it over. The subject never came up again.

That week Papa, Hélène, and I went up to Pouillerel; it was a little excursion that we took very regularly, especially in winter. As we went, we talked about my medical studies. I was still a very long way from that, but I was so fond of the idea that I was quite happy to talk about it. I was very eager to do my semesters abroad in England. Papa had Austria in view instead; the English had an entirely different way of studying; their courses were very different from ours. I had trouble understanding how roads leading to the same goal could be so different. Papa explained that the same concept of medicine was subject to many variations; he spoke so seriously that I felt I had almost become his colleague. Papa had a way of treating you like a grown person; inwardly, I seemed almost to be growing visibly taller while he spoke. As we descended, Papa and Hélène were walking in front, and I was several paces behind them, deep in thought. Suddenly, like a flash of lightning, the thought crossed my mind: What will Papa look like when he is in his coffin? Try as I would to dismiss this thought, it would not leave me, I had to picture the coffin and my father lying in it, pale, all stiff, foreign, a vision we would not recognize. It was ghastly. And Papa, heedless, continued his carefree walk with Hélène.

On Friday morning, Mama told us that Papa would not be going to the hospital that day. He had come home the night before in a lot of pain: he had had a long meeting with the grand council and then had had to perform an urgent operation. When he got home, he was exhausted from the pain; his left shoulder hurt him severely. When we came home from school at noon, he was still in bed, and at four again.

In the small sitting room, our first ball dresses were on display. Saturday, February 9, our first ball was to take place. All the boys in the dancing class had invited me; I would have had to be everyone's date. It was extremely tiresome on account of the other girls and also because I had to make a choice. Papa had given very good advice. I had told him of my embarrassment, and he had asked: "Are any of your classmates among these boys?" "Yes, Bachmann." "Then, accept Bachmann." That I did. Bachmann had said to me, "Very nice of you to accept; I'll send you a big bouquet.

What color is your dress?" "Rose." "Great! I'll send you a big bouquet of rose roses."

I still didn't have a rose-colored silk ribbon for my hair, but that Friday I was so sad about Papa's illness that I didn't buy it.

On Friday evening, I slipped into Papa's bedroom. He said, "Good evening, my little one", in a voice that had changed completely. I believe I had not thought all day long, or even at that very moment, that he could die, and yet I said to him: "Thank you for everything, Papa." And he replied, "Thank you for everything, my little one. Life is not easy for you, but stay as you are." Then, once again, very softly: "Thank you for everything."

That night, I couldn't stand to stay in bed, and yet I was not thinking about his death. I knelt beside my bed and prayed for a long time, and every time I wanted to go to bed, I got up again and went to kneel down and pray.

Early the next morning, I couldn't bear it any longer. I got up very early and sat down at my writing table. There was no way I could work, and it was as if I could not pray. I merely repeated, "My God, my God."

At seven I went down to the kitchen. Mama appeared immediately. I don't know where the maids were. Mama said: "Papa is very ill." Why was Mama saying that Papa was very ill, when he was dead? For one second, I was almost seized with a foolish hope that what Mama said perhaps was true, but the minute after that Mama came back: "Papa has just died." Papa had died at the very instant before Mama came into the kitchen, but she hadn't had the courage to tell me all at once.

Hélène and Willy were still asleep, in the same room; we went there together. Hélène began to bawl, Willy said nothing. It was horrible.

Later in the morning Bachmann sent a big funeral wreath of rose roses instead of the bouquet for the ball.

Grandpapa came to make a five-minute visit to Mama. He had become engaged six weeks after Grandmama's death and had married very soon afterward. His wife had immediately forbidden him ever to have anything to do with his family. Grandpapa had obeyed her, and it had been four years since Mama had seen him. This was his only infraction of his wife's orders, for three years later, when Uncle Constant died, with the last wish of seeing his father just once more, my grandfather did not go, in spite of insistent letters from everyone in the family.

There were visits all day long. My mother, Hélène, and I went off to three different rooms, because there were too many people. We had to "receive". It was horrible. We had to listen to the same phrases over and over and try to respond pleasantly, without a moment left to think; meanwhile I kept repeating to myself just the same: this is too sad, it can't be true, it's going to stop. But it did not stop; it even settled in; it spoiled everything; it took up all the space.

As evening fell, I heard two doctors discussing something I could hardly grasp. I couldn't believe they were really talking about my father. And yet, it was true, and it poisoned many of my nights. They had done an autopsy. My father had died of a perforation of the stomach. The surgeon who had come the night before had been very reassuring, saying that it was probably the beginning of pneumonia and was so painful because it was "badly placed", pinching a nerve. That evening, my aunt Jeanne, who was very worried, had telephoned from the Waldau to urge my mother to let them call in my father's best friend, the surgeon de Quervain. But Mama had categorically refused, fearing she would frighten my father and saying that she had every confidence in the diagnosis of the surgeon from La Chaux-de-Fonds. If it had been done right then—if the diagnosis had been made, and it wasn't a complicated diagnosis, either—the operation would have had every chance of succeeding.

Once I had understood it all, I repeated to myself again and again: he would still be alive if . . . And that "if" was unbearable; it brought an infinitely serious charge against the surgeon and my mother. How difficult it was for me to forgive them!

I don't know how the time passed until the burial. Only the night was left for crying; there were continually too many people around during the day.

Monsieur Junod came; he asked me if I had seen my father's body. No, they had forbidden me to. He did not understand and wanted to insist on the point to my mother and to go with me into the consulting room where my father was. Mama stood firm. I really would have liked to go near Papa, that night when he would be alone, to pray beside him and even to tell him the things I'd never said, to explain things to him, and it seemed to me that there were still so many things to say that to see him asleep in death would at least mean having him for a little while longer, delaying the true departure. But I said nothing, or in any case I did not insist.

The burial service seemed particularly sad to me: cut short, dead in itself of a real death with no hope of return.

All at once, I made a comparison. A few weeks before, a thirteen-year-old girl, a student in the business school, had thrown herself out of the window of the lavatory, right there at the school. She had not done her homework; before class, she had said to the girl who sat next to her on the bench: "If the teacher questions me, I'm going to throw myself out of the window." The teacher had questioned her, and she had answered, "M'sieur, first I have to leave the room." And she had left; her horror-stricken companion had warned the teacher. All he did was laugh, saying, "It takes a lot more than that to kill oneself." And it was only at recess that they had found her broken body in the courtyard. Since she was an obviously sick child, she was granted a Catholic burial. The whole school had been present and had accompanied her body to the cemetery. That had seemed very beautiful to me: and it was the burial of a suicide that had seemed so beautiful to me and the burial of my father that had seemed so ghastly.

The service took place at home, in the big dining room. During the sermon, you could hear the noise of those who were closing the coffin and taking it outside. Then all the men left, except one of the pastors who continued a few prayers for the women, who all stayed at the house; only the men went to the cemetery. I escaped, and, from the window of my little room, I saw the hearse loaded with funeral wreaths, with many vehicles with flowers behind, pass slowly down the rue Jaquet-Droz, followed by a large crowd of men. When the hearse had reached the far end of the street, the men farthest back were not far from the station. I stayed in my room a long time, without understanding, as if in a nightmare.

During the weeks that followed, I continued absolutely and as if bound by some kind of loyalty not to understand anything.

The day after the burial, I went back to school. Mathilde Kocher and Samuel Junod came to my house to get me and go with me and then walked me back again later. This went on for several days. It was very nice, but there was no point in it. I talked them out of it with difficulty. During the day, everything went along painfully but well enough; I did just about everything I was expected to do, but everything had lost its real meaning. Then the nights came; I did not sleep, but they were too short; everything was heavy, filled with responsibility. I would have liked to reflect thoroughly, but that didn't work. I felt sorry for Mama; she was like a helpless child. She often said the same things over and over, and she complained; Papa would not have liked that. She spoiled the baby too much, whom she never left and who she thereby obliged to hear all her troubles, which he certainly didn't understand but which cast a shadow over his early life.

Hélène and Willy were at the Waldau. Until now, I had been bound very much to the house; the only times I went out alone, except on rare exceptions, were the times when I went to Madeleine's. Now, I started to take long walks. I went to the cemetery and then from there to the nearby woods, across the pastures often still covered with snow. Haunting thoughts went with me, but they did not develop: there was this incomprehensible death of my father, and his burial that had looked to me like a thing without hope; and there was, behind the gloomy sky at winter's end, that God in whom my father had believed and who was completely different from what we thought; and often, like a persistent hope, the memory of the Holy Virgin. The Holy Virgin was Catholic, I knew it; did she belong only to the Catholics? And why hadn't I talked about all that with my father? I asked myself: If he were here, would I tell him? But tell him what? That I didn't understand anything? That it was horrible for me that he was dead? That God was different? I went over and over all that in the silence of those long walks. The faithful Mad came over often. I didn't say anything. She got worried. One day, I admitted to her: "You know, I can't anymore." She said simply, "Yes, I see that. Don't you want to talk?" But I couldn't talk about the essence of it. Now she often went with me; she would become a nurse, and I a doctor; we would work together; we would have a clinic for the poor. She thought up a thousand projects to tear me away from my preoccupations. One day, she surprised me: "You really should do some serious studies in theology." My only response was a categorical No. But that evening, when I'd gone to bed, I turned the question over in my mind in all directions. That would be the mission, then: medicine and theology. No. But theology had its advantages; one would understand God and the meaning of life better. And yet, there were lots of "buts". The next day, I told Mad No again. She proposed, "Then talk just once to Louis Perregaux." Again, No. And very softly, to myself: He's a Protestant, it wouldn't work. And yet I was fond of him.

At home, changes were brewing. The first of April we would leave our residence. My father's successor was coming in already for consultations. Another doctor, whom my father had known but whom we had never yet met, Doctor Roulet, came to help my mother with invaluable advice. He was charming. When you tried to thank him, he would say: "I'm sure that if I had died, your father would have come and done for my wife and my children much more than I'm doing for you."

I started looking for an apartment. At number 64 on the rue Léopold-Robert there was one on the first floor with three rooms. The owner, an old Jewish man, at first did not want to show it to me. When he found out whom it was for, he agreed to. When I went back to tell my mother what I had found, she moaned a lot: "Three rooms, after having lived for so long in such a big house!" Obviously, that, too, was going to be painful for her. The first of April we left our home and our servants. And for the first time in my life, I learned what it meant to work; the days of the long walks were over. I did all the housework: cooking, dishwashing, errands, sweeping. And school started again.

TUBERCULOSIS
Spring 1918

When classes resumed, since my mother found the *gymnasium* an uncalled-for luxury, I promised to do the three programs of *gymnasium* classics, *gymnasium* mathematics and the girls' secondary school, without counting the commercial courses in stenography, typewriting, and bookkeeping. I had a bewildering schedule and a whole household on my hands. But it didn't leave too much time to reflect on all that troubled me, and that was a relief.

One day, however, I said to my mother: "You know, it's too much; since I'm doing the housekeeping, one school program would be enough." Mama said, "That's fine, then, take the commercial program, but you'll soon have to be earning your living." "But since Uncle provides everything we need?" Mama got angry, there was nothing to be done. I always got up before 4:00 A.M.; when the lights in the post office were lit at four, I was cleaning the dining room, in which I slept; the next room was a sort of living room; Mama and the baby slept next to the courtyard. In the evenings,

I did homework until very late; besides French, German, Greek, and Latin, I now had English,[1] Italian, and Hebrew; and a lot of mathematics.

Mad was concerned. "This can't go on. Do you want me to write to your uncle?" "No, above all, no fuss."

One Saturday, Mama went away with the baby for a while; I went to my aunt Marguerite's. The first thing she did was to put me to bed, and the second was to call the doctor. He ordered complete rest. The first time I went to sleep, I must have slept close to twenty-four hours. Then they took X rays and set up a schedule: the doctor would allow two hours of school per day and, besides that, as much rest and time on the chaise longue as possible. Often, in the afternoons, I would sit on a chaise longue under a fir tree in my grandparents' old park, and I read. I began to think a great deal again, but with less anxiety. My confidence returned; everything had to have a meaning. At school everyone was very kind; the teachers said, "Take care of yourself; it was foolish to have wanted to work so much", and the students would keep me up to date on what was going on; I think I did only Greek and mathematics. Mad came often to keep me company under my fir tree.

One day Mama came back, a bit like a hurricane. She gave me a choice: either I was really sick and would give up school completely and definitively; or I wasn't sick, and in that case I would resume my school and the housekeeping. Obviously I did not hesitate; I resumed the work. That lasted a very little while, two or three weeks at the most. I especially remember the first day; I was happy to recover a regular life and all my classes; there was a lot to catch up

---

[1] Perhaps an error. It seems that Adrienne received her first English lessons when she entered the school in Basel—ED.

on, because these last few weeks had not been of a nature that would lighten the work. The housework cost me less than it had at the beginning; and many things went more easily because I knew how to budget my time better. I could now sweep a room while the milk was boiling without it completely boiling over the sides of the saucepan, becoming the occasion of an arduous clean-up job. One day, when I got home from school, Mama had finished the dinner and set the table; it seemed like a great feast to me.

But there were also days that were painful; the fatigue that I had had before those afternoons under the fir tree had returned, and often it was overwhelming. Then, too, I would get all depressed and become very painfully preoccupied with myself, a state I had never before known. One day Louis Perregaux telephoned to invite me to go with him to a bazaar in the Eplatures; in former times, this would have been great entertainment, but now, I refused. What good was Louis Perregaux? Mad was at boarding school in Sissach learning German; I was very sad about it and yet, in a way, relieved. I wouldn't have known how to explain to her what was going on, I didn't know, myself; but things weren't going at all well. A doctor who was a widower and a friend of my father's was hovering around my mother; that aggravated me beyond belief. From time to time, he would insist on my going to dine at his house, and, although I liked his daughters very well, I never wanted to go; he disgusted me. One day when he came and my mother was not there, he began to stroke my arms; I became terribly angry; first I gave him a quick slap and then began to chase him out of the apartment, telling him I'd tell my mother and anyone else who would listen if he ever came back; he dashed out rather quickly. I locked the apartment, left the key in the lock, and went to take a bath; I felt dirty, humiliated; I was crying with rage all the time I washed. I heard my mother ring the bell and then try to put her key into the lock. She went away, for I did not budge. Suddenly, an idea came to me: I could kill myself, and all this misery would come to an end; but no convenient way of doing it came to mind. Everything seemed impracticable. But to begin with, since one can't kill oneself decently in a bathtub, I got out of the bath and, I don't know how, suddenly found myself kneeling on the floor, offering God to live for him this life I no longer wanted. Little by little, great clarity came to me: one must never take one's own life, life is worth living, since God is the one who gave it, and since it is worth living, it is worth being offered to God otherwise than as a thing of which one had simply had enough. When my mother came back a second time, I was calmed down. Two days later, my mother left again, with my little brother, to visit some friends in Basel. I was sent to Aunt Annette's. That very evening she received a huge basket filled with cherries, and, while I was helping her to pit them, I began to feel ill. The doctor found that now I was really seriously ill. The pulmonary tuberculosis that he had suspected some weeks before had manifested itself on both sides. I had no idea what that meant: I did not get up anymore; I slept; and, when I was not sleeping, I was exhausted. Aunt Annette took care of me with much kindness; she gave me things to drink and brought me flowers. One day they brought me a pretty rose-colored wool bed jacket, since I would be in bed for a very long time. . . . This "very long time" stayed in my ear; it was rather agreeable, I wouldn't have to make any effort, for this would be for a very long time. . . . I did not read. I coughed a little; it was my sole occupation.

Then came the decision: they were sending me to Langenbruck. I have no memory of the trip. Mama accompanied me. That evening, I found myself alone in a pleasant room with a terrace in the front. The name of the room was Pfauen; there was a peacock painted on the door. I had not seen it when I came in; it was Sister[2] Lina who told me about it. It seemed to me that it was very often evening; from my bed, I would see it fall on a warm, green countryside; it changed it into a night of balmy brown silence. There was a road far off in the valley: but you had to know it was there; it was there just like the other patients were there, even though I could not see them but could only hear their voices. Sister Lina would say: "That's Madame Schmidt"; she was from Germany, but she would never go home, because she was too ill. So, then, one could be too ill to go home. One morning, Sister Lina said: "I hope the noise didn't disturb you; Monsieur Wolf died this morning in the room next to yours, and since he didn't want to die, that made for some noise." One would die in this house; this idea filled me with confidence. The doctor came several times a day. You had to tell him exactly what you had eaten and what you hadn't eaten; and show him where it hurt when you breathed. It was true that it hurt every time you breathed, sometimes here, sometimes there, and there as well. Breathing was just another part of the fatigue of life these days; I hadn't known anything of all that last year, or even six months ago, but Papa had been there then; it was simple to live. There were problems, but they did not become real obsessions. And God was different from what one thought, but he didn't exhaust you so much. One day, I'm not sure à propos of what, I said to the doctor: "In the spring, I'll . . ." "In the spring," he told me, "you won't

---

[2] The word "Sister" in German means "nurse" as well as "deaconess" or "nun"—ED.

Langenbruck. Around 1918

be here." They had said I'd be in bed for a very long time. So this very long time would not last until spring. I asked, "When can I get up, then?" He explained gently, but in a rather hoarse voice, that there wouldn't be any more springtimes for young ladies sick in both lungs. I understood him very well. I was in complete agreement. And I thought, with a new joy: Papa and God will be there. I spent the rest of the afternoon praying, maybe not the whole time, but a lot of it. I offered God my death, since perhaps he didn't need this life. I felt completely reassured, happy, peaceful. Again, I knew with certainty that God was entirely other; but that was just fine; he would explain it all himself, and he would show me.

The next day, the doctor asked, "I didn't frighten you by telling you the truth, did I?" No, he hadn't frightened me.

In all, I stayed at Langenbruck three months. I met several of the patients. Once or twice, when it was too hot, they put me outside all day on a chaise longue, in a forest that came right up to the sanatorium. Since I was too tired to talk much, they had reserved a little out-of-the-way corner for me. It was peaceful, but I still preferred the solitude of my room.

Once the doctor said to me: "You'll be leaving for the mountains in a few weeks; the trip will be painful, but you're not doing well enough here. You're not getting any better on the whole, and there is a chance, all the same, that you might get a little better." I didn't much like the prospect of leaving, but all that had been decided for me, by my doctor, the staff, and my relatives who were physicians.

I had been all alone at Langenbruck but not at all unhappy; life had been as if suspended.

LEYSIN

October 1918–July 1920

On October 1, my mother accompanied me as far as Lausanne; the beginning of the trip was made in a car, the rest by train. We stayed in Lausanne for two days at the home of the Bellevue aunt. Then my cousin Charlotte Olivier, a doctor like her husband, took me to Leysin. She was Russian, very vivacious; she spoke very rapidly with a heavy accent. She explained some things about my illness to me and about the treatment, which would be a long one. She seemed very foreign to me, but, behind everything that appeared strange, I sensed her great kindness. To relieve my mother, they, my Olivier cousins, would pay for my stay at Leysin. When the car finally deposited us in front of La Nichée clinic, I was in a total state of bewilderment. I would be in a room with three beds: one of the girls was an old schoolmate of mine; the other, a young Jewish girl from Frankfurt, had been at Leysin for a very long time and was a little younger than we were. As the result of some confusion, they treated me for the first three weeks as if I had had, besides my pulmonary disease, spondylitis of the neck and left me lying perfectly flat and wouldn't even let me raise my head. It was painful to live like that, especially since I had great difficulty breathing. My roommates spent their days on the balcony, and I in the rather dark room. I was tired, always slightly feverish and very annoyed by everything around me; the days seemed long. When they finally discovered that the spondylitis of the neck had been cured long since, I was able to resume a normal position in my bed. I was doing better than I had been at Langenbruck, but I had frequent relapses, accompa-

Leysin. Around 1919

nied by a rather high fever. Little by little I began to read; it was incredible how much could be found to read in an indescribable disorder. Friends from La Chaux-de-Fonds sent me the homework assignments and long descriptions of what they were doing, thinking that they could make it easier for me to resume classes. Around Christmas, I began to get up a little; for about an hour, on days when I didn't have any fever. For the rest of the time, I could be out a lot on the balcony in my bed. While I hadn't done much thinking when I was at Langenbruck, at Leysin I began to reflect all the more, but my thoughts turned in circles. I searched for God but seemed to find only silence. I liked the silence at Leysin, with its immense calm. Down in the valley you could see the Rhône river and watch the trains go by; those trains took the place of the long road in Langenbruck and signified life, genuine life. What we lived here was set apart, almost outside reality; I understood it more and more as a preparation, but a preparation for what?

This would be my first Christmas without Papa, but I was looking forward to it. It seemed to me that a Christmas away from the world would have a new meaning. Lying on a chaise longue, I saw the Christmas tree. It had a far-away look. The nurses sang; that meant nothing. If I had been alone, I would have wept at all this emptiness. When they took me back to my room; my bed was entirely covered with packages that had come in the mail over the last few days and which they had saved for me as a surprise. There were exactly thirty-six of them. They contained many books and lovely things. Hélène had made me a very pretty little mauve apron, Aunt Jeanne had sent an unbelievably enormous package containing at least twenty small presents and a very kind letter. The unwrapping did not come to an end and I really was happy. But that evening, when I began to pray, I grasped for the first time something that filled me with thankfulness: it seemed to me that love of neighbor, of which I had had a passive experience, had become as though tangible to me. God had, as it were, taken a new form. He was the Father of love of neighbor, but still and more than ever, he was another God than the narrow God of Protestantism. When I thought of the word "narrow" I knew it was appropriate; there was a kind of dualism between God and Protestantism. I don't believe I thought about Catholicism for even a second, but I made, almost unconsciously, this strange promise, which, once made, filled me with a kind of confused concern: I promised God that I would follow the road he pointed out to me, that I would be obedient to him. Then I was a bit frightened by my own audacity and started to limit my promise to the time I'd be in Leysin; but at that very moment the word "narrow" came back to me, and I told God that I was repeating my promise and that I would try not to limit it.

A short while after Christmas, a young girl bursting with health came to visit me. I don't know what good wind brought her. Her name was Jeanne Lacroix; she was from Paris and took turns with her sister Pauline looking after her sister-in-law Emma, a patient in another clinic, Les Frênes. We immediately formed a friendship, a kind of true friendship that doesn't need a lot of explanations and admits what it does not understand through mere reasoning. Jeanne Lacroix was about twelve years my senior. On her first visit, she brought me a book, whose title I don't remember, and some sweets. I refused the sweets; I was never hungry, and for sweets even less than for anything else. She asked me if there were anything edible that I would like. Yes, I had a very pronounced weakness for those delicacies called caviar and *foie gras*, which had doubly disappeared from my life, because of the war and because of my father's death. Some weeks later, I received from Jeanne's brother, who sent them from Marseille after unsuccessful requests to Paris and elsewhere, a tin of caviar and a pot of *foie gras*. I couldn't get over it. But the Lacroix family were all like that; nothing that would give pleasure to their friends seemed impossible to them, and they would let no difficulty deter them from obtaining it. In the meantime I had met Pauline. My new friends were Catholics, Pauline with a great apostolic zeal that I discovered only much later. At that time, they talked with great naturalness about what they believed and claimed to be happy and in possession of the truth. That all really seemed a little surprising to me, and yet I sensed very well they were telling the truth.

One day, the directress of the boarding house, Mademoiselle Schmidt, came to tell me that I would be taking my religious instruction from a French pastor, Monsieur Monin, who would come once a week to the clinic. There would be another girl, Mé-Li-Anne Bouët, the daughter of the owner of another clinic in the neighborhood. I did not have, however, the least desire to take religious instruction; I had been feeling rather liberated by my illness from all my anxiety about the real life of God, his essence. Now, all that had to be brought up again. But I felt so given over to the will of others—I had a very strong need to be obedient, it is true, but that was obedience of another kind altogether—and in short, I was obedient *against* obedience. That's what I felt, perhaps a bit confusedly, but no less strongly. So Monsieur Monin came. He was very gentle and rather boring; we had a French catechism. I nearly counted the minutes until the hour was up. The words he used seemed singularly devoid of content; sometimes, when the lesson was done, I would repeat them quietly, but they rang false. Yes, God was other;

the old anxiety came back; it was stronger than formerly, because now it touched everything that served to create any relationships whatever with God: faith, hope, and charity. Monsieur Monin never prayed with us. He would give us a sort of lecture, require some sort of written exercise, a protocol, and disappear. Mé-Li-Anne disappeared at the same time he did; one day, when she stayed behind for a short time, I asked her: "Tell me, do you find this religious instruction satisfactory?" As far as she was concerned, everything was in order.

During this period—I was on my feet for about two hours a day at this time—Benette de Blaireville, an old schoolmate from the *gymnasium* who was a year older than I, came to see me. She lived at the Chalet Espérance, a clinic founded by my cousin Olivier. There were only girls there. She suggested: "Why don't you come over once a week and give us a talk? We're all falling asleep; we need some life." Yes, I'd go with pleasure. Since I had frequent relapses, I couldn't go there very regularly, but I was there six or eight times. Those were very remarkable, unforgettable moments, milestones in my existence. My subjects must have seemed rather odd: "The Right to Thought", "Obedience and Liberty", "Truth and Its Dosage", "The Expression of Truth in Dostoevsky", "*Raison d'être*", and so on. The audience was composed of workers, young nurses, and a few young students.

Louisa Jacques was there. She was perhaps twenty, with big black eyes in her very thin face, splendid brown hair, tall and slender, with sweet white hands and a slightly husky voice. After the second or third talk, she came back to the house with me. Since I had to lie down, she stayed near me: "You're going to make me become a Catholic", she said as she was leaving. I was shocked by this. Why? "Obedience and liberty are found in the unity you present only in

God and in his Church." A year later, Louisa really dared to take this step: she became a Catholic. She wanted to enter Carmel; no Carmel on the continent, at least none of the ones to which she applied, would admit her because of her lungs. In 1938 or 1939 she entered the Carmel in Egypt and died there as a novice of typhoid fever. When she realized that she had the disease, she offered her life for the conversion of Protestants.[1]

And there was also Solange Sordet. She had been a nurse at the Lausanne Cantonal Hospital and had caught tuberculosis while nursing consumptives. The first time I saw her, a large girl with a deceptively healthy appearance, she explained to me: "I'm too ill to be at the Espérance; I have the bacilli; they're going to put me in the public sanatorium. Now they tell me it's not serious, it's only for a short while. But I know what that way of talking means; at the end of a few months, when it's gotten still worse, they will tell me: 'The mountains aren't good for you, we're going to take you down to the Cantonal Hospital, the air of Lausanne is more gentle. And besides, it's your native air; it will work miracles.' But I will still be aware; I will know that I'm lost. They will put me in a big ward, and when my last days come, they'll stick me in a cell, saying to me kindly, 'You'll see what good the solitude will do you, and now we'll be able to feed you eggs and cognac, which we couldn't do for you on the ward.' But that won't have any effect; I'll comply, but I'll understand. And then, when I can no longer even eat, when I'm half-unconscious, they'll take me out of

---

[1] She did not enter a Carmel in Egypt but rather the Poor Clares in Jerusalem. One can read about her in *Soeur Marie de la Trinité* (Louisa Jacques), *1901–1942: Conversion, vocation, carnets* (Beirut, 1943). [Sister Marie de la Trinité (Louisa Jacques), 1901–1942. Conversion, vocation, journals]—ED.

that cell so they can give it to somebody else, and I'll die all alone at the end of a corridor, knowing very well what is happening. And then, in the pulmonary ward, there's Sister Madeleine, a deaconess, a very sweet person I used to work with; maybe she will tell me the truth, and even if she acts with me like she does with the rest of the dying, I will guess my coming death from the anguish of her expression; she also works in the two adjoining cells and helps those who are dying at the end of the corridor." "So-So", as we called her, left L'Espérance for the Sanatorium; I saw her again sometimes. She was very cheerful and a comfort to those around her. The following spring, 1920, I went down to Basel for ten days. I went by the Cantonal Hospital. So-So, who had been in the pulmonary ward for months, had left that very morning for the cell; she was all pale and transparent, could hardly breathe enough to talk in a whisper. Full of hope, she said softly to me: "Now it will go better. I saw nineteen of them leave the ward this winter to die; not one of them was aware of it; but it won't be like that for me: they are giving me eggs and cognac, it was too tiring in the general ward; I'm going to get my strength back, and very soon I'll be able to come back up to Leysin; we'll take our cure together—it'll be nice!" Poor So-So. I was heartbroken to see her fooled as well. I scarcely stopped thinking of her during my stay in Basel. When I passed through Lausanne again, a week later, fully resolved to tell her the truth, So-So had lost consciousness and was dying, abandoned at the end of the corridor.

The girls at the Chalet Espérance were charming. The ones who came to the talks were always ready for a discussion afterward; I don't know how high a plane our ideas reached, but we were full of enthusiasm and the desire to live.

Mama came to visit me at La Nichée in the spring of 1919. She arrived at the beginning of the afternoon. She found the atmosphere of the house painful. She read all the letters that I had left in my drawer; I felt exasperated. Then, before evening, she left. "Fortunately you'll soon be cured; in an environment like this, one could become seriously ill."

As for me, I wasn't the least bit unhappy. I felt very strongly that this illness was a time set apart, a preparation, but for what? And then, I had one certainty: all of that came from God and was going back to him; it was truly a time set apart for him. How I'd have loved then to have someone to give me counsel, to explain to me how to avoid wasting this precious time! But there was no one. So I arrived at a sort of freedom of spirit and action beyond my age.

One day, Pauline Lacroix said to me: "If you were a Catholic, you would need a very good priest; you are made for obedience." I had no idea what she was talking about. I was not thinking of the possibility of "being a Catholic".

There were a lot of Russians in Leysin, left stranded by the revolution, cured, but lacking the money needed for the equipment necessary to walk again and to lead an upright life. I had the idea of organizing a bazaar; I asked all my acquaintances to make things for the sale; I called on a whole mass of people. It was all very promising; the bazaar would take place on July 12.

All of a sudden it was decided that I was to be confirmed on July 9. I didn't feel in any kind of state to be confirmed, but there was no way of talking to Monsieur Monin: he came at the appointed time and, as soon as his catechism lesson was done, he disappeared with an agility that was as hopeless as it was amazing.

One day he announced to us that, before being confirmed,

it was a good idea to have some kind of examination. We would do it in writing. He gave us, as a subject: "If Christ came back to earth, what would he say of the present state of the world, and what would he say of me?" Good heavens, what a subject! We had to write eight pages, not one more than that, not one less. I have no idea now what I wrote, but, in any case, I put the question to the Lord in all seriousness: Was he not, as I was, of the opinion that I shouldn't be confirmed? I saw everything differently from the pastor; I had completely lost all true certainty, except, of course, that of the existence of one God in Trinity, but strangely different from the one presented to us by the religious instructions, and I ended by asking not to be confirmed unless the pastor saw fit to do it without my inner assent. There was never any discussion of our compositions; only much later did I learn that Monsieur Monin never even read our ideas on what Christ would say.

Hélène was in boarding school at Lutry, where she was enjoying herself enormously. It was probably the happiest time in her life; she was taking home management and dressmaking from a lady named Brun, whom she called "Madame" with an unheard-of affection in her voice; she wrote letters full of happiness; she had friends. She was delegated by the family to come to my confirmation, which was to take place at four in the afternoon. When I got up at two, Hélène was there, and we went together into the village to eat some ice cream; Mama had given her the money for that purpose. I had the very clear impression that I was doing something absolutely indecent by going into a candy store before the ceremony. But as for the "Yes" itself, it had become a matter of indifference to me; I believe I'd forgotten all about it.

When we went down to the village, we came upon two or three posters announcing the bazaar; I took great pains to keep Hélène from seeing them, because what would Mama have said? I suspected, with good reason, that she would have been horrified.

The confirmation took place at the Bouëts', in a big drawing room. All their friends were there. Mé-Li-Anne had a dress for the occasion, but not I, since I was very poor and had really only the basic necessities. The pastor Cavallieri gave the sermon; he was an old apostate priest, much loved in Protestant circles in Leysin and Lausanne; people went in crowds to his sermons, because his heavy Italian accent added one more charm to his character as apostate. I understood absolutely nothing of the sermon; but I remember that afterward, before they served tea and cakes, Pastor Cavallieri said to me in a rather humid voice, "You'll have to come and see me, my child"; and I heard myself saying very clearly, in a tone that did not permit a reply, "No, Monsieur." I had a disagreeable impression, something that added to the emptiness of the confirmation: I felt that I had become a robot. (It was only two years later that Monsieur Cavallieri was run out of his pulpit in disgrace: he had taken as mistresses all but one of the deaconesses at the public sanatorium; he had invited them each in turn, a different one every afternoon, telling each of them that he had to invite the others so they wouldn't be aware of her presence; not only was the thing odious all by itself, but all the details that went with it—prayer before and after— and all the lies. Two of the deaconesses were pregnant. The repercussions at the motherhouse were enormous. When I learned of these horrors, I had already gone to Saint-Loup, but I was horribly troubled by it, and for a very long time.)

The bazaar took place right after confirmation. From morning until evening, I read cards, seated behind a screen. It was great fun and brought in a lot of money. The net receipts were more than three thousand francs, and we were able to buy all the necessary equipment. To look more dignified, I had worn my hair up, and afterward I wore a chignon.

INTERLUDE ON THE PLAINS

I came down from Leysin at the end of the week; I had a ten-weeks' holiday but with a very strict regimen of rest.

First of all I spent a few days with my Olivier cousins at Le Mont. It was a delightful atmosphere; everything had significance, everything had a meaning. We talked about my coming studies; in the winter, since I was doing better, I could stay with the Bouëts and go to school. Mé-Li and her brother were working toward their *bachots*; I could join them. I wouldn't return to La Nichée but to L'Espérance. And my cousins took my vocation as a doctor seriously. They asked me questions and accepted my answers with a kindness that warmed the heart. I really felt somewhat like their daughter; besides, my cousin Eugène, my father's nephew (although older than he), resembled my father, if not in features, at least in personality, manner, and turn of mind. I seemed to relive my childhood in that silent house, full of shadows and memories; I felt at home; it was difficult for me to leave, but I had now also seen, at first hand, the life of a woman doctor: it was fascinating and full of responsibilities. And then, too, there was this: Cousin Charlotte —"Charlotte Russe", as Hélène and I called her, with an obvious lack of respect but not without affection—treated people (even me!) as something very precious; and she did that because she was profoundly Christian. To me, it was not at all disagreeable to be treated as a precious, unique being, because I belonged to God.

From Cousin Charlotte's, I went to the Waldau. There, the common life was rather difficult. I was still too ill to resume it, and I was very sensitive. I got up for breakfast, about eight-thirty; then I lay down until dinnertime. When that could be done in the garden, it was very pleasant, but in the living quarters themselves, although I had a room to myself, it was truly difficult; I would hear the others exerting themselves, and I felt the need to do my share of their work. And then it seemed to me that it was no longer my illness that made so many precautions necessary but perhaps, indeed, a growing laziness. This impression was very heavy to bear. After dinner I had to lie down again until teatime; then I was free to live like the others until 9:00 P.M., when I had to go to bed.

During that vacation I met the Forels: the Forels, and especially Oscar Forel, the young psychiatrist who was very lively, a musician, and infinitely indulgent to the young girl I then was. His wife, Lokit, was more robust, a bit abrupt, but nice to me. Almost every day I spent a little time with them. She taught me all kinds of women's handwork; and he would read aloud, talk psychology, analyze the character of his children, pose psychiatric problems, and play the violin. Sometimes in the evenings, we would go to Mösli, the home for old ladies that he ran; we would sit ourselves down in the nearby meadow, and he would play: for the patients? for us? for himself? who will ever know? But he played well, and this sort of romanticism did not fail to make a big impression on me.

And then, there was Tjotja, who was a close friend of the Forels at that particular time, although, several months

later, heaven knows why, she got into a deadly quarrel with
them. Tjotja was a Russian doctor who had been at the Waldau since we were small children. She had tended our many
childhood bruises, and now she was becoming our friend.
Hélène liked her as much as I did, but Hélène did not like
the Forels. Tjotja used to ask unexpected questions, not always the most tactful but never devoid of a very great kind-
liness. She did not believe in God at all; we used to discuss
that at length; she couldn't believe that I believed, and I, for
my part, didn't want to believe that she didn't believe. Forel
was an unbeliever too; it was frankly disagreeable. I would
explain about God to them but always felt obliged to add:
"He is other than what I'm saying to you, but he *is*."

In spite of all the enforced rest, my life was quite different
from what it had been at Leysin; its density was different;
the hours of solitude were more solitary than those on the
mountain, and, as for the hours spent with friends, they too
had a different quality; for now, I wasn't doing it all alone,
I was with people who had an intellectual life.

Still, I never talked about Leysin. It would have seemed
almost impious to discuss that strange isolation to which I
nevertheless delighted to return. The Waldau, for me, was as
if between two ages; it was only the half-magical and partly
fearsome land; it was not yet the homeland of my second
youth; I would soon be seventeen, and it seemed to me
that nobody had ever had any idea what being seventeen
was like. They were all either healthy adults, or patients, or
small children.

One memory of Leysin stayed with me much of the time:
a young Viennese boy of ten had died there of meningitis,
and I had served as his nurse for several days. They had
found no one else to stay with him while he was in a coma;
he did not move at all, he did not ask for any care, but he

couldn't be left alone. Suddenly, without any way, at least not to my inexpert eye, of foreseeing this change at this precise moment, he had stopped breathing. I had a dead person before me. This transition had appeared so natural to me that for a long moment I had not called anyone. I contemplated this body, no longer disturbed by any breathing, with a real satisfaction. So that was death: to leave behind one this diseased body and present oneself before God with a soul stripped of every other care but the knowledge of God. I envied Paul infinitely. He was a Catholic. I knew that the priest had been there to assist him several days before. I did not know what that meant, it all appeared profoundly mysterious to me, but in front of that child's body I understood that that assistance must have been fine and true, since Paul's very features now expressed peace. I would have liked to talk with someone about all that: I said to myself, at Leysin —it is so easy to arrange the world one is not presently in— I will talk to someone when I'm in the plains. But there was no one, on the mountain or in the plain, to whom I could speak of this assistance from the priest. I thought about it often, and, at the Waldau, where there were about a thousand patients, there was very often a hearse in front of the building, and I would imagine that dead person, stripped, too, in order to live the great hour.

Tjotja knew Doctor Alexandrowska, who had until recently cared for me at Leysin. But as wholly charming as she was, Tjotja was totally lacking in the simplest discretion. She told my uncle things I did not know about. One day my uncle had me come to his office; I was rather impressed to be summoned like that. Besides, although I did not know it then, since my father's death, my uncle, who felt responsible for all of us, had acquired the habit of calling each member of the family who was vacationing with him up to his office, to present to him whatever he considered important. Perhaps we had even all become something like "cases" for my uncle. That is what Charlotte Olivier thought, seeing that the people around my uncle, comprised solely of patients, were imperceptibly robbing him of his ability to perceive as normal the people to whom he talked. As for me, I didn't notice that, I just sensed the inner difficulty my uncle had in speaking; he put off indispensable conversations as long as possible, but, still, he would never let us leave him without having spoken to him. Moreover, I never noticed anything but his immense kindness in these conversations and a great respect for the personality of the other. So, when he summoned me, my uncle asked me to talk about Doctor Alexandrowska, whom I truly considered a friend, although she was perhaps some fifteen years older than I. I told him about the hours spent with her in the afternoons, drinking tea sweetened with jam; I even admitted, without any shame, the few cigarettes I had smoked with her— my first cigarettes, I believe; I told him about the Russian literature she was teaching me to appreciate and about the Russian lessons she was giving me (at this point I spoke a little Russian, that is, with mistakes and roundabout ways I could manage to say just about what I wanted to, and I could easily follow other people's conversations). My uncle asked me several questions, and finally he got around to what he had wanted to say: the doctor had an illegitimate son; he was afraid of a bad influence; however, judging by what I had told him about her, he had the impression that Alexandrowska was someone good; he explained to me that Russians had different morals than we and that he would not at all like to see me adopting them. I had already heard mention of unwed mothers. I had not known that the doctor was one, and, above all, I was ignorant of what one had to do in order to become one. And yet, this whole business upset me profoundly; also because the doctor had never mentioned it to me. Deep down, though, I had a true consolation: I knew that I was finally going to see Mad again and could talk to her both about unwed mothers and about death. She would certainly be able to tell me what was useful. Finally, my uncle said: "I don't see any danger in your continuing to see the doctor." Danger: What did he mean by that?

Without warning, my mother arrived to spend the day at the Waldau. This was a bit like a hurricane. Mama checked over the books that I had brought from Leysin, among which was *Les Contes* [Tales] by Samain. A school friend from La Chaux-de-Fonds had sent them to me. Mama was terribly shocked; she came to find me in the garden and heaped reproaches upon me; one could see what kind of mind I had; she would never dare admit to the family what she had discovered about her own daughter. Since I hadn't yet read the book, I didn't really know what to say. Mama ended by saying: "I wonder if you're still a virgin." I didn't understand the exact meaning of these words, but I felt the insult very keenly. It seemed to me that Mama had just severed irreparably what united me to her; I felt as if I had been thrown out of the family and fallen into a hostile, foreign environment that closed me off from everything that made up my life. It seemed to me that an immediate decision was imperative, but what? And for the first time, perhaps, my illness appeared to me to be a profound handicap; it prevented me from doing anything; and for a long time to come it would mean this nearly nonexistent physical life, this kind of bond and complicity with chaises and rest. But, as so often happens when it is a question of making an important decision, the tiny little everyday decision took its place: it was time to go in to tea. My shortness of breath from the stairs, to which I no longer paid any attention, had still not disappeared when I arrived in the dining room. My uncle and my mother were already there, apparently in a big discussion. When my mother saw me breathless, she began to reproach me for having come too quickly, as if I had been playing some rough game. With his customary impassibility—he emphasized it still more when my mother was there—my uncle declared, "She's always out of breath; it's her illness that does that." Then my mother explained to my uncle: "If her father were still alive, this child would be properly cared for; but naturally, since I'm alone, they've forced me to make her undergo treatments that have only made her worse; when she was still at La Chaux-de-Fonds, it was no more than growing pains, and now, but what is it now?" My uncle tried to make my mother understand that I had a real lung disease, that I was getting much better, but that I still needed to be very careful and to rest. He said all this with great gentleness, wanting at the same time to calm my mother and to encourage me; suddenly I realized: I really did still have a family. With that, I forgave my mother. It seemed to me that she was quite simply too much of a child to understand life; it was always as if someone had just taken one of her toys away, and precisely the one toy she was clinging to.

Several weeks later, for my birthday, I received *Les Contes* by Samain from Aunt Marguerite; I sent it back to her very quickly, begging her to exchange it for another book.

Meanwhile, equipped with a thousand recommendations, I had permission to spend a few days at La Chaux-de-Fonds. Everything seemed both changed and immutably the same. The station looked much smaller, and yet it had kept the same dimensions, the same echoes of railroad noises. A cab took me to my aunt Marguerite's: the apartment was filled with flowers, my cousins had grown, but the atmosphere in the house was just the same as ever, full of my aunt's goodness, her smile, her affectionate care. She immediately saw that I was in need of many rather necessary things, unearthed a little seamstress at once, and when I left three days later I possessed a dressing gown, two blouses, and some underwear. Aunt Marguerite was not wealthy, her husband was very ill and needed costly care; but Aunt Marguerite loved even her niece, and the love she had for her family in its most extended sense made her ingenious.

The finest hours at La Chaux-de-Fonds were the ones I spent with Madeleine. We spent a long afternoon in her parents' park, this time not in endless walks along the paths, but very wisely on a lawn, with me stretched out on an incredible rattan chaise longue, cushioned with a mattress of unheard of softness, and her sitting at my feet. We met again as if we had never parted, and we quickly got to the central questions: God, life, service. She inquired, "Sum up your life at Leysin." But I could not summarize it; the days seemed to me to have been added one to another like an endless string of perfectly matched pearls. Perhaps there were no salient events; there were faces, questions, doubts; no answers and no certainties. Madeleine and I were so used to talking, and not to corresponding, that our letters were not only rather irregular, they lacked content; we sort of stayed on the periphery, talked about everything that held no interest for us, in order to keep silent precisely about all that we were really thinking about. And so, it was a great joy to find we were still such good friends and finally to tell each other about everything that had filled us. But Mad was a little concerned, and she asked: "Are you really on the way, dear? Are you going forward?" I did not know how to answer, for I truly did not know anything. I didn't venture asking the same question, perhaps I wasn't thinking of it, when Mad admitted, very softly, almost as if only to herself: "Since you've been ill, I've often felt abandoned; I've been waiting for you in order to continue." And, with that little short laugh of hers, as if interrupted, cut in half, which was the strangest thing about her—she got it, moreover, from her mother, who laughed in the same way, so you didn't know which of the two of them had just laughed —she said: "When you were very ill, and everybody said you were going to die, I wasn't even really frightened, I was so sure that you have a task to accomplish; it isn't finished, so I'm waiting for you." At that point I realized that Mad had given back to me a certain sense of responsibility that had perhaps been rather dormant that past year but that was not extinguished. She had reawakened it, but what was I to do to become immediately responsible now? I didn't know what I would have to undertake and began to worry, but Mad calmed me down presently: for the moment, I had to get well and yet store away everything that occurred; evade nothing but not hurry. "And what about medicine?" Madeleine asked. Yes, I was still determined, but at Leysin, after my experience with the religious instructions, it had sometimes seemed to me that theology might also provide means for approaching the sick, but theology, for a woman? What did she think about that? And Mad said sententiously, "Either medicine or the convent." Assuredly, she hadn't changed. And soon she suggested: "We ought to go visit Cousin Perregaux; I promised to let him know when you were here." He was her cousin as well as mine. At first, I didn't have a great desire to. What would be the point of stirring up all that again? He had written to me rather often and had occasionally sent me little religious tracts that I had found rather abominable; but as for my cousin himself, I liked him very much. So Madeleine telephoned; we were both invited to tea the next day. We went there together, and, although we had climbed the stairs as slowly as snails on a holiday, my heart wouldn't stop throbbing violently. He came to open the door for us himself and took us into his study, where I'd never been before. It was full of books and old papers. He cleared off a pedestal table on which the tea was served; the silver Empire tea service was lovely. Mad gave me a furtive look; we were full of embarrassment and also the giggles, and it was hard to know which would prevail. But when I refused the cream because my hand was shaking too much to pour it into my cup, the giggles got the upper hand. We stifled them by giving each other withering indignant glares. Besides, subjects of conversation were not lacking, and their plenitude obliged us to be serious, or at least did not discourage our attempts to be so. At the end of the visit, our cousin asked if I wouldn't come back once again. No, I was leaving the next day. Would I come back on my next visit? Yes. Alone? Sure. That second visit took place one year later.

From La Chaux-de-Fonds I went on to Givrins, a delightful village above Nyon, where the Olivier cousins lived on an exquisite family estate. They decided that I must go back to Leysin right away, without a stay in Basel. Mama had been living there for a year, and I had not yet seen her apartment, but she lived on the third floor, which Charlotte thought too far up for me right at that time; and then she found crocheting a little too tiring. And finally, she also said: "I am also concerned about your mother's discussions; you see, you're still truly ill, and since your mother does not wish to acknowledge that, you must take care of yourself."

BACK IN LEYSIN

On October 20, 1919, then, I went back to Leysin, really tired out from life on the plain, even though it had been an invalid's life, fearing Sister Emilie, the director of L'Espérance, who the girls said was incredibly strict, and happy to have a room all to myself. At the station, there was Sister Emilie, with a kind motherly smile that banished my fears immediately, along with Doctor Linden,[1] who was wearing white shoes because the day was marvelous, as mild as a summer's day, with three red roses in her hands to welcome me; after giving me the roses, she left me to Sister Emilie. The clinic was a few steps away; we took them very slowly. She showed me to my room, which was exactly as wide as the bed was long, and scarcely much longer than its width, but very nice. The window looked out on an elder tree; in front of this elder was the front door of a house, perhaps five meters from the window. I had a momentous thought: in order to be able to do without a horizon, one needs to have a horizon within oneself, and immediately this prayer: "Lord, let me share in your horizon."

There was a table in front of the window, and on this table several packages, along with affectionate letters to make the first contact with my new life more pleasant. They were from Aunt Marguerite, from friends, from Aunt Jeanne; and also from friends from Leysin, and of course from one or the other of the Lacroix sisters; I don't remember who was taking care of the sister-in-law right then.

Sister Emilie quickly gave me a little information about the life of the house; all the girls had rooms with two or

---

[1] Referred to above as Doctor Alexandrowska—ED.

more beds and took the cure together on a large common terrace that had been fixed up outside the house; I would have a private balcony. The prospect of all this solitude filled me with true joy; it was exactly what I needed.

I spent ten months at the Chalet Espérance; they figured among the loveliest months of my youth. As a rule, every morning from eight until noon, I went to the Vermont clinic, where I followed a sort of *gymnasium* course with Max and Mé-Li Bouët. Our instructor, an Alsatian named Monsieur Graf, taught us all the subjects, from Greek to mathematics, going through philosophy, geography, history, Latin, and I don't know what else; he was very conscientious and always very well prepared. I was a dreadful student, because the fever very often kept me from going out in the mornings. And Sister Emilie had a real horror of the school; she thought it was much too much for me and that I was already quite learned enough "just as I was", so she made innumerable days of convalescence follow every rise in temperature, during which she would contrive to pamper me unbelievably. They gave me only what I particularly liked to eat, perhaps still more often what Sister Emilie judged worthy of being liked by me. The doctor had ordered injections to build up my strength; she gave them regretfully, declaring that it was much better to fortify oneself by mouth, and always followed the shots with delicacies.

Right at the beginning, while I was still afraid of her, we had creamed carrots for dinner; I hated carrots, and I hated them very especially when they were creamed. Surreptitiously, I slid them into the pockets of my black sheath dress (Sister Emilie herself was serving the meat and vegetables). After dinner, Sister Emilie called me directly from the dining room into her little office. I was really in a tight corner; I thought she had discovered my stratagem. It was about something completely different. While she was talking to me, I felt the cold sauce running slowly down my legs; and, as I left the office, the first drops fell onto the floor. Several days later, after a conversation that made lifelong friends of us, I confessed the business about the carrots to her. Then, I didn't think of it again, and only now, more than a quarter of a century later, Sister Emilie has told me that as long as I stayed at L'Espérance, she had the carrots moved to Saturday's menu, the day I never had dinner in the dining room because school lasted longer.

Thanks to Sister Emilie, the Christmas celebration had a very homey character, and yet, it lacked something fundamental. That evening, when I was in bed, I wept, in a sort of resentment at not understanding. I felt I was definitely on the wrong road; I thought that this lack of understanding was a clear sign of ill will. Suddenly, Sister Emilie appeared. We talked for a long time about Christmas, about God, about prayer; she lived in an atmosphere of transparent peace, and, although she was very intelligent, everything, to her, seemed not only clear but perfectly adequate and proper. I was just about to calm down inside, I had already stopped crying for a minute, when suddenly it seemed to me that an appeasement at this particular moment would be cowardice, one had no right to plug up a hole this way; even if the hole were no longer apparent, it would nonetheless continue to exist beneath that cover.

One day during the Christmas holidays, when I was waiting for Jeanne Lacroix, a telephone call informed me that she would not be coming: she had a headache. The next day or the day after, I went over to Les Frênes to see her; she was lying down in a darkened room with an icepack on her head, moaning softly, and did not seem to recognize me. Very worried, I asked the nurse what was the matter: the nurse explained that there was nothing to be concerned about; it was only an attack of hysteria. Then I saw Jeanne's sister and sister-in-law. They were very upset, there had been a consultation, the doctor had come in haste from Paris, and he and the doctor from Lausanne had found absolutely nothing and agreed with the doctor who was treating her in his diagnosis of hysteria. But that was not in the least way credible to the family, who had always admired Jeanne's perfectly even temperament. I went back up to L'Espérance with some difficulty, really disturbed and upset; and then I began another bout of fever and was confined to bed for several days. The day after my visit to Les Frênes, a short note from Pauline informed me of Jeanne's death. The autopsy revealed a malignant brain tumor. There was a whole succession of extremely troubling things in that for me; added to the sorrow of losing a really dear friend was the error in diagnosis, all too reminiscent of the diagnostic error that had in fact cost my father his life. With Jeanne, it was obviously not the same thing; even if the tumor had been diagnosed and precisely located, it was inoperable; but there was still that suspicion of hysteria. In the vague moments when my friend had been conscious, they had entreated her to control herself, to try not to frighten her family that way, even to remember that she was a Christian and that it was unworthy of her to act out such a comedy. Thus, they had added to her sufferings in a way that was not only useless but cruel and degrading. Would I really have the courage to study medicine, to take upon myself these great responsibilities, to make errors, to endure the inner consequences? For a moment, I nearly had my doubts.

I could not attend the Requiem because I still had a fever, but my thoughts were with the one we had just lost. When I got up, my first outing was to the Catholic church located a few steps away from L'Espérance. This was the first time I had ever gone inside a Catholic church, but it seemed very clear to me that my prayers must be added to those of the Requiem, right there in the last place where my friend had rested. The church was rather dark, cold. Little by little the dancing flame of the little red lamp attracted my full attention; it even gave life to things around it. It was a little as if the church were inhabited, and then you could pray on your knees in this church. I took my place at the very back of the church. I didn't have the curiosity to walk around the pews or go up to the altar or note certain differences with a Protestant church. The life of the flame, the atmosphere of prayer, a kind of communion with an old lady kneeling in front, were completely enough; I was at home; this would become my home. Afterward, without my having seriously thought about conversion for any length of time, I think the idea never left me that one day, I would be definitively at home in a Catholic church. And yet, I never returned to the church in Leysin; I felt I wasn't ready; I did not really see any road, but I think that, deep inside, I knew from that moment on, with a certain sense of peace, that I would find the road one day, that I would find it in a Catholic church. One thing I did know: one had to look for the road, knowing that it was in God; I wouldn't have known how to describe it any other way.

Shortly afterward, Sister Emilie realized that I had not followed up my religious instructions by participating in the Lord's Supper; she invited me to go with her the next Sunday. I spoke with her then about the Catholic church, about the atmosphere of prayer that I had never felt until then, about my usual uneasiness that had been as if dispelled in front of that little living flame. Sister Emilie explained that all that was all only the result of my long solitude, of having read too much, of being away from my family. She didn't entirely convince me, but I didn't stand up to her, and, docile, I went with her the following Sunday. The communion itself affected me like a ceremony that didn't involve me: it passed outside of me.

The days that followed were painful; I felt that I had been unfaithful, but to whom and why? It had a vague connection to the previous Sunday, and, then, there was the visit to the Catholic church; I had felt that it had a great effect, but I could not visualize at all what I was lacking. Some moments I would promise God, very seriously, really to search for him; then great discouragement would grip me again. My uneasiness increased; I didn't talk about it to Sister Emilie, and I believe that the thought of returning to the Catholic church did not cross my mind. On the long afternoons as I took the cure on my balcony that I loved so much, I would look out at the whiteness of the snow; sometimes I would think: one should be white, like that, to reflect God as the snow reflects the sun; to be pure, to think only of God.

Meanwhile Gabrielle Junod turned up, the pastor's eldest daughter; she had come to take the cure. She was very emancipated, engaged, and never stopped talking. She would have liked to share my balcony. Sister Emilie prudently did not allow it; she went even farther and told me: "You must avoid Gabrielle as much as you can." She gave no further explanations. Some days later, Gabrielle called me into her room, which she shared with another girl; she had something to give me, and then suddenly, in front of her roommate, without my having seen anything coming, in two sentences that sounded as if she were telling a joke, she informed me about physical love between a man and a woman. It was so brutal and so unexpected that I was really terror-stricken. At first,

I was very angry with Gabrielle for having unveiled this secret to me in such a crude way; then suddenly I understood: as a prospective bride, Gabrielle was really to be pitied, for no longer even respecting this secret; she would start her married life with a very great handicap.

In the spring, for the first time, I went down to Basel. On the way down and on my way back, I stopped at So-So's home. Willy was in school at Bern. Mama lived with Hélène and Theddy on the bank of the Rhine, in an apartment that was perched very high but was very nice. I felt somewhat lost among my family; during that week, I saw my mother's friends. Mama had a white dress with rose polka-dots and a blue and white tailored suit made for me; Hélène cut out a white blouse that I sewed and decorated with hem-stitching. When I returned to Leysin, I felt very proud of my pretty outfits, and I remember that, the first Sunday, I tried them on each in turn, unable to decide which one to wear.

One Sunday afternoon, a few of the girls and I went for a walk with Sister Emilie. We had sat down under a fir tree to sing together, and, a short distance away from us, three girls, sitting under another fir tree, were singing with us. They were sitting directly opposite us; all of a sudden, the one in the middle fell face forward, rolled a few meters and stopped. Sister Emilie rushed forward, telling us to stay where we were. The girl was dead: she had been hit in the neck by a stone the size of dice that must have detached itself from the top of the mountain and had killed her outright.

This unknown girl's sudden death, coming close after the deaths of So-So and Jeanne Lacroix, made a terrible impression on me. Death was there, it was really in the midst of the living, among us, in those I loved, and in me. But it was not at liberty. It was in the hand of God, it was part of his power; he manifested himself by means of it; it was a sign. A sign for the living. To understand death, to understand God, one had to attend to the living, to love them.

Toward the end of the spring, when Cousin Charlotte arrived, I was again having a bout of fever; she examined me thoroughly. Then, looking very sad, she told me that since autumn I had stopped making progress; I would never have the health required for doing medical studies; and right away, without letting me have time to think, she asked: "So what will you do?" And I answered: "I'll be a nurse." "Well," she said, "you can try; it is much less exhausting at any rate."

After this decision, made in haste and without the idea of it ever having occurred to me before, it appeared to me that life had lost its meaning for me. I would live life as if it were a task; I would strive to make it easier for others. But it was clear that, if God was other and life other and death other, that complicated everything in a strange way. Obviously I had to find God first. One evening, when Sister Emilie had come to sit by my bed—how I loved those moments in the evenings when she came in, so softly that you didn't hear her walking down the corridor, and when we spoke in low voices so as not to wake the girls in the adjoining rooms—I told her I would serve my apprenticeship with the deaconesses. She was very pleased. "That way you will become a deaconess." No, I didn't believe so, because I believed that God was really different. She explained then that when one was with the deaconesses, one lost any concern about God's essence; one simply served him, and it was good that way. I, too, really thought that to serve was more important than to understand, but I could not bring myself to give up understanding.

One day, I was asked to fill in for the pastor at Sunday school. I don't remember what was at issue, but this occasioned a lot of trouble. One of the participants accused me of not having declined to speak; I should have done so, since I was a Catholic. Max Bouët said, "It sounded rather like the Salvation Army, but I was captivated." That afternoon, several of the monitors came to L'Espérance to speak to me. As for me, I was rather bewildered by all the commotion. I had not dispelled my inner uneasiness; I had shared it with others.

Since it was obvious that I would not be studying, I had no more classes at all in the summer. I took a more consistent and regular cure. Moreover, I was doing much better. Very early in the mornings, I would sometimes walk toward Prafendaz; from there, one could see a little tip of Lake Léman. How unreal and far away the world looked! I had not the least desire to rejoin it, but I knew that that fearful moment was drawing near. I tried, nevertheless, to accept whatever was offered as coming from God.

Toward the end of July, I went to spend about ten days at Gryon with a cousin; she had two sons about my age. Charles was very nice, but every time his mother, Marianne Masset, saw him in conversation with me, she would call him away; she was serious and strict with me. I had the impression that I displeased her beyond measure. One day she took me for a splendid walk all the way to Plans. It was a stormy day. I don't know what I said about God, but she said to me: "One does not speak of God." Then I no longer knew what to say. On other afternoons, when she was invited to tea at the homes of elderly ladies, she would take me with her, but she carefully warned me: "In our family, young ladies are not to speak." That wasn't difficult; I was silent and ate some excellent snacks. I reminded myself of a cumbersome object: it's deposited on an armchair and picked up again on leaving.

After that communion, I had again been keeping a journal. One evening, in my big room that smelled of a fresh forest, I don't know how, I splattered ink on the floor. The floorboards were pure white. In vain I scrubbed with my handbrush and soap, nothing worked, and the stain was indelible. I tried to use a penknife to remove the few stained slivers of wood, and the damage got worse; I had to give it up. But it was terrible to have to announce that to Cousin Marianne; when morning came, I had to resign myself to it. Her reply was something like, "I had really thought that your visit would cause damage to us."

Then, I went to meet my mother, my brothers, and Hélène at Langenbruck. Hélène and I got along very well; she wore a narrow black velvet ribbon around her forehead; I immediately copied her hairdo; I don't know what we did to amuse ourselves during that vacation. There was a young Russian doctor there—Hélène and I dubbed him Sascha—he was a bit ill, and from time to time he took walks with us. At Leysin, with Doctor Linden, I had learned enough Russian to make myself understood and follow a conversation; it was fun to speak with Sascha. Then we went back to Basel. Those were very mixed weeks. I was supposed to enter Saint-Loup in September; this plan gave Mama no pleasure; she would have much preferred, since I couldn't return to school, that I set about earning my living in earnest, but because Charlotte found the plan sensible, and since I had been absolutely dependent on her for a very long time, no objection was possible. Hélène helped me to make my wardrobe; she sewed underwear and smocks, while I embroidered the smocks and knitted—I had already begun them at Langenbruck—a prodigious number of woolen and cotton stockings. Mama bought me a ticket via Neuchâtel and said that Uncle Willy was very displeased about my intentions, so I had to avoid the Waldau on my journey.

SAINT-LOUP

September–December 1920

I arrived at Saint-Loup one evening; it was a scant half-hour's walk from Pompaples, over a path that to my mind was exquisite. When I got there with my small suitcase, a kindly, rather chatty old sister welcomed me; I was immediately struck by this very special atmosphere of the houses of deaconesses. I felt as if everything fit together like clockwork; perhaps I would like it. The Sister Superior, Sister Julie Lotz, was from Basel; she had a very deep, rough voice, and her little white bonnet poorly concealed the fact that she was almost completely bald. She told me first thing that I had been accepted to please my cousin Olivier, who was a friend of the house, but, obviously, I was much too young, and probably, since I was only eighteen, I would have trouble adjusting to the spirit of the house. Their work was designed for stronger shoulders, we would have to see. . . . She, as if showing ancestral portraits, had me look at huge paintings depicting the founders of the house; there were also a few of them in the parlor with the red plush furniture. They had a rather severe, sad look; they looked vexed at being seen there. No, all this was not encouraging. I almost wanted to cry. In my room, which I would share with a roommate

from Zurich, who, like me, was there as a volunteer and
not as a novice, there was a little note of welcome, sent by
Sister Emilie. Sister Julie explained to me again that there
was no distinction made between novices and volunteers:
the religious and work programs were exactly the same for
both. Because I was still so young and had been ill for such
a long time, I would have an hour free each day after dinner,
I would be excused from what they called the *corvée*, that
is to say, from having to help with the housework, doing
the dishes, peeling vegetables, and so forth. We went into
the dining room. It was an immense room; the novices' table was on the side where the door was; on the other side
was the table for the sisters working at Saint-Loup, and the
biggest table, which appeared to me to be of immense dimensions, was reserved for the Sister Superior, for the sisters in retreat, and for sisters on vacation. Sister Julie walked
me around all the tables, introducing me to each one: I had
become Sister Adrienne. Sister Adrienne was horribly intimidated, she didn't understand any of this business, and
she wished she could disappear, it didn't matter where, just
disappear.

This was a peculiar period. There was never any way to reflect; one had absolutely no time to think at all. In the morning, rise at 5:30; clean your room; at precisely 6:00 A.M., a
half-hour Bible lesson, then ten minutes to memorize Bible
verses, in a room whose temperature, in my experience, was
never above freezing; novices' breakfast with Sister Julie,
who read a passage from the Bible first, and then you gulped
down some toast and café au lait. Prayer. Hurry off to begin
work at 7:00 precisely. I had the nursery; six; you had to
give them their first bottle, bathe them, and put them into
their bassinets in the dayroom, not without having weighed
them first and taken their temperature. At 10:00, they all

had to be in the large room, and there you gave them their second bottle. Then you had to make up their six beds using a special system for folding the sheets that I never succeeded in mastering; wash the floor, dust, and prepare the buckets of dirty diapers. Meanwhile, at 10:00, when you got the signal from Sister Vic, the floor nurse, there was a snack that you took with her: porridge and tea, accompanied by Bible reading. At precisely noon you had to be back in the main building for dinner, but first you had to make sure that none of the babies was wet. I had no luck: I checked, I changed, but whenever Sister Vic slipped her hand into their diapers, she always found one who had just relieved himself: they did it on purpose!

We would arrive out of breath at the Motherhouse, for the long prayer before dinner, followed by religious reading. The novice mistress was very nice. She ate at our table and claimed that Sister Vic mistreated us: perhaps she was not completely wrong. After dinner, prayer; rush back to the babies; bottle, change diapers. At 2:00, *corvée* and, for me, return to my room. In less time than it takes to say it, I would go to sleep on the chaise longue installed by Sister Julie; I would awaken with a start in order to be at the anatomy lesson at 3:00 or the lesson on medical treatments. At 4:00, prayer, Bible reading, tea, and bread. Then another bottle, change diapers; put the babies back into their beds. Straighten the bassinets, sweep and clean the dayroom. Then from 6:00 to 7:00, worship in the chapel. At 7:00, supper, prayers, Bible reading. Then the last bottle, care, and change of diapers. Then came the most fatiguing time of all: I had to wash, unaided, the diapers of my six babies as well as those from the six "big babies" from the other room, and in cold water. My hands, unused to such work, cracked open and were soon covered with abscesses. Once done, I went to

join the novices in the corridor, and we would go all together to the vigil. For the others, I think, the vigil began
about 8:00; for us, generally about 9:30. Someone would
read aloud, and, for us, it was terribly disconnected, since
we never heard more than about the last half-hour of the
pious story. While we listened, we mended or sewed. At
10:00, last official prayer, then return to our rooms to finish
some job, polish our shoes or sew on a button; I don't think
our light was ever put out before 11:00. It was obviously
an exhausting life.

On Sunday afternoons, we had an hour-long Bible lesson
with the Sister Superior. It was something like a puzzle: each
of us, during the week, had to find the number of times one
or two given words appeared in such-and-such a gospel or
epistle; for example, "baptism" in the Gospel according to
Saint John. Then we had an hour free, which we used to
discuss our impressions. There were some charming novices
whom I liked very much: Sister Emilie Junod, Sister Marguerite from La Chaux-de-Fonds. I told them once that I
understood nothing from all these Bible lessons; I didn't
remember anything from them, except an inexpressible impression of emptiness; the words themselves seemed to me
to be devoid of meaning; God was not in them but was as
if hidden somewhere behind them. Love of neighbor also
seemed to me to have been abolished from their explications
of the Gospels; I no longer found it anywhere but in action.
Further, all that did not touch me profoundly; it reached
a certain surface level, and then the truly extreme fatigue
erased the impression, removing from it any real interior
contact.

On Sunday evenings, the novices and the youngest ones
of the sisters played stupid games with the pastor: two
blindfolded novices would try to feed each other whipped

cream. These obligatory games annoyed me; I would have preferred, and much preferred, some conversation with a novice.

It seemed to me that the entire life was mechanized, that a certain strength of the will collected what was left of my energy and made me move like a robot. Worse still, the entire prayer life seemed to me to be seized by this inertia. But I wasn't really uneasy, because I had too little time to think.

One fine morning, Sister Vic said to me: "It's easy to see that you're ill, all the other girls are complaining about your cough; even Sister Julie has spoken to me about it, but you are big enough to tell the Sister Superior yourself that you are ill; no one else can do it for you; it's your own responsibility." I was terribly embarrassed. What should I do? I saw clearly that it was not working, but I would have liked for it still to work out for a while. That evening, I had a brilliant idea: I put in a thermometer with firm resolution: below 38°C (100.4°F): I would wait; above 38°: I would admit defeat. The thermometer registered: I had to admit defeat. Which I did the next morning after breakfast. Sister Julie was very nice and sent me to bed. The instant I lay down, I had this feeling that I've had all my life, no matter what my illness was, the first time I went to bed: that I could have gone on a little longer. The doctor diagnosed bronchitis. It was delightful to be ill; for the first few days, however, I didn't have much chance to surrender to these delights, for I slept almost continuously. When I had slept enough, I recovered some consciousness of being alive; I could pray, freed from the meaninglessness of the words. My companions kept me up to date with charming visits. Sometimes, it almost seemed to me that they had inherited my past uneasiness. As for me, I was no longer troubled; I was waiting. At the end of a week, I was able to get up and, two days after that, to resume the work. The first time, I had worked for three weeks; the second time, it was at the end of only ten days that Sister Vic gave me her little speech again. This time I set 39°C (102.2°F) as a limit for the fever; it was attained. Again, after breakfast I went to Sister Julie. When I got into bed, the same initial disagreeable feeling of having given up too soon. The doctor was not at all of my opinion. As soon as I was able to get up again, I would have to take another cure. At first, I nearly gave way to despair at this verdict; besides, I didn't really know where to turn. The Olivier cousins had suffered grave reversals of fortune; Mama would be very angry. In the end, I sent a few lines to my uncle at the Waldau; he answered in a not very encouraging fashion; he had not understood why I did not come to see him before going to Saint-Loup; he thought it was cowardice that had kept me from doing so, that I knew he would be against this idea of nurses and Saint-Loup; finally, he was expecting me.

I stayed in bed at Saint-Loup for three weeks. What disturbed me most, basically, was that I could pray again, while during the ten days when I was working I had felt profoundly hindered from doing so. What was the reason for this constraint in the community? Yet it was by definition a Christian life. Real anxiety tortured me whenever I thought about it, and I thought about it a lot.

I felt absolutely sure that God wanted my life, without any reservations; I was ready to give it to him, only I didn't see how this gift would be made. I had believed that Saint-Loup would be appropriate, if not to become the road, at least to show it to me. When I was alone, I could pray and think about God, but in company with the others, that became not only empty but dead, like a routine.

While I'd been ill, my cousin Charles Masset had occasionally come to see me. His visits had been charming; he was very simple in nature, he didn't seem to be prey to any insoluble problem; he would bring a book, some chocolate, and his very good humor. Suddenly he stopped visiting; his mother was afraid he was getting attached to me, and she wanted a rich wife for him. Poor Charles; he obeyed immediately and never married. Moreover, I don't in the least believe he had any intention but to spend a few pleasant moments with his young cousin. And, in connection with my cousin's visits, what surprised me particularly about the deaconesses was their conception of renouncing marriage. It seemed somehow provisional: they avoided discussing the subject in depth; it remained unsettled. Every one, or at least several, of the young sisters left a void in their lives that nothing, for the present, filled. If, however, a sister suddenly left the association and got married, it was not without creating a certain scandal; they talked about it at length, made comments on all the ups and downs of the romance; the event left deep and slightly pernicious traces in the life of the community. And yet, there was no such thing as a vow of celibacy. It was a little as if they had two sets of weights and measures to judge the marriage of a sister that had already taken place and that of another that was still in the future. As a problem, this question interested me very much, but, as something personal, it was a matter of profound indifference to me. When I thought about it, I felt some anxiety: Wasn't it necessary, before setting out on one's path in the diaconate to know exactly how God intended to direct lives? He could only want one, sole and unique solution for every person. As long as one road did not make another impossible, there had to be a compromise there. I didn't think for a moment that God liked compromises.

At Saint-Loup, one called the novices and volunteers as well as the deaconesses Sister. It became difficult for me, perhaps due to lack of time, to call people anything else but Sister, and more than once I surprised myself by saying Sister to a patient or a child; this happened during the weeks when I was working. During the weeks when I was ill, I remembered these mistakes, and I then asked myself very seriously if Sister could become a real title, which was more than a simple form of address appropriate for any Christian, if there was not some essential spiritual work accomplished in order to merit this title in some way. Sometimes I talked to one or another of the novices about these questions, but they were totally dazzled by their vocation and so overtired that they didn't grasp the point of what was bothering me. Perhaps, of course, I didn't know how to make myself clear enough. It sometimes seemed as though the whole life at Saint-Loup was an error, an immense error, that would have a tendency to grow and become worse to the degree as long as it was not recognized.

I had, however, experienced some very fine moments there. One evening, but only for a few hours, I had been given night duty at the chalet. I had to go from room to room, give an old grandmother some tea, put another one on the bedpan, empty the chamber pots, change a bed, change the babies, and in the meantime sit in the corridor alert to the least noise, while knitting away on an endless stocking reserved for the night nurses. That night had a special character. It was oppressive and cold, it somehow seemed to have swept down over the whole house, to have covered it with a strange power that one had to fight against, even to protect from it the patients so abruptly entrusted to me. To me? No, to God. Then not to me? Yes, even so, to God and me, perhaps even to God through me. The idea was a revelation: since there seemed to be a union between God and me in this care of souls in the night, it was therefore necessary for me to pray. No just for the patients in the chalet—except for the infants, they were mostly arthritics and chronically ill people, all incapable of moving, only women. By day I had hardly seen them, except one or two who remembered my father and had asked that I go to say hello for them. I particularly liked this unique half-night's vigil, in spite of the impressive battle I had to make to keep from going to sleep as soon as the actual work was accomplished; the knitting, by the way, helped in the battle.

One morning, I was "on surgery". That is to say, from seven o'clock on, I had to go to the operating room to learn how to observe, to help, and also to endure. The first patient to be operated on was a Madame Golay de Sentier, whom I knew from Leysin; she had been in the room next to mine at L'Espérance. Now they had to operate on her for appendicitis, and she was two months pregnant. As soon as they opened her abdomen, I fainted, bang, and that was that. But it was very brief. As soon as I came to, the surgeon, Doctor Curchod, who was to care so kindly for me when I had bronchitis, gave me a man's leg to hold up while he operated on some sort of tubercular disease in the region of the perineum. He made it very clear that I must not drop the leg, for, if I did, I would risk great harm; the lancet could then slip and grievously wound either the patient or the surgeon. I drew myself up straight then, but I thought the operation would never end, and the leg was really extremely heavy.

Now it was a matter of taking my leave of all that, the work, the atmosphere at Saint-Loup; it wasn't very easy for me; I was leaving too many things behind me, too many vital questions that had not received answers: and my life again was cut off from any promise of tomorrow.

I had kept my journal at Saint-Loup; I dejectedly threw it into a burning furnace; I didn't want to risk its falling into the hands of my family. I wrapped my ink bottle up in my underwear in my Japanese suitcase. Alas, it came open, and the novitiate staircase was completely blackened; I didn't see it at the time, but I learned later on that it had taken many months of scrubbing to wipe away my traces completely.

THE WALDAU

December 1920–August 1921

In the train, I suddenly discovered the damage caused by the ink; my suitcase was dripping nicely; my underwear was soaked. It was impossible to put right any of it.

This time, the welcome I received at the Waldau was not extremely warm. Aunt Jeanne had no joy in checking the contents of my suitcase; the tiny ink bottle seemed to have held as much as a carboy and had spared nothing. Aunt Jeanne, who was so good, was totally lacking in humor in situations like this. And Uncle Willy had not forgotten that I had not stopped by the Waldau on my way to Saint-Loup. I never explained to him that it was my mother who had wanted it that way. However, after a few days, everything was once again absolutely at peace between us.

The two first weeks, I lived more or less as if I were on vacation; but for the first time, perhaps, the future weighed heavily on me. My health was still in danger; it had been necessary to give up medical studies, and I would never be a nurse; I could see absolutely nothing I could ever be any good at. On the other hand, the peculiar experience of Saint-Loup had set something new in motion within me; I truly thought that I would never succeed in understanding what God expected or even required of me. My illness no longer seemed to me to have any meaning.

Christmas was coming; my mother was expecting me in Basel. When I spoke to my uncle of leaving, he would not hear of it; first, he would send me to consult Professor Sahli at Bern, and we would abide by his decision; but in my uncle's opinion, no work could yet be considered.

So I went to see the Professor, with the Waldau's barouche, which had played such a big role in our childhood, since they always sent it to meet visitors and, sometimes, even us, in special circumstances. Rolli, the coachman, although taciturn, was our good friend; he had often even let us sit up on the box with him. The Professor's waiting room was a large, bare, cold room, with the special odor of poorly heated third-class railway carriages. He was a heavy man who moved clumsily, stiffly, and painfully. When he had finished examining me, his recommendations were exactly what I had least expected: a strict, well-regulated cure, but taken at the Waldau itself, since the mountains had not seemed to have done me any particular good. He set up a schedule for me that rather resembled the one I had been on the summer before, when I had spent several months at my uncle's between the two stays in Leysin. When I went back with Rolli, all tired out from the expedition, my uncle was already informed and in complete agreement.

It felt funny to be starting this life of unknown duration between my uncle, who appeared only at meals, and Aunt

Jeanne, who was hardly enchanted by the prospect of this
cure, for she correctly foresaw that it would be more trouble for her to undergo it than it would be for me. She had
a sort of innate horror of a regimented life and had visible
trouble being on time for meals; generally, she arrived at
least several minutes late, always with a new excuse, which
never failed to vex my uncle a little: his punctuality was
legendary, but he never complained in front of us about the
loss of time my aunt forced him to put up with: he never
began to eat until she was there. On the other hand, she
had the habit of sending her nieces off, at every moment,
to do errands for her all over the place, without concerning
herself about whatever occupation they might be busy with
at the time. It was as if the idea that took possession of my
aunt at that very instant was of an extreme importance and
the execution of it would brook no delay. Perhaps, though,
my sister and I were somewhat negligent and forgetful, and
thus Aunt Jeanne might have been afraid that her wishes
would not be accomplished if we didn't carry them out immediately.

But Aunt Jeanne really went to a lot of trouble, and, besides, with my chaise longue so far away from the room
where she usually was, everything went along fine, more or
less.

The only thing that Aunt Jeanne never really succeeded
in comprehending was that, in the first few months, I was
supposed to sleep for exactly twelve hours every night, no
more and no less. At night, I went to bed at eight-thirty, and
appeared for breakfast at exactly eight-thirty every morning.
I would spend two hours, three times a day, on the chaise
longue and take one or two half-hour walks. I read rather little but kept my hands busy with embroidery or knitting that
Aunt Jeanne intended for the poor. I had no desire to read; I

had read a great deal at Leysin and lived, in spite of the lack of time, very intensely at Saint-Loup; now, I would have liked, somehow, to make a synthesis of God and the world, finally to understand. But understand what? Perhaps, above all, the meaning of life; indeed, I supposed that every life, as life, had a meaning in God himself; but that, on the other hand, each life had received a special, individual meaning as its reason for being, which, in order to be accomplished had to be understood.

On Sundays I sometimes went to church at the Waldau. I understood nothing of the sermons because I spoke no German, but I tried to discover from the face of the pastor or the patients some manifest sign of their participation in the divine life. If that occurred in any way at all, it must have been very interior, because it was not at all evident; the people left the church just as they had entered it; their expressions and their gestures were the same.

On Mondays, from time to time, there was a worship service in French in the women's ward. Pastor Morel coated all his words in a sort of sickly sweet mush; I was incapable of getting any substance out of them. The congregation was nearly the same as that of the chapel on Sundays, whether or not they understood French; so the worship services were rather obviously a kind of diversion for the patients; perhaps they were for me as well.

Winter passed slowly. It was a succession of similar days that stretched along without marking any notable change. I did not feel ill but tired, with a kind of steady, heavy fatigue that I was well used to; it would have seemed odd to me to be able to work or walk for any length of time.

When early spring arrived, they put me out in the garden on a chaise longue; I scarcely ever left it except at mealtimes, perhaps because the fatigue had increased somewhat, perhaps because it was really pleasant to watch new life being born, life without problems; that filled the monotony of my existence without disturbing it.

For May Day, the secretary in the bursar's office, Mademoiselle Bähler, had invited all the children at the Waldau —children of the gardener, the chauffeur, the plumber, the joiner, and I don't know how many overseers—to take a carriage ride across the Bernese countryside. She invited me to join them; it was strange suddenly to change environment and landscape. I greatly enjoyed being among the children, almost all of whom I knew from our vacations in the past, but whom I now saw only at long intervals, for really I was living a secluded life, in an atmosphere of great calm that I also liked enormously. The trip was very merry; it made me regret my habitual isolation a little; it was somewhat like diving into the world, but into the world of childhood; although I was much older, I felt like a child among these children.

When I went to bed that evening, I had a high fever and painful glands all over. I stayed in bed for several days; the doctors who came to see me did not arrive at a diagnosis. But when I got up, that time, it was a genuine convalescence; I got my strength back, real strength; I was happy to be alive and full of plans that all seemed capable of being realized because I truly felt I was getting well.

I will never forget that month of May, the walks all in bloom, the green of the meadows, the smell of the gardens, the sounds of the night, the fountain and the spring that I heard singing from my bed, which had the merriest voice. More and more, I abandoned my chaise longue and began to take ever-longer walks across the fields or in the woods. Sometimes Aunt Jeanne would go with me, and together we would go all round the forest, which was a delightful walk, especially at the end of the afternoon. I would tell her of my plans or revive childhood memories. My very deep understanding with her dates, I believe, from that time.

At the end of the month, my uncle sent me back to see Professor Sahli. He heard nothing more in my lungs and advised me to stay at the Waldau for a time, while allowing me to resume a more normal life.

I went back once more among the patients; since I no longer lay down except for a moment after dinner, I had a lot of spare time, but I did not use it in a very consistent fashion; rather, I just enjoyed it, like a brand new gift.

Little by little a new form of future presented itself to me: I would go ahead with my medical studies all the same, and perhaps it would work, since now, even if I wasn't strong, I was at least cured.

In July I went to spend a few days with Aunt Marguerite, who had lost her husband at Easter. Aunt Marguerite was a sort of fairy godmother for the family. She had very limited means at her disposal, but she always managed to give pleasure to everyone, never forgetting a birthday, remembering everybody's likes and dislikes. I very much enjoyed being with her, and my two cousins, very lively and, especially the older one, rather undisciplined girls, made life full of surprises. From my earliest childhood I had been very attached to the older one, Madeleine, who carried on a conversation like a grown person, very sure of the world and of herself. At this time, my schoolfriends were graduating and receiving their *maturités*. As soon as they saw me arrive, they absolutely insisted that I pass the examination with them, and in spite of my protestations—it had been a long time since I had worked in a consistent way—Charles-Henri Barbier went to see the director Lalive to ask his permission. Apparently he ran into a refusal, which distressed him very much, but I consoled him by telling him that in August I would be going to stay with my mother in Basel, and I would start school again.

The few days spent at La Chaux-de-Fonds had brought me back into contact with student life; now I was happy to think that it was going to be mine once again.

After Saint-Loup, my religious life had undergone a slow-down. I prayed some, but I had stopped worrying about the subject of God; it almost seemed to me as if it were up to him now to worry about me, especially about putting me on a feasible road. One thing, though, seemed to me to have been decided: I would be a Christian doctor. I would try to lead my patients nearer to God.

PART TWO

THE BASEL GIRLS' SECONDARY SCHOOL
August 1921–April 1923

In a most vital way, Basel embodied my homeland for me. My father had always spoken to me of his ancestral city with great affection, which is the main reason why I was so happy to return to Basel. For three years my mother had been living there with my sister and my younger brother Theddy while Willy was finishing his schooling at a boarding school in Bern. I never understood why my mother moved to Basel, since she had always felt like a stranger there, never learned the language, and considered the local customs odd.

I arrived late one afternoon. It was hot and humid, and a thunderstorm threatened. The streetcar ride from the railway station to 44 Florastraße, where we had a fourth-floor, five-room apartment, seemed to last a long time. I could not help but notice the women passengers in their summer dresses and wondered whether I would soon become acquainted with them; in La Chaux-de-Fonds, we were known to everyone, to far more people than we ourselves knew, and I thought it would soon be the same in the big city. It would not have taken much, and, even on this first streetcar ride, I was seeking to make friends, at least in my mind.

I moved into a very small room, unpacked my suitcase, and soon went to bed. It was not easy to fall asleep, for the weather was really oppressively hot. Unfamiliar voices could be heard from neighboring houses, women talked to each other from one window to another, nearby a newborn child was crying. I was a bit confused: the three years of illness seemed to have vanished, and, since I was once more living the life of a normal young woman, my mind reached back to La Chaux-de-Fonds for a point of comparison—perhaps it would be possible to begin where I had left off there. The pain of losing my father was less intense; some sort of change had clearly occurred. All at once I left my bed, went to the window, gazed at the night-shrouded roofs, and, when it suddenly began to rain heavily, I began to pray: "My God, love this city and grant that I might love it." Yes, the love of God, God's love in this city, his city. It seemed to me as if God, in his incomprehensible magnitude, held something very tangible in his power: a city, nocturnal and drenched in sticky air. He was now sending his rain to this city so that it might think and know more fully that it belonged to him.

The next morning I arose early and put on my white dress with red dots, together with my huge red hat, the one that looked like a broad wheel. I followed the Rhine as far as the Middle Bridge, then walked through the middle of the city to the girls' secondary school. I dawdled along the way, taking possession of my surroundings, inhaling, as it were, the city's nooks and crannies. Everything was unfamiliar, yet the strangeness was attractive. I was happy, I had a future. The pending interview caused me no anxiety whatsoever, for it could result in nothing else than the opportunity to resume my schooling, to gain my diploma. When I arrived, classes had just recessed. Hundreds of young girls rushed down the steps; it was rather difficult to swim against the stream and climb the steps. The woman who met me in the office, Georgine Gerhard, who would later become my friend, was hard of hearing but spoke fluent French, so there was no problem communicating. A moment later I found myself in the rector's office; his French was as defective as my German, so it was difficult to establish the extent of my knowledge and, even more, that of my ignorance, so diffi-

cult in fact that he was much more generous to me than I
had hoped: I was to spend six weeks of probationary status in the next to the highest class, after which the faculty
members would decide whether I might stay. Since I had
been ill, I was given a dispensation from physical education
classes; French instruction was likewise ruled unnecessary,
since I already knew more than enough; and I was excused
from singing class so that I would have more free time.

The gaps in my knowledge proved to be frightfully large:
I had learned neither English, chemistry, nor physics; although I could read simple German sentences with effort,
at best I could only employ a simple subject, verb, and pred-
icate in German sentence construction. I was about three
years behind in the normal course of Latin, mathematics,
botany, and zoology. The overall assessment was not encouraging, yet I was happy: I had been accepted, and the
word "provisionally" caused me no anxiety. I was curious
about the class I would be joining.[1] It was agreed that the
rector would pick me up at seven the next morning and
accompany me as I met the teachers and girls. Much later,
after we had become good friends, he confessed to me that
he had accepted me without raising questions because I had
shown courage and independence in coming to the school
by myself. Actually, the only reason I arrived by myself that
morning was that it never occurred to my mother to accompany me.

Finding myself on the street again, I soon forgot about
school. It was as if the city were absorbing me into itself. It
seemed beautiful to me, and I was ready to love it, not as
a totality but as it appeared in each individual person. As I

[1] Not a class of instruction, but the cohort of girls who entered together
and stayed together until graduation—TRANS.

made my way home slowly, with frequent detours, I looked at the faces of one stranger after another and thought, "Perhaps some day I shall learn to know you, help you; how I will love you!"

Since we had the services of a maid during that period of my life, there was no housework for me to do, and I was free to go out again in the afternoon. I wandered for hours through the inner city watching people. Occasionally, almost incidentally, I might realize that I was standing on a street corner or looking at a window I had seen earlier in the afternoon. But I had eyes for people and people alone. After all, during the long time I spent at Leysin and the Waldau, I had had contact with a very limited circle of people. Everything was different now, as if the entire city had been offered to me. I would be able to choose people, to choose people to love, and, until that came about, I could at least pray for them. It was all so blissful. My praying knew few words but nonetheless carried all these unfamiliar faces with their unknown joys and sorrows to God.

Then, the next day, the world of school began. I entered a very small class of eleven girls, making it a complete dozen. The rector introduced me in a kind manner, then left me to my new classmates. They were completely different from what I had anticipated. Or had I had any expectations at all about them? They looked like tiny, shy children; they said little and giggled all the more. I understood neither their words nor their giggles, and, as they were a year younger than I, I soon nurtured something like motherly feelings for them. That I was anything but shy perhaps made the difference in age even more marked.

That the school in La Chaux-de-Fonds had an entirely different character about it from the one in Basel soon became apparent. At La Chaux-de-Fonds, not long after entering the *progymnasium* program (at age eleven), we were acting like responsible young people. Whether in relationship with our teachers or among ourselves, we were treated both as individuals and as a group. The teachers had never scolded us; at the most, there were discussions, arguments for and against. A reprimand from a teacher would have been unthinkable. Their attitude toward us was perfectly polite; when they said something to us, they expected a response; and this obligation to reply soon awakened in us the sense of our own indubitable though still childish human dignity, and it was only natural for us to behave in accordance with it. If we did not know what to say, we asked quite candidly for a suggestion. In the best sense of the word, I think we were being brought up in freedom. The focal point of that education was located above all in the awakening of a sense of duty toward our inner person. Of course, one or another pupil might occasionally prove unworthy of the trust being extended, but, when that happened, the others felt the responsibility to work on him until he came to his senses. Such an approach seldom failed.

My new schoolmates lived in a completely different relationship with the teachers. They were apparently given no opportunity to prove to their teachers that they were grown up—should someone neglect some assignment or other, she was afraid of the teacher's scolding, of the consequences of a reprimand. This was all strange to me. At first I simply did not grasp what was happening; as I slowly caught on, I tried to defend myself against such an attitude. In doing so I do not think I was being less childish than the others; it was simply that the school in French Switzerland had brought me up differently, and the years of solitude deepened my sense of personal responsibility.

The material we studied in school also seemed to me quite

different from what I had expected; it was as if it had lost its inner cohesiveness. Earlier, I had always had a sense of the relationship between the various subjects; here things seemed almost arbitrarily to develop in different directions: the various subjects were to be considered in isolation; the English authors remained foreign to the German, to say nothing of the Latin. None of them had anything to do with mathematics; chemistry floated somewhere above it all, having nothing to do with botany. And assignments, too, were to be completed individually.

Yet all this school business was nice. Without exception my schoolmates were friendly girls who rapidly endeared themselves to me, and they too accepted me well. I sat next to Hanna Huber. She spoke only standard German, free of any local dialect, and was probably the most talented of them all but also the most calm and composed, objective about everything. She introduced me everywhere.

A deeper friendship soon linked me with Hanni Liechtenhan and Bethli Schaerer. Both of them had a sense for what I called the problems of life: one's neighbors, their questions, their concerns. God played a large role in Hanni's life, and she was much occupied with him. We had an enormous pile of things to discuss. Since Hanni lived on Florastraße too, we took the same route to school. Occasionally we took real walks together. I felt very close to her. Remarkably enough, my friendship for her suffered no inward damage from the fact that Hanni somehow looked down on me a bit. She readily came to me with questions, often sought advice from me and even followed it, yet still she had a slight bit of scorn for me because I was "French" and did not quite fit into any given framework and because it did not bother me that others quickly developed entrenched opinions about me.

Hanni had great difficulties at home. She could never get anywhere with her father. So, although it was not easy for me, I decided to attend services at the Matthäuskirche regularly in order to get to know him through his sermons. When I thought I had a good sense of who he was (I think it cost me about a dozen sermons), I explained to Hanni where, in my opinion, the difficulties lay, encouraging her to pluck up courage and ask him to take an afternoon's walk alone with her. She did that and the next day said to me only, "You've given my father back to me, thank you!" She never told me anything more about her father, which was probably a good thing.

Bethli and I talked a lot about love, marriage, our fellow creatures, the sick (she also wanted to become a physician). To find time for what seemed to us to be such important conversations, we often skipped school together. It was usually English or math period that paid the price. We almost had to run away from the school to avoid getting caught. Once we escaped, we went to the Battery.

The English lessons from an old teacher named Dick[2] were really badly taught, and to miss them did no harm; but either way I was learning no English, a language that, under the circumstances, really would have been useful. So I decided to take private instruction. An old friend of my family, Miss Jachmann, was an English teacher by profession and lived at the Baslerhof. She was most willing to take up the task of tutoring me. Her lessons were certainly excellent, but she asked so much of me that it soon seemed to me I had no time left for any other subject. She gave me a lot of homework; if I didn't know it thoroughly, embarrassing scenes would take place, and so, for better or for worse, I

[2] A Germanic surname, not a nickname for Richard—TRANS.

had to keep up. For three weeks I worked on my English as if nothing else existed in the whole world. Then the program was over, and I could adopt the comfortable pace of my classmates with a good conscience.

About the time Miss Jachmann's reign of terror ended, the prescribed six-week period of probation also concluded. With some anxiety I went to see the rector: Would I be permitted to stay?

The rector was very gracious. As he had heard no complaints about me, he would assume (and I with him) that everything was fine. I was overjoyed and went straight to the music school to sign up for piano lessons. The director told me that, if I promised to practice three hours a day, I might take lessons from Conductor Münch. I gladly promised, and with that, yet another bliss began to unfold within the general blissfulness of school.

For me, school (including playing hooky) was a real delight. I greatly enjoyed being able to learn, and I especially liked math: the formulation of the problems was almost more stimulating to me than their solutions. I would have loved to have taken philosophy and religion classes as well, but they were not offered at all at the secondary-school level.

In those days a custom existed that has long since completely disappeared: at irregular intervals a woman author would come and conduct a reading from her writings. I do not think that we came into contact with very significant literature in this way, but we did experience the author in the development of her work or with a finished book. I sensed an unusual human enrichment on each occasion— it was as if we were participating in some great event, and the most personal mysteries were revealed to us.

At home things were going quite well. My mother's circle of friends was a rather lively one at that time, and thus she had enough variety in her life to avoid being dependent on her children's experiences.

THE RAILWAY BRIDGE

Still, one thing happened that left a lasting impression on me.[1] Cousin Charlotte showed up for a short, very short, visit on a Sunday morning. I returned from services at the Matthäuskirche a few minutes after Cousin Charlotte arrived, and she immediately interrupted the conversation she had begun with my mother, telling me that she was going to abduct me, as she put it, for she had something to say to me. From my time in Leysin I retained a certain fear of her unannounced visits, for, although she was very nice, she possessed the undeniable gift of spreading a degree of unrest. She formed her judgments rashly and then insisted on corresponding changes. So, on this occasion we walked along the Rhine. She thought I seemed pale and emaciated, although I felt quite healthy. She began the conversation with these ominous words: "I have reprimanded your mother a bit about you; she does not understand you, and it is essential that she learn to understand you."[2] I never had much of a chance to speak, and I have forgotten what the topic really was. Only her opening has remained in my memory. She left me standing at some unexpected corner, since she needed a little solitude to master her agitation before embarking on

[1] The motivation for this episode becomes clear in vol. 7 of Adrienne's posthumous writings—ED.

[2] This was written in French in the text—ED.

her next visit. Expecting trouble, I returned to Florastraße. Mama was furious with me, and I was completely unable to make her understand that I had had nothing whatsoever to do with the entire matter, for I had had no contact at all with Cousin Charlotte since I had come to live at home. Mama would not be persuaded, and I began to weep in a manner that is most unusual for me: for hours on end, incessantly. My entire life seemed a mess, I would never be able to do anything sensible; school, education, piano lessons, all the new people—none of this meant anything to me anymore. My hands were empty, I had nothing to give to anyone, the whole picture was black on black. I was alone in my little room. Schiller's early plays lay on the table, for I had planned to read them for the first time that Sunday; but reading was impossible for me. Finally, in order to occupy my hands, I began to sketch myself—my disconsolate expression, my face in tears. But this did not help; all I could do was cry.

No one was stirring in the apartment. Hélène and Theddy had probably gone out; Mama was in her room, making no sound. About four or five in the afternoon, the flood of tears dried up, but I felt no better inside, and I knew very well that no one could help me. I hadn't the slightest desire to go and tell one of my friends. There was nothing to tell. The white *voile* dress with the bright blue collar that Aunt Jeanne had given me the previous summer was so rumpled I had to iron it. Then I left the house. I followed the Rhine as far as the Railway Bridge, walking alone, with rather slow steps. At first I spoke with God, asking him somehow to bring order to my life, to show me the path I was to follow. Gradually, however, my disconsolateness began to turn into a kind of anxiety: There must not be any path for me; without realizing it, I had now lost my way entirely. My plans to study medicine seemed meaningless; I should apply again to Saint-Loup after all, despite the certainty that I would be turned away. I didn't know how to deal with my own family, how could I deal with other people? It had all been a game, and God does not let people trifle with him. I searched my entire past, trying to find one promise I had made to God and really kept but came up empty-handed. Finally I reached the bridge. About one-third of the way across, I stopped and gazed down into the deep, rushing, swirling current. Suddenly I decided to hurl myself into the river and put an end to my misery. But as soon as I had had this thought, and it seemed inescapable, a sense of dread seized me. I turned back and once more walked along the Little Basel bank of the Rhine. A few minutes later I found a bench and sat down with a sense of relief. But then my cowardice seemed outrageous to me; one ought not be afraid of death! At that moment I was no longer talking to God but only to myself, to my despair, to my useless life. Once more all I could think about was me, that my life was nothing but a burden to me and to others, that it no longer fulfilled its purpose, that it perhaps had no purpose at all. Slowly, filled with great sadness, I went back to the bridge and stopped at the same column. A train rumbled across the bridge. Everything trembled. Death's power must be like that. Again I gazed down into the swirling water, and then, all at once, I knew precisely: *this* would be cowardly, this choosing of death for myself. I have to remain, stick it out; God lets none of his creatures out of his hand. It was hard to go back, but there was no other way. I walked back more slowly than I had come. I was unable to make my peace with all the heaviness that seemed to fill my life. Perhaps it would simply not work, but, in the end, that did not matter. No one asks us if we are able to do it; and if we are not asked, we ought to go on without asking too many questions. Going on could only mean, so it seemed to me, staying with it, sticking it out. But staying with what? School alone could not be the object; certainly something else, something greater, was intended. School was only one point within a totality, a transitional stage, a necessity, that seemed to lead not merely to medicine but to everything that God had in store for me. It was wonderful to think of God at that moment, to know in my innermost being that he was close. But the darkness was still there. It was not merely something reserved for the future but was included in the immediate Now. Despite the certainty that I was not permitted to end my life, the great uncertainty of my relationship to my life, to my mother, to my fellow creatures, remained.

My homeward path lay along the Rhine. The riverside was filled with people taking Sunday strolls; I did not glimpse a single familiar face. By the time I reached home, it was time for supper. No one asked me anything, and at first I felt horribly lonely and estranged; I wanted to feel estranged; I wanted to live like a stranger among them, since I could live nowhere else. Suddenly I was pierced by a realization: No, not that, for that would also be a form of suicide. I must take part in their life, I must truly live in communion with whatever we might have in common. And it was there that the difficulty lay.

During dessert, which was a rhubarb cake I had baked the previous evening, Hélène suddenly said, "A young woman jumped off the Railway Bridge this afternoon. They pulled her out by the Garrison, but it was too late, they couldn't do anything more for her." I shuddered terribly at her words: Had God's voice, God's will for her, become inaudible for her? I sensed the awakening of my responsibility for this woman, for all women on every bridge.

When I returned to my room, I picked up Schiller's *Die Räuber* but could not read. I decided to go directly to bed. After getting ready for bed, I knelt at the edge of the bed—normally I did not pray kneeling—and prayed. I never finished praying. It was as if the whole world of prayer opened up to me in a new way, as if it were so immense that each prayer could merely be a beginning. I fell asleep praying and only awoke when all the church bells were striking six o'clock; it was time to get up. I went to school with rather stiff joints; along the way I could not stop thinking about God's love, and, since I walked part of the way with Hanni, I had to tell her something of this love that awaited her, me, all of us. Hanni said that she, too, knew of this love.

From this point onward, for extended periods, death took on a face I had never imagined it to have: it was almost as if death had acquired some kind of inimical and threatening character, quite unlike the death one anticipates in illness. At the same time, death revealed to me the immediacy of a clearly formed, rescuing love of God.

The experiences of that Sunday, however, were something I could not discuss with anyone.

ACQUAINTANCES, GRADUATION

That same week I participated for the first time, with my mother, in a formal dinner, held at the Wenkenhof.[1] I was enthused about everything all at once: the numerous guests and

---

[1] The Wenkenhof was a palatial eighteenth-century estate located outside the old city and known for its French-style gardens—TRANS.

their elegance, the beautiful and well-apportioned rooms, readily flowing conversation in French, marvelous flowers, a beautifully appointed table, and fine cuisine all left a deep impression on me. It seemed like a fairy tale. After dinner the hostess, Madame Burckhardt-Passavant, suddenly came up to me and said in a rather loud voice, "You have such wonderful eyes. One can see all the purity of your soul in them; stay pure like that always." I was more than a little astonished at being addressed like this so suddenly, but I understood it as something of a polite comment made at a rather awkward moment. Mama was quite indignant, for on the way home she scolded me roundly for appearing to have been pleased by the words. However, my joy at an otherwise so successful evening was too great to permit myself to be upset.

A few days later there was another, similar dinner hosted by Professor Wieland-Burckhardt. I found it equally exciting and thought how wonderful it would be, someday, to have charge of a house like that, to receive as guests people who without exception had things to tell.

The next morning, however, when I had to be at school at seven in the morning, regardless of the fact that I had been up late the night before, lack of sleep made me realize I was not cut out for that sort of life. As an occasional diversion, it might be fine, but my life would have to unfold at the workplace, among a much more diverse group of people thrown together by common work. After all, I really wanted to live for people.

At school we had neither religion nor philosophy classes. I missed both, for it seemed to me more and more that the knowledge we were being taught consisted of mere coincidences, whereas I still thought some unity must be possible. My schoolmates were indignant when I mentioned this to them: How could anyone wish for additional classes? Is that perhaps the way these French-speaking foreigners are: they always want something more? I tried to explain that a few classes in philosophy and religion would be a relief, at least an inner relief, for many things would then slide into place by themselves. I had no success with this line of argumentation; nor do I know if, had the schoolgirls stuck together and asked for these additional classes, we would have been granted them. And so each little piece of knowledge floated merrily along in its disconnectedness.

In order that I might not give up completely, at least inwardly, I began to read a bit of philosophy on my own. But the books that were available to me were too difficult. I did not understand most of what I read, and I had to put them aside with little real gain. On the other hand, once I did attend a lecture on Plato's philosophy that made a great impression on me. To be sure, the lecturer's complex sentences were hard for his listeners to decipher, but they seemed to arise from the depths of his heart, seemed to come forth so simultaneously with his very thinking process, that I could not shake off the conviction that I had witnessed a vital act, that I had attended a genuine philosophical birth. So I was enthusiastic and even retained a few things I thought I had really understood. On the way home, I was so full of what I had experienced that my elderly cousin, who had accompanied me to the lecture, absolutely had to share my enthusiasm. I was so truly enthusiastic, however, that I also felt it necessary to bring up some reservations, as if to support my enthusiasm. How surprised I was when Heinrich Barth called me up the next day and offered to meet with me to discuss his lecture. The two days that preceded our appointment were perhaps the days in my entire life in which I was most a teenager. I acquired an entire library of works about

Plato and his philosophy, stumbled around in the most profound treatises, went to the hairdresser, had my schoolmates
point out for me my chief errors in speaking German, and
undertook most earnestly to behave as a young lady should.
Sunday finally arrived, bringing with it an utterly grand hour
of conversation that began with a few words about Plato but
soon turned to the meaning of life and the meaning of my
plans to study medicine. From that point onward I had a
friend to whom I owed many happy moments. Since he
lived on Rheinweg, in a house on the corner of Rheinweg
and Florastraße, we often walked together to the school,
where he taught a class in Latin. Even if our conversations
were a bit awkward, still, he always knew how to give them
a content that corresponded to my thirst for knowledge.

This friendship with Heinrich Barth occasioned a remarkable confrontation with another student at the girls' secondary school, who was two years younger than I. Once,
during a break between class sessions, she introduced herself
to me and explained that she had a claim on Professor Barth.
Her name was Agnes,[2] and she had had private lessons from
him, because for a time she had been unable to keep up with
the other students in Latin class. She had fallen in love with
him and reached a quite unilateral agreement: she was going
to marry him. That he had no notion of her intentions did
not in the least detract from the firmness with which she
held them.

A series of confrontations with Agnes followed, developing in mid-course into a strange sort of friendship. She
could be perfectly friendly on one occasion only to be cold
the next. She threatened to kill herself—it would be all
my fault—but then again she made me the sacrifice of her

---

[2] The name has been changed by the editor—ED.

love. My repeated efforts to convince her that my friendship with Heinrich Barth was even more platonic than his book failed to remove her suspicion or quiet her jealousy. This often made me anxious: inwardly I was struggling powerfully with the question of marriage. I believed firmly that I was intended never to marry but could not see the form this would take. A commitment seemed absolutely necessary; I considered this, just as in marriage, to be a commitment to God. But how? Something like Saint-Loup was not even in the picture anymore, for it would have to be something immense and definitive, so immense that one would thereby come very close to God and so definitive that eternity alone could confirm its irrevocability. This preoccupied me a lot, but I made no headway: it was as if one were circling round and round the same mysterious point.

Yet I would have very much liked to have children, lots of children. People in my circle seemed to have incredibly few children; often I thought of marrying a working-class man who already had many children, to whom I would then gradually add my own. In my thoughts about this working-class existence, laundry day seemed like a sort of high point.

At the Waldau we had always helped Aunt Jeanne hang up the laundry. She never entrusted this work to the servants, for she wanted it done very carefully and always hung everything up so that it was perfectly straight. This all had its ceremony, which seemed very mysterious to me: the linens had been washed and placed in huge baskets. Clean water was poured over them one more time before taking them out, wringing them slightly, and hanging them on the clothesline. When everything had been adjusted to hang perfectly, the linens were rinsed with water yet another time and only then permitted to dry in the breeze and the sun. To me this always seemed to have a connection with our souls, which also longed to be thoroughly washed and then rinsed still further. Somehow I connected all of this to sacramental confession, although I knew very little about it at the time. Still, even then I experienced the need to confess, although I seldom brooded over my mistakes for very long. I tried to recognize them and then simply to hand them over to God.

Before the summer vacation my schoolmates took a three-day trip into the Alps; I was not permitted to participate. Mama came up with the idea to send me to spend a day with my friend Bethli Christ at Langenbruck. That was a very happy day. It was now Bethli who had to lie in bed at Langenbruck, but it was expected that her recovery would be rapid. I rejoiced to find everything more or less as it had been when I was staying there four years earlier; frequently I sensed a certain yearning for those years of solitude and repose. They seemed to me to have been pure gift, a gift I had not known how to use as God intended.

Bethli surprised me by declaring that one ought to use life mainly for oneself, that it makes no sense to live for others when they wouldn't understand anyway. She believed in God only intermittently and even then only conditionally; she saw in him above all an image of the Good. My joy at seeing her again was so great that her thoughts were incapable of making me unhappy, especially since I was not convinced that she really believed what she said.

As always, I spent summer vacation at the Waldau. More than ever before the physicians extended invitations to me, but my friendship with the Forels was occasionally rocky: I certainly loved them very much, but various things that I can no longer recall[3] led to a degree of estrangement. More-

---

[3] See *Geheimnis der Jugend*, vol. 7 of Adrienne's posthumous writings —ED.

over they continually insisted that God does not exist, that
people invent God in order to reduce their own account-
ability and to constrict the range of their experiences, that
so much of what God ostensibly prohibits would be most
useful as a means of expanding human horizons and bound-
aries. I probably did not understand it all but was somewhat
impressed by the certainty with which they presented everything. Still, the idea that God did not exist never had any
impact on me at all.

Before vacation one of my classmates, Eva Bernoulli, had
withdrawn from school. She had a great predilection for
the theater and was always organizing plays at her house in
Arlesheim. She had assembled something of a small theater
company; the entrance hall, the double staircase, and the balcony on the second floor together created a very practical and
multifaceted stage. I spent many Sundays at the Bernoulli
house; even if no play was performed, there were always
convivial gatherings at which Eva's father, Carl Albrecht
Bernoulli, always seemed to lend a very personal touch to
the conversation. Guests came from the widest possible variety of backgrounds; people arrived more or less around tea
time, and about half of them stayed until the evening meal
and late into the night, until the final streetcar announced
its inevitable arrival. Once several professors and I missed
the tram; we walked home through the cool autumn night.
I loved these impromptu social occasions greatly, and they
made me more and more familiar with the essence of Basel.

About this time I began to find it very difficult not to be
able to intervene in situations. I always felt that I must be
able to help, by deeds, by words. Slowly I began to sense that
prayer could turn this inability to intervene into permission
to do so. But this sense was so faint that it did not help
me banish my inner difficulties. I would have liked to talk

with Eva's father and with Eva herself about her future, to have helped her discover the most sensible way to shape her talents, at least as far as her choice of profession was concerned, for she had reserved her more personal gifts for her leisure time and tried to shield them from her profession, in order that her professional work might retain a sense of clear purpose. Perhaps it was precisely my inability to act, in what seemed to me to be a clear-cut case, that permitted me to understand a little better the side of God's reality that always remains beyond our grasp. Slowly the evidence of a power of prayer that was beyond my control but nonetheless effective impressed itself on me. There was a kind of surrender in it, in the sense that I had to give Eva up to God in prayer.

My own physician's calling remained clear and delightful to me. The only problem was that neither my mother nor my uncle wanted to hear anything of it. If I talked to my mother about it, she quickly lost patience and told me I must find employment in a lucrative position immediately after graduation. This was not necessary, for I knew very well that my uncle had repeatedly emphasized that he wanted us to have a proper education. Since he was the one who gladly and generously was paying the expenses of the entire household, the financial question was not in doubt. However, when I talked to my uncle about studying medicine, he wanted no more to do with it than did my mother. On the one hand, he agreed that it was high time to decide about my career; on the other hand, he did not think the medical profession suited me. Since the idea of practicing medicine would not leave me, there arose within me a confused attitude toward the uncle I otherwise loved so dearly. Any conversation with him that had any real substance seemed to me to lose its reality and truth because what for me formed the basis for it—my medical studies—did not even exist for my uncle. If a conversation turned to this subject, my uncle always knew how to turn it aside, so that I constantly felt as if I had no solid ground under my feet.

I turned twenty years old on September 20 of that year, 1922. My schoolmates prepared a huge surprise for me when they all assembled at my house that evening and sang all my favorite songs. They had arranged with my mother to be smuggled quietly into the room next to mine; suddenly I heard singing: "*Wie schön ist die Jugend von zwanzig Jahren* [How lovely youth is at age twenty]." We had a very joyful evening, although in the midst of the festive mood I became a bit downcast over the transiency of these twenty years: how quickly one reaches this age, without even the slightest hint of accomplishment. On the other hand, the next years would probably also be gone before I knew it; one ought to make the most of the time. There was also the whole question of God's love, which, although often very insistent, somehow still remained distant. I knew beyond doubt that I belonged to him totally, but the shape of this belonging, its strength, the aspect of commitment, remained question marks over which I repeatedly stumbled. I prayed much and thought constantly about God; these were the only signs of my devotion. I carefully avoided what the church offered in the way of preaching and worship, as if they might interrupt and delay the decision that lay ahead. What seemed most odd about Protestant church services was that they either stimulated vehement contradiction from me, which seemed to lead to nothing positive and thus appeared unprofitable, or some little corner seemed to captivate me, which only made my inner situation all the more uncertain, since these things all seemed to lead into increasing falsehood. I had no thoughts of Catholicism at that time. I was simply filled with an increasingly powerful sense of longing for God; I knew that he was hidden not merely from me but from the entire Protestant church, not because he wanted it that way, but because of our fault. God himself wanted to be permitted finally to reveal himself.

On the exceptional occasions when I went to church, if communion was being celebrated, I, too, would go to the front, although with great uneasiness. This made me unspeakably unhappy; I was increasingly convinced that something was false but could see no way around it. I thought the falsehood had to do with me and regretted my lack of trust and preparation. When I received communion, it was as if I had received the dry skin of a peach as nourishment and missed out on the fruit itself. Frequently I thought about the taste that the fruit must possess. I never made it beyond this point; my many uncertainties kept me from progressing farther. The only thing I was sure of was that Protestants lacked sacramental confession, that they refused a powerful grace. Yet, although I knew that confession was Catholic, I took no initiative at that time to approach Catholicism.

Making music occupied a growing place in my life. I virtually luxuriated in it, hoping to reach God through music, to understand something of God so that I could then offer my life to him unconditionally. It was clear to me that we must be completely at God's disposal; something stood in the way of that, but what the obstacle was, I could not figure out.

At school things were fine. Studying languages and mathematics really made me happy. For the first time history also began to fascinate me, for Rector Barth knew how to present it in such a way that I eagerly anticipated each new class. A certain kind of friendship linked me with the rector because he treated us as human beings and understood our questions. It often seemed to me as if his dealings with us were based directly on the command to love one's neighbor. Our immaturity did not annoy him; he let us know that time and our growth would bring about many transformations in us. He listened to our wildest statements and rashest assertions calmly and with a sense of humor.

As I have said, Bethli Schaerer and I were very close friends. We took walks together, and I would rather not have to count the number of times we skipped classes together; the total would be incredibly high. We had endlessly long conversations about the meaning of life, about marriage, about men, about love's constancy, about women and children. I don't know where we got all our wisdom, but we were never short of arguments. We shared a great need to help people, to place ourselves completely at the service of people. Since I knew of no other way to do this than the practice of medicine, I tried to convince Bethli to study medicine. My joy when I finally succeeded at this was great.

After Hanni Liechtenhan had been completely reconciled with her father, she distanced herself from me. I never knew why. She also warned Bethli repeatedly not to become too deeply involved with me. I often sensed the impact of these warnings in Bethli and felt uneasy. That Hanni kept her distance from me also saddened me.

Once Bethli told me that she believed one could become totally absorbed in service to others without believing in God, or at least without raising the issue of God's existence. Although I did not at all doubt God's existence, I did feel inhibited and thwarted in my search for him, undoubtedly because of a growing awareness of human imperfection. This made me uncertain enough interiorly to avoid directly contradicting Bethli; I merely insisted that, without God, I could accomplish nothing and that I would constantly ask him to reveal his truth to me in such a way that it would give shape to and ultimately take over my service entirely.

There were days when I was indeed very restless. That I was to study medicine was clear. I loved the sick, and it seemed in keeping with my essential nature to choose this profession and none other. Basically, no other profession ever really registered with me. Very sporadically the thought of studying theology occurred to me, for it seemed to me that I might gain personal relief in and through a more exact knowledge of God. But the relief I needed more urgently could never be conceived of in a purely personal fashion; it would have to be given away, and then, perhaps, through its complete potential for being given away, that relief might finally return to me. My experiences at Saint-Loup still pained me, and I sensed that the same false premise that had made Saint-Loup an impossibility for me might turn up again at the basis of theological studies. Occasionally, though only very briefly, in fleeting moments, I even gave a name to this false premise: an untrue interpretation of God's words.

Once, while on a walk with Willy, we went into the Heiliggeistkirche [Church of the Holy Spirit] because we, or at least he, was tired. It was already twilight, and at first we could make out only dim outlines. Bit by bit the sanctuary lamp shone more brightly and more vitally. I befriended it, for it seemed that the lamp must have some connection with the Holy Spirit, with the church's name. I was sorry that the Protestant church buildings had no constantly burning light, I even thought that this lack symbolized their lack of vitality. The Holy Spirit also seemed to me missing [in

Protestant churches], to awaken no comparable notion. I was becoming very sad.

Outside the church we encountered our elderly von Speyr cousin. I explained to her that we had just been inside the Heiliggeistkirche, which made her indignant: it was, after all, a Catholic church, and we had no business there. Willy, with whom I had already shared my newfound insights, was deeply impressed by the encounter with our cousin. He did not want to resume our conversation. That saddened me all the more.

Two of my schoolmates were Catholic. One of them had an incredibly dirty neck, although she otherwise appeared to be well groomed. Her neck completely matched the view of Catholicism that had been inculcated in me: from my earliest childhood I knew that this was a constituent element of Catholic faith. My schoolmate's neck thus confirmed what I already knew and was no cause for any surprise.

These two girls were by no means unpopular, but they participated only marginally in our discussions. They always stood somewhat apart. I assumed this was a consequence of their faith; only much later did I realize that the other schoolgirls, with their low opinion of Catholicism, had certainly pushed them into this position.

During the last Christmas season of my school years I heard for the first time, at least the first time that I was aware of it, about midnight Mass. I wanted so badly to attend, and I spoke with Mama about it; it seemed to me I simply had to go, for I hoped that it would enlighten me; I believed I would suddenly comprehend something that could not really be so far from me, that I could grasp it and take it home with me. But Mama had little appreciation for the eccentricities of her daughter, and so I did not go. On Christmas Day I traveled to the Waldau. Several Englishwomen were on the train, and I prided myself not a little on being able to carry on a decent conversation with them.

I joined in all the festivities at the hospital. The celebration in the church came first, with my uncle playing the organ, as he did every year. Celebrations followed in each ward. It took four or five days to make all the rounds. My uncle planned each ward's festivities himself, called the patients together by ringing a bell, lit the candles on the tree, and made music. His patience was unbelievable, for—fine musician that he was in every fiber of his body—he nonetheless accompanied every song, every novice violinist, even the most impossible flute solos, either at the piano or the harmonium. When genuine musicians came forward to play, he was most grateful.

These celebrations were, like all the church services at the hospital, subject to interruptions: patients might have seizures or become excited in unusual ways. I asked myself in all seriousness whether, despite my love for surgery, I might not rather become a psychiatrist.

Until now I had had more love for than medical interest in the patients at the Waldau. I spent a good bit of time with them, even though less than when I was a child. I had always been more fascinated by their fate than by their "case". This began to change somewhat. I tried to provide diagnoses and prognoses and noticed the related characteristics of illnesses affecting individual patients. Still, it seemed to me that the personal characteristics of the sick ought to be more important to a physician than the illness that linked them together. During this Christmas vacation, I tried to convince my uncle to agree to my plans to study medicine. All he said was, "You haven't even graduated from school." I could do nothing more about it.

During my last quarter of school, our teachers eased up on us. We were assigned almost no homework, so that we might enter the final exams well rested. This considerate treatment was particularly pleasant for me, since it meant I could spend a lot more time playing the piano, but this was also a farewell. It seemed clear to me that I could not accomplish both: medical studies and music. Something I could not entirely define was involved. At the Waldau I had often experienced the necessity of making some small, interior sacrifice in order to help the sick. Such sacrifices seemed to me to be as effective as the prescribed therapy. Thus I wished to sacrifice my music for the sake of my future patients. I imagined that I could thereby draw closer to them, that it was better to approach them having given up something. Moreover, I feared that, if I continued to play my dearly loved piano, I might neglect my more urgent obligation to study. Thus my decision was based on two different grounds, at different levels, but even that did not make giving up music any less painful. And so I played with all the more happiness during these last months and enjoyed music to the fullest, refusing to be driven into a mood of farewell. I still relished music in long drafts.

Our mathematics teacher used to say to us, "Don't get the idea that someday you will wake up in bed with diploma in hand." Despite his warning, we did indeed awake one morning and found ourselves graduated, all of us together.

THE BEGINNING OF MEDICAL SCHOOL
Easter–October 1923

The day after the examinations were over I talked with Mama about medical school. She did not want to discuss it. I was free to take a vacation at the Waldau, but after that she expected me to find a position, say, in one of the banking companies, where the daughters of good families were gladly hired as executive secretaries. She had already made some inquiries; there was no doubt about my being hired. If I refused to go along, it would be out of pure egoism.

I had to fight my way through a fairly intense inner struggle that day. I really had no standard of measurement; I did not really know how urgent it was that I study medicine—and the permission to do so was bound up with this obligation—or how much my wish to study medicine might indeed arise from an egoism I had never admitted to myself. Until now this goal, unlike all others, had been much more substantial and utterly unambiguous.

The other, ever urgent matter was to come to God—by means of a decision I could not envision at all. This made me most uneasy, although I was unable to locate even a trace of the path I needed to follow.

I prayed for a long while, asking God not to permit me to take up the study of medicine out of pure selfishness. Soon I sensed the same peace I had known before talking to Mama: medical school was the right thing to do, the reasons for it were solid. About the essential thing, however, I could gain no clarity; everything remained doubtful and uncertain.

And so I traveled to the Waldau the next morning. I had two and a half weeks ahead of me. I hoped to talk imme-

diately with Uncle and then discuss matters more exten-
sively with him later. I would have been happy to spend the
first semester at the Waldau, traveling from there to study
at Bern. Things were too difficult at home; I could hardly
imagine what it would be like to begin medical school there.
I was afraid I would become impatient with my family. I
badly needed rest, needed to recover a sense of balance.

Uncle welcomed me cordially, congratulated me on my
examinations, thought I seemed a bit tired, and recommended a thorough rest. When I tried to steer the conversation toward my future studies, he cut it off immediately,
though not ungraciously, telling me that there would be
plenty of time to talk about that. When the occasion arose,
I was to explain to him the reasons that had convinced me
to study medicine, for, until now, it had appeared to him
as nothing more than an impossible, childish dream. In his
eyes I lacked both the necessary health and the capability
for such an undertaking; I probably also lacked the stamina
it would require. Moreover, he feared that medical school
would destroy the personal qualities present in me: I had
no idea how rough the course would be. He would send
for me sometime in the coming days. I assured him without
hesitation that I had made my decision, irrevocably, but it
made no difference: the conversation was over.

The next two weeks were really torturous. I saw Uncle
almost exclusively in the company of others; he was nice
to me but acted as if my problem simply did not exist. He
talked about books and ideas, told about all sorts of experiences, including some from his own student days, was generally very kind and gracious and in a good mood, offering
his niece genuine signs of his affection, but nothing else.

At one point I gathered all my courage together and went
unbidden to his office. He was giving me no opportunity

to present my concern, so I thought I had the right to create one. Uncle was somewhat surprised at my sudden appearance and asked what had happened. I said simply that it was already Friday and the semester would begin on Monday. At that point he said he had to go into the city and invited me to accompany him as far as the streetcar. And so we walked down the long, tree-lined lane. The trees were covered with buds that had only begun to swell; no leaves were out yet. We encountered all sorts of people from the institute; Uncle greeted them all most personally but without permitting himself to become involved in any conversations. His seventy years had not slowed his step at all and, as always, walking next to him meant a quick pace; one never had to slow one's own to match his. It seemed as if we had always strolled together down this long lane. Yet it was also sad. I could not talk about my request, which still had no importance for my uncle, and perhaps, on the whole, no reality. Mostly he talked about his fellow students who had taken up medical school without any sense of inner necessity and then later, equally without visible reasons, gave it up, thereby wasting the time they had spent at it. He talked about others who indeed earned a diploma but never felt at home in the profession and hence never accomplished much in it. None of this was encouraging to me, though my uncle was almost talking to himself, as if everything he was saying applied only indirectly, or perhaps not at all, to me. I was more than a little unhappy. As the streetcar came into view, Uncle said, with kindness yet as if from an unapproachable distance: "Perhaps you wanted to say a few things too, but there is plenty of time before Monday. I shall call for you."

My walk back to Waldau was a slow one, completely devoid of enthusiasm. It was almost as if I were saying a final farewell to the landscape of my childhood. The large pasture with its multitude of sheep was still there; how often Aunt Jeanne had taken me there when I was younger, since I felt a special attachment to the sheep and had always somehow confused the shepherd with our Lord. On the other side of the tree-lined lane, on the green, soldiers rode past. The dirigible hangar was open, with an aircraft in front of the building, and I thought, almost with melancholy, how much I longed someday to be able to fly. This walk to the hospital, a path I had strolled so many hundreds of times, carried within it all the day-to-day realities. Yet it seemed to shrivel up, and my previous life shriveled up with it, as if it had all been for nothing. It seemed to me as if medical school were floating away, leaving me nothing to hold onto, at least nothing comprehensible. I thought about God, firm, perseveringly; suddenly I knew that all my difficulties were really small when measured by God's. That brought me consolation. Back home I took my handwork to the fountain and happily crocheted away on an orange-colored pillow with large black chimeras, as if this pillow were enough to fulfill my life. All of a sudden Doctor Wolf was standing next to me, suggesting we go for a walk. We walked together through the slowly darkening landscape. It was a remarkable walk: though he was normally very quiet, he talked about Goethe's relation with Schiller, about the relationship of one man with another, of talent with talent, then he talked about the loneliness of a gifted person, about the misunderstandings in which he has to live, and about the necessity of these misunderstandings, which keep the gifted person from claiming special status. It was like a monologue; I was welcome to listen but not to converse; but then, what would I have said anyway? Frequently it flashed through my mind: I am an adult now, my sudden farewell to childhood this afternoon was substantial and genuine. Now Doctor Wolf began to talk about music, which is the only thing that can give real inner meaning to life; without music there is no giftedness, no individual life; and only an individual life, in his view, was worth living. Everything else was a leveling and had no right to exist. I did not understand everything, but it was beautiful and sad at the same time.

We returned right at supper time. He ate with the patients in the private quarters, something he did not like to do but which was expected of the unmarried junior physicians. I ate with Aunt Jeanne. We were alone, for Uncle had not yet returned. As soon as possible after supper, I left to visit Doctor Wolf in his bachelor's apartment. I knew very well that it was not entirely acceptable, that Aunt and Uncle would not have liked it. Yet I had to see him, for I was driven by an immensely powerful uneasiness, an uneasiness that dwarfed all my concerns about my medical studies: Did Doctor Wolf not know about God? I had to talk with him, thoroughly, and even, if possible, accurately.

At that time it was especially hard for me to talk about God, for I knew all too well that God was completely different from what any of the Protestants imagined him to be. Yet even though I prayed a lot and searched for him a lot, because of my general uncertainty about his manner of being, I felt unqualified to speak about him. I feared I was not capable of answering specific questions and might thereby cause more confusion than good.

The room in which Doctor Wolf received me was remarkable; only a few pieces of furniture were to be seen, and they were nondescript examples of institutional furnishings. Yet the walls were covered with a large number of modern paintings. I could not have said whether they were beautiful or not, for they seemed to be driven by ideas that could not come to expression, like sentence fragments devoid of any syntactical frame. Yet they did not make me feel uncomfortable; they were part of the strangeness of that evening. Doctor Wolf did not seem at all surprised that I had come. He offered to make tea. I declined, for I did not want to shorten any further the tightly rationed moments available. Then he said, "If there is to be no tea to introduce this precious hour, then music." He took up his violin. I had never heard him play, and I no longer know whether he played well or merely adequately; it is hard to assess musically the sort of improvisational performance he gave. After a short prelude that introduced the theme, or rather, uncovered it, came something of a long, vehement outcry that very slowly unveiled the soul. Not the soul but the lament dominated. It was an endless lament, which, through its expression and only through it, revealed a soul born in and living in lamentation, a soul that lacked the strength for freedom. Occasionally he stopped playing for a moment and looked at me inquiringly, struck a chord, and the lamentation resumed. A small lamp in the corner cast fantastic shadows; there was no overhead lighting. Doctor Wolf was pale, paler than usual. He, his playing, the sparse light, everything altogether made the whole scene more ghostly. When I could hardly stand it any longer, he suddenly stopped himself: "I've been doing all the talking, now it is your turn." I began to talk about God, began to talk to a little child about the loving, merciful God. The words came out slowly and with difficulty, but God was alive; he was present among us. After a short while, everything had been said; we both rose, he took my hands in his, very gently and cautiously, and thanked me. Then he said, as much to himself as to me, "Don't believe in demons; even if they are powerful, they exist only to be overcome. Yes, I shall overcome them. This was a beautiful time."

I never spoke to him again. Two weeks later he was arrested in the woods nearby for sexually molesting two young boys. He later came to Basel to practice medicine but was repeatedly committed either to mental institutions or prison, always for the same offense. When we encountered each other, he would quickly avert his face. In 1943 he committed suicide.

As I returned to the main building, I was rather confused. I could not tell whether the evening had had any purpose, everything seemed both unreal and disturbing at the same time. I wanted to help but could not see how. Aunt Jeanne was alone; Uncle had returned from the city but had already gone to bed. As far as I can recall, apart from special festive occasions, he always retired about nine o'clock. Aunt was mending socks at the dining room table; I sat next to her with my handwork. She asked no questions, which meant I was not expected to explain where I had been, let alone to explain what had taken place. I let myself be as though taken in by the quiet evening atmosphere of the dining room. Suddenly Aunt Jeanne said: "I think you are tenacious enough to succeed." This almost startled me; yes, that is what I had to do: succeed with Uncle, Mama, and so many others. But to succeed might mean above all having to succeed at what God wanted accomplished. And would I always be able to understand what that was?

Sunday passed like all Sundays at the Waldau: a bit festive and very quiet. No one said anything about the semester that would begin the next day. In the afternoon, Aunt Jeanne and I went for a walk in the woods. We followed the edge of the woods, saying little. The spring afternoon's light made the landscape especially peaceful. I could no longer tell if any peacefulness remained within me, or whether it had disappeared. The world I had known up to this point seemed to be constantly shrinking; a new world had not yet opened up. I could not tell whether the new would suddenly break in upon me like a catastrophe, or whether it would turn out to be linked to my present and my past.

After supper Uncle played the piano briefly, then came into the dining room and played Patience with me. He took me to task for playing too rapidly, for not taking time to survey the entire game and so improve my chances.

The next morning, Monday, someone knocked vigorously at my bedroom door at about seven o'clock. The chief attendant of the women's department of the hospital announced that my uncle was expecting me in his office. I dressed hastily and went to the downstairs office, which was normally off-limits to us. There Uncle told me that he really could not oppose my wish to study medicine, since I was of age and no one could legally object; I would have to discuss it with my mother. He could not understand why I wanted to do this, hence he would not be able to provide financial resources for it. Moreover, he thought it better that I begin my studies at Basel rather than Bern—I had chosen the harder path, and I would have to walk it in a place where I could not take any detours. With that he shook my hand in farewell, and I found myself dismissed. It was not an entirely pleasant experience.

I went back upstairs, said goodbye to Aunt Jeanne, and packed my small suitcase. I would have to hurry in order to catch the next train, so I ran down the long lane as fast as I could, stopping occasionally because my luggage was so heavy. I had never had to carry my own bags down this lane, and so this departure from the Waldau was unlike any other, but I had no time to brood over it.

Only after I was in the train did I realize that my mother did not even know I was coming. She did not enjoy surprises of this sort; that would undoubtedly not make the beginning any easier. Still, at heart I felt a touch of joy: in a few hours my medical studies would begin, for real. I was going to be a medical student, one among many others.

At Basel the weather was more springlike: hot and humid. The leaves of the chestnut trees were already completely unfolded. I picked one off, planning to insert it in my first letter to Uncle, to show him how far ahead the city was.

When Mama caught sight of me at the door, she was not very delighted, something she made abundantly clear to me. After that no one talked to me for weeks. I came and went, but no words escaped her mouth; I could not even get a response to a question. At first this was very hard to take, later I became so accustomed to it that it almost seemed perfectly normal.

I registered at the university that same afternoon, then went to the girls' secondary school to discuss my situation with my friend, Georgine Gerhard, who was secretary at the school. I was going to have to earn some money, and the thought of tutoring had occurred to me; nothing else came to mind. Georgine got a great many students for me, indeed, so many that at some points I was spending twenty hours a week tutoring. A few of these girls were very gifted and needed tutoring only because they came from other schools and had to catch up in one subject or another. Others had fallen behind, and it was no fun trying to feed them a bit of wisdom drop by drop. But I learned how to deal with people and to figure out all kinds of ways to achieve my goals. Mostly I tutored French, but also Latin, English, mathematics, and several other subjects. At the time I had no doubt that I was earning my five francs an hour; today I am less certain.

Having significantly improved my financial situation by

means of my conversation with Georgy, I confidently entered a shop and bought a rose-colored dress made of durable but attractive material, white hose, and white shoes, topping it off with a white cloth hat. Dressed in this outfit, I went to my first laboratory course, inorganic chemistry, taught by Professor Fiechter. It was marvelous; from the start we really went to work, and it was there that I gained a serious foundation in chemistry. After a good textbook introduction, we did all the experiments ourselves, we had to note everything down very precisely, and even had theoretical problems to solve. It made me very happy. Later Professor Fiechter said that I was the best student he had ever had, which made me more than a little proud, especially since this was not the case in all areas of the curriculum.

In the botany lab I never really caught on to how things fit together. I had no difficulty preparing and drawing the slides and was able to see in the microscope what we were supposed to observe, but the conclusions to be drawn from our observations remained hazy and disconnected in my mind. Most likely we simply needed to spend much more time at it in order to arrive at satisfactory results. The lectures in botany were very uninteresting, and I followed them, too, only with difficulty. The same was true of physics. In both subjects the gaps in my schooling became apparent at their worst.

Our daily lectures in zoology were quite remarkable. Old Professor Zschokke spent the entire morning memorizing his lecture; from the hallway we could hear him practicing. As we entered the lecture hall, he would always be standing at the door, extending his hand to each of us and saying something nice to those of us he liked (which was always the great majority of us). The others received at most an indifferently proffered hand accompanied by a stiff gaze that

lacked any personal engagement, only to brighten into amiable kindness for the next person. If you were the object of
his coldness, you never had the faintest idea what misdeed
had brought it on. Often he would go so far as to withdraw
his hand in irritation and say in a clearly audible voice: "No,
not for you, no, no." The whole performance was odd and
disgusting, for both the rebuff and the friendliness seemed
artificial. He was always nice to me, since my father had been
his student and apparently a very good one. When the hour
had struck, Zschokke himself closed the door, and woe to
anyone who dared to enter after that; he would have to endure a torrent of verbal scorn from the professor and would
certainly be among the recipients of Zschokke's cold stare
at the door when it was time for the next class. Zschokke
delivered his lectures in a remarkably choppy rhythm, and,
in order to get it started, he often had to resort to the end
of a sentence, so that his lectures seldom began with a complete sentence. The entire lecture was sung rather than spoken, and newcomers usually needed more than one class
session before they began to comprehend even a few bits
and pieces. With time, the whole of it became understandable, but even so most of what he said was just words to fill
up space. Zschokke and his two assistant professors[1] also
taught the zoology laboratory course. Though it was very
specialized in topic, it was quite interesting, especially because Adolf Portmann, who later succeeded to Zschokke's

---

[1] In the German university system, the title *assistant professor* does not
refer simply to an untenured faculty member in a collective rank but des-
ignates a person who has completed his doctoral degree and is assigned as
a personal assistant to one of the relatively few full professors. Thus each
professor has in effect his own staff of assistants. See n. 3 in the chapter "The
Broken Leg" for corresponding practice in clinical medicine departments
—Trans.

professorship, was one of the assistants and managed, at least in part, to expand the parameters of the course a bit. Portmann would bubble over with ideas and insights that all had something to do with the material at hand yet also reached over into new areas we had not yet encountered, uncovering for us new approaches and research methods. A fine, deep friendship soon developed between him and me, a friendship that was never disappointed.

In my naïveté, I had registered for yet another lab course, one that was called "Electromedical Equipment". Its instructor was one of the most vain people I had ever encountered. The class had only a few participants, and none of us had the slightest idea what the empty, elegant phrases meant. Since we students were too few for an absence to go unnoticed, we had to do semester-long penance for our incautious registration, sacrificing one evening a week, from six to eight o'clock. I never quite forgave this instructor.

Only one course, a three-hour lecture in osteosyndesmology offered by Professor Ludwig, gave me a faint reminder that I was studying medicine. The classes would have been extremely dry and boring had he not been exceptionally gifted at drawing. He could take a piece of chalk, aided by an indescribable rag, and, in a few seconds, produce from ordinary strokes the most lifelike rendering of a bone. When, by adding connective tissues, he linked one bone to its nearest neighbor, one was almost surprised that they did not suddenly begin to move. We all hoped fervently that some day we might be able to draw the way he did. It was this skill of his, I think, that inspired in me a great personal affinity for Ludwig, so much so that, although we never had any personal contact and I never really absorbed much knowledge of his specialty, I felt certain that a bond of friendship linked us.

Adrienne with fellow medical school students

I felt fortunate to be able to study with boys, for it gave me a greater sense of freedom than I had known in the society of girls alone. Since I was the only girl among the new students that semester, it was natural to associate more with the boys. Of course, two of my former schoolmates were studying botany: Hanni Liechtenhan and Hanna Huber, and we saw each other in several of our classes. Bethli Schaerer had also decided to study medicine but was spending six months at the hospital in La Chaux-de-Fonds in order to learn about nursing from a very practical perspective.

My best friends during the first semesters were Adrian Sutermeister and Willy Roessiger. Neither of them entered medical practice, for both died a few months after completing the government board certification exams.[2] In later semesters, my friends included Edwin Wilhelm and Hans Mast, both of whom became general practitioners in Canton Aargau. Our times together were very easygoing and happy; we sat together in various lectures and labs and journeyed together from one building to another, for the distances were considerable in those days. We talked a lot about questions we had regarding our future careers, about how to relate to other people, about the strong desire we felt to understand and to help others. We always agreed about things, and, even where this did not seem to be the case at first, we soon came to a common, amiable solution. None of my comrades loved discussion for discussion's sake, which made them quite different from the friends I had had while attending *gymnasium* at La Chaux-de-Fonds. We all had a very definite sense that we were already entering upon our place in the medical corps.

---

[2] *Staatsexamen*, roughly equivalent to an M.D. degree in the U.S.— TRANS.

Several times a semester we made field trips with our zoology or botany professors. The first zoology excursion took us into the Jura mountains in order to search for salamanders. I brought a bunch of them home and kept them in an open aquarium, where they did quite nicely, growing impressively. I was proud of their development. How shocked I was one morning to find most of them crawling all over my bed. Completely unprepared for their migration from a wet to a dry habitat, I held a bit of a grudge against them for a while.

The Zschokkian excursions were renowned for always concluding with a properly boisterous drinking spree. Since this did not appeal very much to us, Adrian and I usually left early and took another way home.

When most were well inebriated, Zschokke would choose a few students who suited his fancy at the moment and pledge his friendship with them. The following day, however, at the door to the lecture hall, he would say to each of the previous night's select few: "Now, my friend, just so there is no misunderstanding, I'll use '*Du*' [familiar address] with you while you will once more address me with '*Sie*' [formal address]". Most of them had known that it would turn out this way; those who did not were quite disappointed.

One morning, at my first class, a second-semester student (how far in advance of us the second-semester students seemed to us then!) brought me a huge bouquet of lilies of the valley. I thought it a splendid bouquet, but I was more than a little embarrassed at having to wander from one building to another with this white magnificence in my arms throughout the entire morning. I never forgot that August Meyer had spent an entire Sunday afternoon picking lilies of the valley for me in the woods of St. Chrischona.

At home the silence had suddenly been breached: Willy was no longer attending school in Bern and had begun to attend the Minerva in Basel. He needed tutoring in English, I was permitted to give it to him and thereby to resume my normal place in the family. This restoration of my right to speak made scant impression on me, for all that was happening to me in my studies left little room for anything else, especially since I had to spend many hours tutoring for income. I was able to get by on little sleep in those days—four or five hours a night was plenty, although I did make up for it somewhat on the weekends: I would sleep for fourteen to sixteen hours at a stretch from Saturday night to Sunday.

I traveled to the Waldau on the first day of the summer vacation. For the first time in my life I was not really looking forward to it, since I had never really digested the events of my stay there the previous spring, and I was afraid of falling back into an atmosphere of indecision once more. It was not so much that I thought I would have to struggle through my own decision all over again; rather, I thought the atmosphere, the conversation, the whole setting, might be full of remnants of those uncomfortable Easter vacation weeks and that Uncle might still be angry with me. But there was no hint of all that. Uncle and Aunt received me amiably, and I found myself asked to tell Uncle about all sorts of experiences from the summer semester. It seemed as if he had virtually forgotten how much he had once opposed my plans.

After a few days, it occurred to Uncle that he had not heard me playing his wonderful grand piano since I arrived, and I had to confess: one of my first errands in the summer semester had been to my piano teacher, where, with heavy heart, I informed him it would be impossible for me to carry on two such demanding preoccupations as music and medicine; yet to continue with music as a sideline, as relaxation, was simply not acceptable to me. I said nothing about the fact that this sacrifice was hard to make, but one thing I knew for sure: medicine, at least as I imagined it, demanded sacrifices of me, sacrifices whose meaning might not even be immediately apparent to me but which, by their very sacrificial quality, were required by God for use as it pleased him. In a certain way I believed most firmly that he asked this sacrifice of me so that I could give myself more to other people.

At the outset of the vacation I learned what had happened with Doctor Wolf. It burdened me greatly.

Something else weighed me down during those weeks: anxiety about the dissection course. I was really afraid of it. The thought of human cadavers, as an expression of death, frightened me; and even worse was the fact of having to live with these cadavers, learn from them, and cut them up. I lacked the imagination to portray these scenes graphically in my mind, yet I could not rid myself of a painful preoccupation with the dissection course. I counted the months, weeks, and days that separated me from this fearful first day of classes. I could not believe that I would be able to put up with it any more than I believed my comrades would be able to do so. Reasoning it out did not help, nor did the knowledge that generations of physicians before me had managed to survive it.

Nor could I understand how a body could be subjected to this after death. I could, with great effort, understand the necessity of an autopsy in order to clarify a diagnosis, but not this slow butchery down to the bare bones by inexperienced hands.

I mentioned this once to Uncle, but he entered into the conversation only superficially, talking as if dissection were the least important thing in the world. I lacked the courage to tell him how much the very thought of it tortured me.

I spent very little time during the vacation on my studies, apart from reorganizing my notebooks, copying portions over into a cleaner form, where I had not already done so during the semester; I didn't do much else. It may have been at this time that I became aware how much I loved the Waldau; I no longer experienced it only as the place where Aunt and Uncle lived, but altogether, as an institution and as space. Each place in the garden, in the woods, on the lanes, and in the building itself was not merely familiar but also dear to me. Memories surfaced everywhere, not merely as isolated instances but as part of the whole network of my life. And I loved life just as I loved people: as an unconditional gift of God. Perhaps that is why the dissecting room loomed as such an unbridgeable chasm in my mind.

Watering the garden was one job that I loved to do when I was at the Waldau; it was one time when I might have the best chance of not being interrupted, since Aunt Jeanne possessed an undeniable gift for interrupting anything one might be doing. She lived so much in her own world that she had difficulty respecting the world and the work of others. She was constantly calling; I had never noticed this as much as I did now, since I was eager to have long hours at my disposal. Only brief moments were ever available, so I saw no other solution but to work in the early morning, between five and eight o'clock. For my study I had been given a room that faced north, overlooking an inner courtyard that led to the kitchen. One could watch the awakening of the entire institution taking place in this courtyard as the stillness of the night gave way slowly to noise and movement. Since patients worked in the kitchen as well as various other outbuildings, everything was noisy enough. Cooking and delivering food involved all manner of busyness, yet, how I loved—half-working, half-dreaming—to watch the patients' lives in front of me. Handcarts arrived from each unit of the hospital and from the more distant buildings, each cart accompanied by a member of the staff and a patient. The carts rumbled and the canisters rattled loudly and sharply; no sound failed to echo in the covered porticoes. In the kitchen the huge kettles were steaming, some of them even whistling, while lids and even entire canisters fell on the floor. From the nearby attendants' stations, shrill cries could be heard; in the middle of the courtyard a fountain splashed softly and steadily yet audibly. My room, normally occupied by one of the junior physicians, reeked of stale smoke. I never felt any attachment to this study room, but I did feel an attraction to the courtyard. Beyond the courtyard one could see a few fir trees from the woods. My solitude ended after eight o'clock, when I went to our common breakfast; if I managed to sneak a few moments for studies during the day, I did so at the desk in my dearly beloved bedroom, number 17. Located above my uncle's official office, it had a window that looked out on the garden and the beautiful tree-lined lane.

That summer I learned how to sew my own clothes. One of the patients taught me all sorts of things about sewing, but I never really became adept at it. It always seemed as if a dress was long overdue to be finished before I ever really got a good start on it.

Since the Forels were gone and, as mentioned above, Doctor Wolf too, I saw few "normal" people apart from my aunt and uncle. I spent much time in the hospital wards with my handwork; I felt comfortable among the patients. I had a number of long conversations with many of the young women, most of whom were ready to decide they liked life in the institution, at least compared to the harsh existence they had known outside. I tried to give life outside more vital meaning for them. Such attempts may have been unsuccessful, but I felt obliged to try.

Pastor Henzi preached at church. He was a nice old man who delivered his sermons most earnestly. I was more fascinated by the patients, by their facial expressions, than by his words. I always walked back with several women patients, wanting so much to give them what I lacked: certainty in faith.

THE DISSECTION LAB

Winter Semester 1923/1924

My return trip to Basel was quite remarkable. It seemed as if I faced another choice. Medical school seemed endlessly long —even if I did not miss a single semester, it would be at least five years until the board examinations, five years without any real effectiveness. Yet my wish to be able to help was so powerful that it became irrational: What would the patients at the Waldau, the ones I had really related to in the past months, do while I was finishing medical studies? What did the conversations with these patients—conversations that had brought real relief, perhaps even real help, to them— have to do with the dissection lab? Would it not be better to become an attendant in a mental hospital immediately than to waste years of time on studies that would only block any possibility of immediate effectiveness? These thoughts were not merely an escape from the dissection course.

Adrienne during medical school

A small occurrence near the end of the trip gave me back my unshakable confidence. A woman was traveling with two small children. While she took care of one, I watched over the other, which showed me that there were people everywhere whom one could help in small ways; I would certainly have no difficulty finding some of them during my studies.

During the last week of vacation, we moved to very spacious lodgings on the Sevogelplatz. To my great satisfaction I was able to settle into an attic room on the floor occupied by the maids. The kind of independence and seclusion pleased me; I would be able to work in peace, away from the commotion of family life. Everything in my room was reddish-orange: the carpet, the sheer curtains, the block-printed fabric of the couch's cover, the upholstered seats of the chairs. Tall bookcases flanked both sides of my tiny desk. The room had only one disadvantage: the screeching brakes of the streetcars that stopped directly in front of the house. Only gradually, after the initial impressions of the room had worn off, did I realize a second disadvantage: the Rhine's distance from me. As long as we lived in Little Basel, all my departures from the house had begun with a walk along the river, and, from my room in the house on Florastraße, I could always glimpse a bit of the river between the trees of a nearby garden. In our new home, the Rhine was farther away. One almost had to search for it to see it, and I did not have time to spend doing that. My strolls through the city also diminished sharply, for the distances were so much greater that the only reasonable way to manage them was to take the streetcar, especially since it stopped right at our door. In all the years that I rode the streetcar, I don't think I ever learned anyone's name, yet I felt a great deal of commonality with these people, some of whom I saw daily: the woman with the deep-pile velvet coat, who always spread it out behind her to avoid sitting on it when she seated herself; the bank employee who always read pious tracts to himself, a new one almost every day (years later I once received Communion next to him in the Marienkirche); the young girl who briefly looked into her mirror at nearly every stop; the student from the girls' secondary school, whom I helped with her French homework and who was always upset if I happened not to be on the streetcar when she needed my help most. The twelve-o'clock tram was always fun, for a goodly number of the "Dalbe"[1] were always aboard, and, since they were blessed with very loud voices, one overheard many but not especially interesting secrets made public in this way. Illnesses, domestic servants' escapades, and menus, together with their recipes, made up most of the chatter. At other times of the day, the streetcars were usually not enlivened by a lot of talk, but they were lively nonetheless.

The semester began with the course in dissection; the other lectures and labs came on the second day of the term. When I entered the anatomy and dissection class, I had not seen my friends since the end of the summer semester. Sutermeister and Roessiger were standing at the top of the stairs. The sight of their faces, which seemed remarkably pale, reawakened in me the fears that had diminished somewhat while we were busy moving into our new lodgings. The pain was sharp, penetrating: "My God, I'll never be able to do it", I thought. Yet I managed to put on the white apron and black oilcloth sleeves—how I did it, I don't know. No sooner was I holding my father's dissection kit in my hand than Roessiger, opening the door for me, announced

---

[1] Inhabitants of the Sankt-Alban district, where many old, distinguished families, called Dalbanese, once lived—ED.

festively in English: "Ladies first!" From here on everything
happened with uncanny rapidity. Two cadavers lay there in
the middle of the room, dark gray, like moist mummies, one
on the right, the other on the left. Tall, dry, a bit sinister,
Professor Ludwig, from whom I had taken osteology in the
summer, led us to the cadaver on the left. He tested the
sharpness of my scalpel, appeared to be satisfied but not enthused about it, and made a precise incision in the middle of
the neck, lengthwise, showing me how I had to dissect the
skin in order to expose the main neck muscle. It was called
the *platysma*. I've never had as much trouble remembering
a name as I had with this muscle. As I recall, it took me the
entire afternoon; I was constantly forgetting it and having
to ask Roessiger, who had been assigned the same dissection
project on the right side of the head and neck on the same
cadaver and so was also struggling with a *platysma*.

I never had any success with anatomy. Professor Fiechter
may have announced at the end of the summer semester that
he had never had as gifted a student as I, but Professor Ludwig probably had nothing but the saddest memories of me. I
could never understand how the various tissues fit together,
had great difficulty impressing their names on my mind, and
the function of each muscle or nerve remained shrouded in
utter obscurity for me. Yet it was not the human corpse
that blocked my access to the dissection of cadavers, for I
grew accustomed to dissection very quickly. My dissections
looked good enough, I was able to carry them out precisely
enough. But the whole business remained something of a
secret code for which I lacked a key.

In order to receive a new dissection project—during a
semester we were expected to do three to five of them—
we were supposed to hand in the results of the current one.
This meant asking Professor Ludwig for his signature of

approval, which he granted only after a short examination. These quizzes were always dreadful experiences for me: once I failed entirely and on the other occasions passed so narrowly that I was ashamed. Today, since many aspects of anatomy were clarified for me in the process of studying surgery and traumatology, I can no longer understand why the study of anatomy was so infinitely difficult for me. Despite all this, in the end I loved the dissection lab, but certainly more because of the company of my lively friends than that of the cadavers. During most of two winter semesters I was with Sutermeister or Roessiger while doing dissections; they were good friends, and our time together was always joyful and natural.

During this first winter semester, in addition to anatomy class, I took nothing except lectures in the natural sciences, together with a lab course in zoology with Professor Zschokke. I enjoyed this lab greatly; I had no trouble remembering the anatomy of animals; we also sketched the dissections, which perhaps made it easier for me to understand. It never occurred to me that this work had any similarity to my other anatomy class and that difficulties might somehow arise from a common source. As far as I was concerned, human and animal anatomy were unrelated.

Since the beginning of this semester, my schoolfriend Bethli Schaerer had also become a medical student. She was not part of the dissection course, but otherwise we had the same classes. On the first morning, I met her in the Küchengasse. The later sunrise of autumn illuminated the area around the railway station in a very unusual fashion: it had just rained, and now the pavement shimmered dazzlingly. One had difficulty seeing anything but this brilliant light from the ground, and I was virtually blinded as I approached my friend. She was happy about her medical studies yet also a bit apprehensive about working with so many male colleagues. From my time in the *gymnasium* at La Chaux-de-Fonds, I was so accustomed to associating freely with boys that it was not the slightest problem for me; I was not at all uncomfortable with them. A few days later, Bethli disappointed me by insisting that the female medical students should stick together more. I simply could not go along with this, so I most often joined the male students when walking from one building to another, although occasionally I walked with her, depending on the circumstances.

Since I was still doing a lot of tutoring, I often worked on my medical studies at night in my beloved attic room. I had secured an orange lamp shade, which I had dyed myself with a batik design. I re-covered the chairs in the same fabric and embroidered them with mythical salamanders of my own design. When I think about all that orange now, it seems hideous, but at that time I apparently thought it was pretty. The fine little wood stove that I myself tended kept the room warm well into the night. Normally I worked until about two in the morning; since I got up at six, I would certainly have suffered from lack of sleep had I not made up for it on the weekends. Immediately after supper on Saturday, I would take a bath, go to bed about eight o'clock, and sleep uninterruptedly until the bell rang for Sunday dinner about twelve-thirty. I had more trouble getting out of bed then than at any time during the week!

Sunday dinner was always boiled beef, for that had always been the custom in my grandmother's house in La Chaux-de-Fonds. My mother had resumed the practice in Basel.

When in Basel I no longer went to church services on Sundays at all; I felt more and more out of place there, and more than ever I was convinced that everything ought to be different. Something very basic prevented me from experi-

encing God's presence in church, and the sermons only left
a void in me. At the Waldau I went to services almost every
Sunday, but I knew very well that I did it only because of
the patients: I wanted to have a part in their worship and,
through this worship, to pray for them.

I was already praying as a rule, not excessively, but several
times a day. I prayed for the most impossible matters, for
strangers I knew only through their worried faces, for the
cadavers in the dissection room, even though it took all the
effort I could muster to imagine that they had ever really
been alive.

There was probably no time in my life when I took science—every science—more seriously than during this winter. I was of the opinion that a real physician should have
mastered the natural sciences to the point that he understood all their problems. This led to two remarkably naïve
steps. The first was that I joined the Society for Scientific
Research, having heard from another student that student
membership cost only five francs a year. I attended the first
lecture given after my membership had been accepted, only
to discover to my astonishment that the audience, except for
a few junior faculty from the university, consisted of nothing but gray- or bald-headed men and not a single woman.
This did not keep me from attending meetings regularly,
since my five francs had earned me my rightful place. Although I understood little, to this day I have not come up
with an adequate reason for dropping my membership. It
has been years, however, since I attended any meetings.

My second step had more serious consequences. A botany
student once commented, in the course of a discussion, that
medical students really did not understand botany at all. Either they understood it merely as a study of medicinal herbs,
or they confused it with art, perhaps because of the beauty

of many of the flowers. Real botany was to be found, not in the lecture halls, but in the colloquium. I don't know how he managed it, but by the time we parted we had agreed that he would take me to the colloquium the next day. Having completed only one semester, I had no idea that this colloquium was really a sort of society of doctoral candidates. When Professor Senn caught sight of me, he congratulated me for my courage and assigned me a research project related to phototropism in plants. At the end of the semester, I was expected to present my results in the colloquium. There was no way out. These two experiences made me a bit more cautious in the future.

By mid-November we found ourselves rather discouraged in our dissection course. Mast announced that he would never, ever be able to master those hideous, heathen names for the muscles and that he would finally give in and follow the advice of one of his lower *gymnasium* teachers and become a street sweeper. We decided to take steps to make his decision easier. By "steps" we had in mind a celebration. But how could we stage a festival at two o'clock in the afternoon? Suddenly we had an inspiration: we would go to the fair. The hardest part was to escape from the dissection lab. We managed to prevail upon one of the members of the second class to preoccupy Professor Ludwig by calling him over and showing him some aspect of his dissection project. While this was going on, all eight of us silently disappeared. We spent the afternoon most enjoyably. To be sure, we had to be careful about riding on the roller coaster, since it emptied the contents of our wallets rather rapidly, but we had enough for two rides each. To make the fun last longer, we took turns in twos, while the others waited underneath and waved. Suddenly my mother appeared with Theddy. She was more than a little surprised to see that the location of my dissection lab had changed, but in the end she took it well. By evening we had come to one conclusion: it would be better for all of us, together, to become street sweepers. The only remaining question was whether the bursar would refund the fees we had already paid for the semester. The question remained unanswered, since the following day found all of us once again laboring over our dissection exercises, learning how to pronounce *omahyoideus* without stuttering.

We sometimes asked ourselves if one could justify in God's eyes this process of slowly cutting human bodies into pieces until only the bones were left. We came to agree that there simply was no alternative, but we never felt very good about it. Once when I was walking with Jenny[2] down the Blumenrain, he expressed his conviction that science, and nothing else, required the practice of dissection. Suddenly he became very excited and stopped in front of the "Three Kings" and refused to go any farther. He thought he had the solution: to demonstrate his belief convincingly and to show that he really meant it, this very day he would bequeath his body to medical science, as both a sacrifice and an expression of gratitude. All medical students should do the same, for it really was ignoble to ask such a sacrifice of people who had no active interest in science. One had to do it oneself, today, for love of science and for love of the future generations of physicians who could then dissect us. Before long, however, his enthusiasm experienced a severe blow: he could not possibly ask such a sacrifice of his future wife, that is, he could neither ask her to marry a man who had made such a pledge before his marriage and hence without her consent, nor could he ask her to take the same fate upon

---

[2] A surname, not a woman's given name—TRANS.

herself. So it was necessary to give it up and leave things as they were, which discouraged him. At the time the whole business seemed to me to be unworthy of further discussion, and we decided not to talk about it with the others.

In the dissection lab, or, rather, in the cadaver rooms adjoining it, something quite odd was happening. An alarming number of the cadavers supplied by the hospital and other institutions seemed to be satisfied with only the briefest stay in our anatomy course. No fewer were delivered to us than before, but after a few days, or sometimes weeks, outraged family members or acquaintances would demand them back, long before they had served their purpose. Something mysterious was going on, but no one could figure it out. We began to suffer from a real shortage of cadavers. Only after several years had passed was the mystery unraveled, permitting a return to the previous state of affairs. It seems that the attendant who was responsible for preparing the cadavers for dissection had taken the job only because he belonged to a sect that was opposed to the practice. Each cadaver was tagged with the deceased person's name. The attendant would launch investigations, often very difficult ones, to find friends or relatives of the dead person; then he would portray in emotional language what happened to a corpse on the dissection table, convincing people to come and claim the body. When necessary, he himself paid for a proper burial with flowers. When all this became known, Attendant Schweizer had to make a quick search for a new job; but before the discovery, he had managed to secure a dignified burial for many dozens of cadavers.

One morning one of the students failed to appear. We had never paid much attention to him, for he was quite introverted, seemed intentionally to avoid our conversations, and wandered with either frowning or haughty demeanor (it was hard to tell which) from one lecture hall to another by himself. At first his absence was hardly noticed, and when someone began to ask if he were sick, the word began to make the rounds that he had switched to the study of theology. This subject caught my attention. Theology had always been a temptation for me. I would have eagerly pursued a religious ministry and just as eagerly searched into the mysteries of God, but the key to this search always seemed hidden from me. Moreover, I seriously doubted whether the pastorate was a proper profession for a woman. Hindenlang's departure from medicine into theology preoccupied me especially because it seemed to echo my conversation with Jenny, whose words had revealed a new aspect of the bond between a man and a woman. If both man and woman were supposed to have such identical thoughts, which was obvious, then a lasting and profound union would have to be achieved, a union that would at the same time have to be in the process of development. Suddenly I found it hard to imagine the marriage of a theologian. Celibacy alone seemed appropriate, as a sacrifice for the man, but equally for his wife. But how could that be? It was clear from the outset that my fellow students all intended to marry, even if only sometime in the distant future. What would Hindenlang do now?

From time to time we talked about marriage in general. Some of us thought that, at least theoretically, it would be good if physicians remained unmarried. But then a number of questions arose, questions I did not entirely understand, that revealed to me that it was much harder for men to remain unmarried than I had thought. I was not surprised when I received two marriage proposals that winter, but I was careful not to mention them at home. Mama would not have understood my quick, ill-considered, so to speak, refusals. Ill-considered inasmuch as, at the time, the problem of marriage simply was not of personal concern to me.

In February Hanna Huber, my former schoolmate who was now industriously studying botany, and I were invited by Doctor Witschi to the Professors' Ball. It happened that my cousin Professor Fiechter, with whom I had had the opportunity to attend the two previous years' balls, was not going this year, since he had moved into a new house and, with his ringing laugh, was proclaiming to one and to all that he simply had to economize and could therefore not afford the costs of attending. Witschi was giving an unspeakably boring course on genetics in which I was enrolled: I think I agreed to go to the ball largely for the sake of Adolf Portmann, with whom we always had interesting conversations before and after class. He thought no more highly of Witschi's lectures than we did. I really was not at all pleased to go to the ball with Witschi, but Hanna, who had few opportunities to go dancing, was willing to go only if I went. So we went, both of us. It seems, however, that we had been invited in order to ensure that Professor Witschi's brother-in-law, Hans Mühlestein, would have a dance partner. More talking than dancing took place. Mühlestein was not uninteresting, but he jumped from one extreme to another and could speak only in antitheses, making him simultaneously tedious and entertaining. He asked me in passing whether I might not like to marry him. When I firmly declined, he posed the same question, about an hour later, to Hanna, who likewise had no fancy for it. How we laughed over the good man who, at the time, was in the midst of a divorce (at least so I was told) and was offering one marriage proposal after another.

Another festival took place as spring approached: the *Zschokkefest*. Each winter semester old Professor Zschokke customarily invited all of his students, at least those who were more or less in his good graces, to supper in one of the pubs. For weeks we had been working on the "*Schnitzel-bänke*".[3] Since all sorts of people attended Zschokke's lectures, in order to hear him at least once, he never noticed when we smuggled the theater's hairdresser into a lecture in order to make a sketch of Professor Zschokke's head. At the supper, then, Roessiger played an incredibly authentic Zschokke giving a zoology demonstration that made use of "live" animals constructed of cardboard and painted in a variety of colors. Although the mood became more and more liquid in the course of the evening, we all had a really good time without anything turning sour. Perhaps Zschokke's personality was basically so refined that he was the one who kept anything off-color from surfacing, despite the fact that enough alcohol had been consumed to remove any sort of inhibition.

THE BICYCLE TOUR

Summer Semester 1924

The break between semesters, which I spent at the Waldau, was like it had always been: uneventful but pleasant days. Gradually the penetrating smell of the dissecting room wore off, which brought a sense of liberation. Only my anatomy books retained that odor, and they do so to this day. From

---

[3] Humorous couplets composed on the occasion of a celebration, the subject of which is the person or event being commemorated—TRANS.

time to time there were short walks with Tjotja, who could never get her fill of hearing stories about my semester, about what had been easy to learn and what had not. During this vacation period I worked very little.[1] Instead I prayed a lot. I felt enriched by all I had experienced in recent months, but I also felt a powerful need to spread everything out before God, to present it to him, to give it to him, in order to receive it back again from his hand, to receive it in a more ordered, easier, more secure form. The spring seemed especially warm. My favorite spot was the wobbly little wooden bench in what was known as the "little street". Nearby the cows and their calves grazed; on summer evenings they lowed constantly, "Taaannte".[2] They had always done so— Hélène and I had never heard anything different from them. Only Aunt Jeanne insisted that they said "Muuuuuh" rather than "tante".

The day before the semester began, I returned to Basel and bought a new English bicycle with three gears. I could have danced for joy with my bicycle. It meant an end to the streetcar, at least for the summer, and it gave me a new independence, since I no longer had to adjust my schedule to the twelve-minute intervals at which the trams ran. Moreover, the bicycle was splendid to look at: gleaming, with tires full of air and faultless brakes. I rode it much more than I needed to, especially in the evening, along the

---

[1] The Swiss university schedule, like that of most continental and British universities, allows for a relatively long vacation period (six to ten weeks) between each semester, with vacation understood as a break from classes but nonetheless a time for study, writing seminar papers, preparing for exams, etc. Degrees are awarded, not on the basis of having passed a requisite number of classes, but rather for having prepared adequately, both within and outside the classroom, to pass the examinations—TRANS.

[2] *Tante*, meaning "aunt" in French—TRANS.

Bicycle Tour

neighborhood streets fragrant with blossoms or along the Rhine, beneath the soft lindens. Yes indeed, I had regained the Rhine, including the ginkgo tree beneath the Wettstein Bridge. How I loved those summer evenings. I seldom went farther, preferring to round the same favorite corners again and again, usually by myself. From time to time I would go for a walk with Portmann and Obermeyer. Obermeyer was a young zoologist, a friend of Portmann. He was quiet, almost melancholy, but kind and inspiring. When Portmann was not there, he talked enthusiastically about Portmann; how I enjoyed listening to him.

That semester I had fewer lecture courses to attend than in previous terms, for I had completed the required classes for the first *propædeuticum.*[3] The extra time went into zoology, where I had a half-day lab, in which I learned the entire process involved in making microscope slides. Since this was so time-consuming, I usually left for the zoology institute at six in the morning. It so happened that there were an unusual number of early morning thunderstorms that summer, taking my bicycle and me by surprise on many an occasion.

One afternoon a week, I had a course in histology with the feared, but, to be honest, dearly loved Professor Ludwig. I liked this much more than anatomy. It was held in the same room where the dissection classes were given during the winter, but the cadavers were gone. Even the odor had disappeared and, with it, the gloominess that had seemed to hang over the room; indeed, now it seemed almost cheerful. And that cheerfulness extended even to the tissue patterns that lay under our microscopes; it was as if the tissues

---

[3] The first level of preliminary studies, which concluded with the "*erste Propæ*" examinations as described below—TRANS.

now had real meaning, a clear connection. For me, histology had the same significance as ions had had a year earlier in chemistry: an inner necessity. Just as learning about ions had suddenly given a clear and comprehensible structure to the obscure chemistry of my school days, so, too, histology seemed to make the essential difficulties of anatomy fade.

Although I took my indispensable walk along the Petersgraben less frequently during this semester than in the past, once I did walk over there with Obermeyer and explained to him what it meant to me to walk along the hospital's garden: for me it was a mortgage on the future, a means of contact from a distance with hospital life. He understood completely. Medical school often seemed devoid of any direct connection with the reality of sick people. But when I looked at the illuminated windows of the hospital during evening walks along the Petersgraben, I often saw shadows moving. It was then that I knew: inside are people who are indeed sick, and someday I shall make my way into that building and find my assignment. Especially during the difficult years we spent living on Florastraße, this consolation had been essential for me, but also at this later point I needed it from time to time. I could not imagine how beautiful hospital work would be, and I looked forward to it with joy. Yet so often I seemed to be making such slow progress toward that goal.

Even though they were only a preparation for something more important, I enjoyed my studies, especially now in the summer, since the dissecting room seemed to have vanished into thin air. Life with my fellow students was pleasant and rich in human experience. My schoolfriends had perhaps retreated a bit into the background, and I saw them less frequently. In the evening, I sometimes, though too rarely, went to visit Pauline Müller, who always knew how to make our time together a bit festive. She lived in an old house on the Heuberg, and the walls of her large room were painted with hunting scenes, giving the place an unusual, slightly unreal ambience. Since she loved people greatly and had a lively interest in them, each conversation with her took on meaning for me. At the time I may not have fully understood the source of this significance, but I enjoyed it, and our evenings always came to an end at a very late hour.

I visited Georgy Gerhard often, for she lived at Rennweg 55, quite close to Sevogelplatz. My visits there were frequent and usually brief but always characterized by a warm cordiality.

At home very little had changed. Mama had still not made her peace with my medical studies, which meant that I had to learn more and more to keep quiet, something most difficult for me, especially on days when, in my opinion, much had happened, and I would have liked to talk about it. Hélène was home very little; she divided her time between social work and gardening. In addition, she was beginning to establish her friendship with her girlfriend Zellweger, a friendship that already at that time seemed to make heavy demands on her, leaving her little time for other people. Willy was attending the Minerva. He was not very pleased with the operation there but was happy enough to be living at home and to be left more or less to himself in pursuing a program of university preparatory work, even if slowly. Theddy was growing up, happy and unconcerned.

When the university vacation began, I first joined the others in the trip to the Waldau but spent only a few days there, for I had planned to take a bicycle tour by myself, financed by money laboriously saved from my tutoring income. Actually I had as many pupils as I wanted, so I had gradually

become a bit selective and had turned down from the outset those who seemed to lack basic industriousness and the
necessary motivation. My main expenses were the course
fees; I needed few clothes and often wore hand-me-downs
from my immediate and extended family. Sometimes people
gave me fabric, or I would buy it, and I would make myself
the sack-dresses fashionable in those days, which required
no great skill as a seamstress. Mama always was a bit taken
aback when she saw me on the floor, with large shears in
my hand but minus any pattern, cutting out fabric for a
dress or blouse I would later wear. I was never any good
with money: it no sooner made its appearance than it had
vanished. But that did not worry me much.

So it was that I mounted my bicycle early one morning at
the Waldau. My belongings were in a Japanese basket that
I had strapped to the frame over the rear wheel. On top of
the basket was a canteen. Uncle accompanied me as far as
the garden gate, which was still closed at this early hour. He
was a bit worried, afraid that I would overexert myself or
do something stupid. I promised to be careful and to write
frequently. I shall never forget the beginning of my tour: it
was a bright day, but the city seemed like a ghost town as I
rode to the railway station by way of the Kornhaus Bridge.
(I could never cross the Kornhaus Bridge without recalling
my first wager, with Pastor Pfisterer.) Not far beyond the
station, the Murtenerstraße began, a very fine road that offered splendid scenery. I was so enthused about it all that
I often sang at the top of my lungs. I could not imagine a
greater joy than to ride a bicycle through the countryside
in a world made so magical by the morning. I had so much
energy and was in such a good mood that I rode all the
way to Saint-Loup without a break. What a homecoming
my arrival seemed to me, how good it felt to reenter this

institution that I both loved and feared. I wandered up and
down, talked to the sisters I knew, until it slowly began to
seem to me like a museum that preserved the past but did
so precisely as an irretrievable past, a past that was no longer
alive, a past that had only been a stage in my life. I knew
there was no place in my heart for service understood as it
was here. I entered the chapel, which was empty, and sat
for a long time in the little choir. At first sleep threatened to
take over, for I was rather tired from the long ride; then I
realized suddenly that, precisely now, I must not under any
circumstances sleep here; instead I had to reflect and pray.
Praying in a chapel had become very strange to me, and,
moreover, I was very restless inside. I had the very definite and, at precisely that moment, real sense that now, at
once, urgently, something was to be understood, something
was to be unveiled, to be grasped directly. In this chapel, I
thought, one really ought to kneel to pray, but there was
really no place to kneel. Then it dawned on me: Saint-Loup
really ought to be Catholic. I almost laughed out loud at the
thought, for it was a solution to what burdened me in regard
to Saint-Loup yet at the same time was absurd. What did
I know of Catholicism, about Catholic service? A Catholic
version of Saint-Loup would be a monastery with absolute
obedience and with a devotion that took no holidays. And
with the Mother of God, who belongs with any monastery.
At this point the memory of my vision of the Mother of
God in my little bedroom in La Chaux-de-Fonds stirred to
life. Yes, the Mother of God! . . . I started to pray, perhaps tentatively to her as well. Finally I calmed down a bit.
The choir filled up with people, for it was time for evening
prayers. Sister Emilie Châtelain played the organ, and she
played gloriously. There was something remarkable about
Sister Emilie Châtelain. She had exceptional musical ability

and loved God; having entered Saint-Loup, things did not go especially well for her, for she was asking for something total, and she did not find it. If she was nursing patients in some city or another, she would perform long periods of the most intensive service, sacrificing herself and doing far more than was required of her. But then she would suddenly fall apart, run from one concert to another, wanting nothing but music, neglecting her ward and handing over the most urgent tasks to the other sisters. But she suffered greatly because of this; she despaired of being able to give her life the character she had envisioned. Since it was greatly feared that she might one day make contact with a real monastery, the director decided to transfer her, entrusting the running of the laundry at the motherhouse to her, since as long as she was at Saint-Loup, there was no possibility of going to concerts. And so she lived in the laundry building and was responsible for the organ and directed the singing. Once we had a long conversation, during which she more or less said that she had not found the freedom that should be a part of any definitive commitment; that something basic must be wrong; that she knew it must be unconditionally possible to give oneself to God totally but that she had never discovered how this was possible. All her disquiet arose from this. She did not look on the laundry as punishment—any sort of work was fine with her if it could be carried out in the spirit of the Lord. But there was something in or around her that was not right. I felt myself to be a kindred spirit with her precisely in regard to this invisible but nonetheless effective impediment.

And so Sister Emilie Châtelain played, the sisters sang, something was read out of a book of meditations. The longer the worship service lasted (perhaps half an hour), the emptier I felt. It was as if a deep, monstrously deep, chasm had opened between reality and what was happening here. Only God was real, only God existed—everything else only through him. It seemed like that which I otherwise perceived to be an unknown obstacle were becoming something tangible; it consisted in the fact that we, in a certain sense, overlooked God, we transformed him, prevented him from approaching us. Our unwillingness was the obstacle; perhaps it was often more of an ultimate nonunderstanding, nonlistening than nonwilling, at least in many instances and certainly in this one, where a huge amount of good will could be presumed. But then where was the willingness, the true willingness that is united with understanding?

There was no opportunity for lingering after the service, since it was time for supper, which was very pleasant and unconstrained. The atmosphere of the chapel was left far behind. I had no trouble changing moods; perhaps the mood was mine alone—I could not determine for sure if it was. I entered into the happy chatter readily and spent an enjoyable and unconstrained evening. I saw Sister Emilie Châtelain only briefly; she was very pale, transparent, tired. Outwardly calm but obviously having chosen her moment carefully so as not to be noticed, she whispered fleetingly what was obviously very important to her: "I myself have given up; it is too late to do anything else. But you must never give up. You are still young, but don't wait too long."

I did not forget those words, but they had more import for me with regard to her than to me: the challenge that they contained seemed to have no immediate weight for me. But I felt sympathy for this sister. Still, her words did not burden the evening for me. Things were uncomplicated and good; people told me about the sisters I knew, about the new assignments they had undertaken. I was knitting a bright, multicolored scarf for myself, while the sisters were knitting or mending stockings. Sitting in their midst, it seemed almost comical to think of wearing such a colorful piece of clothing. This may be the reason why I felt somewhat distant from them by the end of the evening, much as I had felt earlier in the chapel.

After a refreshing and dreamless sleep in the same residence where I had once lived, I ate breakfast by myself so that I could get an early start. However the area around Saint-Loup, with its many cliffs and deep gorges, captivated me. I scarcely knew the area, for there had been no time to take walks when I had lived there. For several hours I pushed my bike along remote pathways, gazed in rapture at the brook below, and finally ended up at the sisters' little cemetery. A very aged sister was hauling a watering can around, stopping here and there to attend to the graves. I avoided entering into conversation with her. Even the cemetery could not reconcile me to life at Saint-Loup. Yet it seemed as if I had taken something new, something vital, with me from Saint-Loup, something I had to carry around with me until, matured and certainly taking on a completely different form from what I had ever expected, it might later come to birth in me.

Toward noon I arrived in Morges. There, and in a neighboring sanatorium, I visited two former Coccinelle members of my group.[4] These visits were deeply disappointing to me. I had expected to meet people who were sick but living. Both of them had been cured, but they continued so to live their earlier illness and all the little complaints connected with it that to me they seemed to be dead.

I ate nothing at all that day on my journey; the ride was

---

[4] A devout society of (former) patients at the Leysin Sanatorium founded by Adele Kamm, who also suffered from tuberculosis—ED.

too hot and strenuous; I had frequent resort to my canteen, however; while in the morning it had contained plenty of molasses-water, by evening it had been so frequently refilled that nothing remained but pure water.

By evening I arrived at Madeleine's house, in a suburb of Geneva, on the chemin de la Colombe. She lived in a pleasant house that needed a good bit of repair. There, for the first time, I met her husband, who was a distant cousin of mine and hers. A few months earlier I had been alarmed when Madeleine informed me of her engagement, but my alarm had had no effect on her. About twenty years earlier, Jules had been engaged to marry Madeleine's aunt, at whose request the engagement was later broken. He took it very hard, lived for many years outside Switzerland, and, in a sort of permanent state of despair, he led a life he basically abhorred. While Madeleine was attending a nursing school in Geneva, she visited our mutual cousin Adrienne Montandon one Sunday, where she more or less by chance met Adrienne's son Jules. He immediately fell in love with her, glimpsing in her a striking resemblance to her aunt (a similarity that had until then escaped the notice of everyone else), and, employing his mother as intermediary, proposed marriage the same day. Madeleine refused, but the entire family joined forces to make her change her mind. They made it clear above all that Jules would certainly resume his gloomy Parisian life, made worse by this second rejection that could only discourage him more deeply and lastingly. So Madeleine gave in and married a man almost thirty years her senior. I believe she knew full well throughout the engagement that this marriage could be nothing but a sacrifice for her. The sacrifice, however, was more difficult than she could have imagined.

That evening we talked very little about that. Whenever

Madeleine and I were together, no estrangement could enter the picture. Our friendship could not be broken by silences; the conversation simply picked up where it had left off. At first we talked about the activities we were busy with, then we talked about God, about what he wished, what he intended, about the ways of a Christian physician. Almost in passing—which is how Madeleine said even the most important things, in an almost childlike voice, punctuating her sentences with short, almost hoarse, bursts of laughter—Madeleine said, "You know, I feel such a sense of resignation. But you must never give up."

Coming barely twenty-four hours after the words of Sister Emilie Châtelain, these words quite naturally had quite an impact on me. Shaken, I told Madeleine about the strange coincidence. She was not surprised but merely took note of it as a confirmation of what she had said.

Jules would not put up with long visits, so, although I had actually arranged with Madeleine to stay several days, it now seemed better to leave the following afternoon. We agreed to meet again early the next morning; I was unable to sleep during that night in that tiny house. Madeleine's fate troubled me. Could one really be resigned, at the young age of twenty-four, to want nothing more, to become a mere observer of the lives of others? And what could *I* do? Both the sister and Madeleine had placed in my hands something definite, something that, for them, had a meaning and a form; yet my hands seemed to me as empty as ever. Long before, perhaps always, I had had the conviction that I possessed a real, even if as yet unclear, mission in life, and I wanted to carry it out as best I could. Yet I never really viewed my time as a medical student merely as years of preparation for a career, rather, I also considered them a kind of human pause inserted into my life. Yet now I seemed to be thrown out of kilter, especially because until this point I was sure that every mission in life stemmed from God and therefore would be completely nontransferable. In between, I groaned, "Oh, Madeleine, why do you give your guests cotton sheets?" Sleep was completely out of the question. I also felt a bit humiliated to have to leave so soon, for, after all, Madeleine had belonged to me long before this impossible Jules had intervened. I wanted all men banished, along with bed linens that were not pure linen. But that did not prevent the fact that the real problem lay elsewhere.

Early in the morning we met in the garden, which was small, though delicately laid out and extremely well tended. It led directly into other gardens, so that it almost felt like being in the country. Madeleine and I sat in the garden until breakfast-time, talking at length about the mission that I still envisioned no more clearly than before. Madeleine said that it was completely clear to her that the strong must take up the mission of the disappointed or the weak; in the failures of the weak lay a lesson for others. All they needed was to find the right place to begin: they should begin where others had ended. I did not want really to understand this: Did we not have to struggle along side by side? Madeleine said, perhaps not side by side, but certainly together, which would not exclude the possibility of one being occasionally in front of the other. During our school days, we had certainly been side by side; now it was time for one to go before the other. This, too, would be beautiful, for it would give meaning to her failure, which would become a point of departure, perhaps even a beginning indispensable for the continuation I was destined to undertake.

Still I asked, "Must I somehow retrace my steps to find the trail and make a beginning?" "No," she said, "the beginning remains hidden from sight."

We ate breakfast with Jules in the dim dining room. He seemed to regret my departure. I studied Madeleine's face, which remained impassive. All right, then, I would go. In the little courtyard Jules had thoroughly cleaned my bicycle and pumped up the tires before breakfast. I understood nothing at all. Now, while he fastened my little basket to the machine he seemed concerned—he thought it a bit risky that a young woman should travel alone through the world like this. When it came time for farewells, Madeleine said quietly, "Everything is all right, dear."

I made a detour through the city; I really did not know my way around. For a few kilometers I rode along the right shore of the lake, then the road began to climb, and I had to dismount frequently because the road was steep for a considerable distance. The sun burned brightly, but rows of trees or small wooded areas repeatedly interrupted the heat. I concluded my ascent about noon, at the Col de Saint-Cergues. Everything was so beautiful that I let myself be captivated by the landscape, and the concerns and conflicting impressions of recent days seemed to vanish. I could hardly believe it had been only two days since I had left behind my familiar Waldau and my whole, well-ordered existence. I rested for a while under the firs at Saint-Cergues; although the view of the lake was now behind me, the scenery was still glorious, peaceful, and liberating. Then after a quick border-crossing [into France] I was on my way to Bois d'Amont, where Pauline Lacroix lived. How I looked forward to seeing her! During the winters she was a social worker in Paris, during the summer she turned a house owned by her family into a child-care center. I had not seen her since I had been at Leysin. She had invited me to stay for the entire summer—a magnificent generosity was apparently something she shared with all members of her family. I had arranged for a friend of mine from Basel, Esther Geßler, to work as Pauline's assistant. Esther was already trained as a teacher but was glad of the chance to gain some experience. The way Pauline ran her child-care center astounded me. I arrived just as the afternoon snack was beginning. Pauline made her way through the garden with a large box full of chocolate bars, giving each child one of them, while Esther was distributing large sweet pastries. The open cartons then sat on a table in the garden, and the children were permitted to help themselves to as much as they wanted, under the sole stipulation that whatever they took had to be eaten right away, not set aside for later. The meals they served were like one might expect to find in a good hotel; dessert always consisted of a sweet dish of some sort, followed by marvelous fruit, real first fruits. I asked Pauline if the fees the children paid were correspondingly high, to which she laughingly responded that most of them were paying nothing at all and the remainder only a pittance. She was of the opinion that nothing was too good for such children. And in fact the children put on weight in an incredible fashion; to mitigate the difference between their winter fare at home and what they had been fed during the summer, she would send food packages to many of them throughout the winter.

I was forbidden to help out. Pauline's temperament brooked no contradictions to her insistence that I was to rest or go for walks. I spent a lot of time lying in the shade in the garden, reading, reflecting, marveling. During the day I saw little of Pauline, for she had a lot to do, but after dinner, while the children were resting (Esther would read to them), Pauline would join me for a coffee break, and again after supper, late into the night. Although our conversations lacked continuity, they were significant in many ways. In one matter I felt somewhat perplexed, for Pauline had told me early on, almost vehemently, that she still was expecting me to make a life decision. At first I did not understand what she meant and told her that I had made my decision: I was irrevocably committed to a career as a physician. Pauline responded that that was not what she had in mind, rather, it was a question of Catholicism. A feather could have knocked me over: I had never seriously given any thought to that, indeed, I had never thought about it at all. Now it was Pauline's turn to be astonished: My entire life had been nothing but a circling around this question. I conceded that all questions of faith somehow unsettled me, but more in the manner of a growing alienation from Protestantism without any alternative direction emerging. To this point it had all been a very slow growth, a development, a reorientation. But Catholicism? No, certainly not that. Pauline shook her head: "Okay, if you really don't want to." Then more softly, "Perhaps I spoke too soon. I'm not very patient."

Pauline was small in stature, and I would have liked to give her a little hug to make her feel better, but that was absolutely impossible; she would have interpreted it as an evasion. Earnestly I promised her I would never reject anything that might present itself without first genuinely examining it in prayer.

The remarkable thing was that through this conversation I experienced a confirmation of the fact that I had an obligation to assume, but, even so, I felt no uneasiness at all. In an expanded sense of readiness, I knew with precision that I must do what God willed, but I had at that time no thought at all of conversion. That would indeed have meant a turning for me, while I was expecting an enlargement, something like a constant contact with God that would not be altered by a creed.

We did not talk about it anymore, though we did talk a

lot about Christ's love and human love, about the hunger
for love that people have, about the meaning of our life. But
it was all rather interdenominational. I believe that Pauline
was very intelligent; it was through her I learned that Catholics could be capable of truly giving their lives. Until that
conversation, I had thought that Catholics were even more
inhibited about this than were Protestants.

On Esther's afternoon off, we went by bicycle to Le
Rocheray on the Lac de Joux [in Switzerland]. We were
incredibly joyful and laughed the whole time. Nothing was
off limits to our high spirits. We swam in the lake and then
sat under the firs on the shore and devoured the provisions
Pauline had sent with us. Esther thought it was odd that I
had not told her in advance that Pauline was Catholic. I was
a bit surprised and excused myself by saying that Pauline's
Catholicism was an interior matter, something so private
with her that it was understandable that I had not thought
to mention it. Esther was of the opinion that she would like
Pauline even more if she were not Catholic. I became angry: without her Catholicism, Pauline would not be Pauline
at all.

I saw one's confession as an absolute given. One is what
one is, and one simply has to be whatever one is to the best
of one's ability. God does not require us to choose, rather,
we are supposed to grow from wherever we are. Toward
what? Obviously into God. It was completely clear to me
that I was not a very good Protestant. Then it suddenly occurred to me: perhaps I am not Protestant at all. But I want
God, and he won't let go of me.

That evening I would have liked to have talked with
Pauline about this, but since she did not raise the topic,
I said nothing. I was a bit afraid of her, perhaps more afraid
of myself, of my impulsiveness. Precisely on this matter it

did not seem good to say too much and certainly not to be carried along by one's own hasty and unexamined words.

Pauline went with me once to the stream, where she taught me how to catch crayfish. I thought it was fun and brought a whole kettle of them home. Pauline cooked them herself, and we ate them late that evening, accompanied by wine. I thought the wine was dreadful. After about ten days, I set out. Pauline wanted to keep me there, but I had all sorts of things planned, and, in the distance, my first exams were beckoning. The thought of them was not pleasant.

As I rode back down from Col de Saint-Cergues, suddenly my brakes gave out completely. I had a wild and really terrible ride, taking each curve as best I could, hoping for the best. It was like this all the way to Givrins, where I arrived completely exhausted at the home of my aged uncle. Perhaps it was fear more than exhaustion that I felt in my bones. Life at Givrins with my elderly aunt and uncle Olivier von Speyr was rather odd, as if time had stopped at a point many years earlier. There were seasons still, but they did not seem to take their course anymore, nothing was hurried. My aunt and uncle lived in the ancient rural tradition. With a paternalism that seemed most natural, they presided over their men- and women-servants of many years' standing. Life as their guest was splendid. You were given a room supplied with any sort of book you could possibly need as well as with pictures and family albums; the current crop of various ripe fruits in the garden was pointed out, with an invitation to help yourself; and, after this introduction, you were left to make yourself at home in whatever way you pleased. We met for meals, lingered together for a bit after eating, and then went our way. This sort of hospitality pleased me extraordinarily well. That night as I lay in my candlelit room, I thought back over the wild ride down the

pass. It seemed most remarkable that I had made it without
an accident. And then I realized very emphatically: I would
not have liked to die now. I made a bit of a promise to
God that I would henceforth be more grateful for the life
that seemed to have been given to me all over again. The
next morning I made the *tour du propriétaire*[5] through the
outlying property with my uncle. He showed me the tiny
orchard where the most beautiful apples to be found anywhere in Canton Vaud were growing—he won prizes for
them whenever he entered them in competitions. There was
no one in Givrins who could repair my bicycle, so that afternoon I rode over the slowly descending road into Nyon,
took the bicycle to a repair shop, and spent the night with
some cousins. In marked contrast to my relatives in Givrins,
my Nyon cousins had completely lost contact with nature.
Even though their house was surrounded by a large, nicely
tended garden, they seemed to have no relationship with
the trees or flowers. For them, life seemed to be confined
to their house, to the softness of an armchair, to an agreeable
meal, to impeccable clothes, and rare jewelry. But I liked
them. They had arrived without having ever left, but this
suited them well. I felt no need to change them, indeed, I
would have been a bit alarmed if I had found them different.

The comfortableness of their life made an early departure the next morning unthinkable; moreover, I thought
the route along the lake would be very easy and quickly accomplished. Thus I left Nyon late in the morning and soon
received an education about the pleasantness of the lakeside
road. It was really difficult, with its constant climbs and de-
scents, and, since I was traveling at midday, tremendously

[5] A tour of the property, a stock phrase in French, with a facetious ring
to it—ED.

hot. I filled my canteen at different springs, and Aunt Charlotte's molasses was soon merely a memory. It was already completely dark when I reached L'Etivaz, where Hélène was running a children's camp. Hélène was rather upset over my late arrival, for she had not had precise word about its timing, only about the date. She described the superb dinner she had eaten with the children, but her story alone could not satisfy my hunger. When she finally realized that my lateness was not the result of ill will on my part, she whipped together something delicious to eat out of blueberries that she and the children had picked. We lingered for a very pleasant while together. I admired the careful and practical way she had arranged the entire house. However my announcement that I would be leaving the next day for Leysin saddened her. I was scheduled to be at Leysin and had understood that my sister had expected only a brief visit from me. Actually, it was only after my departure the next day that I realized the extent of her disappointment. At home, we had simply lived side by side, while our paths seemed to have almost nothing in common. Later in life, I often thought that my visit in L'Etivaz might have served as an occasion to strengthen the ties between us, to establish an intimacy that never came into being in Basel. I probably acted thoughtlessly, and, even if my departure for Leysin could not have been delayed (at the time it seemed as if it could not, although I no longer know why), I might at least have visited her again on the way back.

In Leysin I stayed in the chalet with Sister Emilie. I think it was the first time since my illness that I had been in Leysin. She had turned her office into a very nice little bedroom for me during my visit of several days. During the first few days, everything was pleasant and good. I felt happy, visited friends and acquaintances from the old days, and sat for

Adrienne behind her sister Hélène

hours by Sister Emilie with my work. We talked a lot about God and faith, about the possibilities of living a life of faith in which faith, more than life itself, would come to fruition. Then she told me about the aforementioned scandal, which made an immense impression on me. To have wanted to serve God (for that, after all, was the purpose of the pastorate as well as the life of a deaconess),[6] and then to end up like that! That night I was so deeply frightened that I tossed and turned in my bed. I saw no possibility of ever regaining a sense of peace. The impression this story left on me was very similar to the time in 1916 when Madame Motta told me that Doctor Walker had committed suicide in the belltower at the Waldau. With every peal of the bell, I thought of his corpse hanging for days next to the huge clockworks until it was finally discovered on Sunday. Back then I had been frightened and hurt by the suicide of a well-known and respected man; now the same effect came from hearing of the shameful acts of a pastor whose colorful sermons I had enjoyed hearing; and then these sisters, some of whom I still knew. It was as if the ground under my feet had completely disappeared. I knew, of course, that all sorts of evil things happened in the world, but never had I encountered evil in the guise of the good.

I did not speak with Sister Emilie about this again, and basically I was quite sorry to have had to hear of this whole

[6] In the Lutheran and Reformed churches and in other Protestant denominations, communities of deaconesses developed long after the Reformation as a form of dedicated service by unmarried women, somewhat parallel to Catholic orders of nuns. They are not identical with the isolated instances of pre-Reformation convents that became Lutheran nunneries in northern Germany, with Protestant orders of nuns that have emerged in more recent times, or with the order of deaconesses in the very early Christian church. The latter contributed to the development of women's religious orders in the Western Church—TRANS.

thing at all, for it seemed to me to be so terribly brutal that I could not see how I could draw any profit from it for myself or anyone else. The story tortured my sleep for some time. Somehow it seemed as if God had abandoned his own people. Then, suddenly, something occurred to me: Pastor Cavallieri had once been a Catholic priest, and part of the reason people had made so much of him was the fact that he had converted to Protestantism. People liked to praise a man who had exchanged the priest's cassock for the Reformed pastor's neckbands. I had never been entirely comfortable with this praise for him. Now I thought: perhaps he really had abandoned God first, already then preferring human reasons to divine ones.

At Leysin I saw my beloved physician, Doctor Alexandrowska, once more, although Sister Emilie never appreciated my visits with her and always tried to create some obstacle to them. She did not like me to spend time with unbelievers.

After about a week at Leysin, I went to Lausanne for one day, where I visited my various relatives, one after the other. That brought me to the last day of my trip. I had spent the night in a small and noisy inn, the *Pension des Etrangers*, which had used up the last of my paper money. I had only a few coins left in my wallet and, by early afternoon, no more molasses in my canteen. I rode by way of Chalet à Gobet to Moudon. Rain was pouring down, I had to push my bicycle uphill because the ascent was too steep, and I was getting wetter and wetter. Even when I was riding it in normal fashion, I was no drier and began to feel freezing cold. I decided I would have to change clothes in Moudon. But where? Several drunken men were standing in front of the first pub I came to, since it was market day. That was not particularly inviting. Not far away I saw a letter carrier, which gave me an idea. I drove up to him and asked if there were a physician in the vicinity. Certainly, in that house over there. Is he married? Yes. Is his wife at home? He thought she was. Fine. I went to the house. As I rang the bell, I was much less sure of myself; what I planned to do began to seem a bit audacious. The door was opened by the doctor's wife herself. I introduced myself, or, more precisely, began to recite a long list of my various relatives in the medical profession, beginning with those who were professors, all in the hope that she might recognize a few of the names and thereby not be too quick to dismiss my request. I finally ended by asking her—and I knew at that moment in my heart what it is like to be a beggar—if I might quickly change clothes in her bathroom; although I was soaked to the skin, I did have dry clothes in my traveling case. I shall never forget how Madame Guex received me. She prepared a warm bath for me, and, as I came out of the bathroom, a splendid breakfast was waiting for me, as if she had guessed that my finances that morning would not have permitted me the luxury of stopping for tea. Then, while I hungrily consumed everything, she said several times: "This will work out splendidly."

I was a bit curious to know what it was that was going to work out so well. It turned out she was having a family dinner that day, and I was invited to imagine just how welcome I would be. At first I really did not want to stay for dinner but gave in when I saw that I would genuinely offend her by refusing. Her husband soon returned home, then twelve guests appeared. In my entire life I have never experienced such a meal. There must have been seven or eight courses, each of which had some specific link to the guests: here is the trout that you like so well, dear; here is the pastry made from your dear godmother's recipe; the chicken in the pot is the one you yourself gave me; I think I recall that this is your favorite roast, and so on. Remarkably enough, none of this struck me as bourgeois. Instead I saw in it nothing but an expression of love, of goodwill, which grew out of the same spirit that had received me with such naturalness.

Only the wine bothered me. When I first arrived, I had been given a glass of wine, something we had never had at home, for my father was a teetotaler, as was my uncle at the Waldau. Perhaps because I was not used to drinking, I did not enjoy it. Seeing the full glass of wine in front of me, I decided to drain it quickly so as to have it over with. No sooner had I done so than it was refilled for me, so I emptied it once more without delay. Only with the second refill did it finally dawn on me that the refilling was necessitated by the emptying; that was most certainly the custom there, I was never going to have it over with, and so I did not empty the third glass, which accompanied me through the remaining courses of the dinner.

Five years later, my husband and I visited the Guex family. Almost in a confidential tone, Doctor Guex told my husband that what had pleased him more than a little about me was my candid love of wine; therefore he would like to fetch a particularly good bottle for us now!

The meal lasted almost until evening; when I took my leave, I was wearing one daughter's shoes on my feet and another's hat on my head, for my hat and shoes had not yet had enough time to dry out. I took the train to Bern, carrying with me enough provisions to undertake a little trip around the world without any fear of going hungry.

I did not stay very long at the Waldau, for family life there was simply not compatible with studying. After about a week of vain or partially vain effort, I returned to my attic room in

Basel. But I accomplished little academic work, for, despite spending long hours in front of my books, I lacked any real eagerness to learn. The natural science that was going on in these books seemed boring, and I could not see how it had anything to do with life and even less with medicine. Despite my love for zoology, already having had to work so hard at anatomy and histology had alienated me a good bit from it. My exams were scheduled to take place late in September, in the evening in the botany institute. There were two of us, Brunner and I, one of us waiting in the antechamber while the other was being examined. I was fully prepared to fail, especially since I had been making new "discoveries" each morning as I reviewed my various textbooks; much, even if not everything, seemed completely new to me, so new that I could never begin to take it in and make it my own. And so, now we were in exams. Roessiger and Wilhelm, who were on deck for exams the next day, came by to see us, even bringing pastries and fruit to give us some strength. They seemed infinitely well prepared, as they indeed were. After each exam I was sure that, at least in that subject, I had failed, and with finality. The physics exam left me especially devastated, and probably the kindly examiner, Professor Hagenbach, no less so; he led me from one area to another, from optics and acoustics to electricity, the laws of gravity, and X rays. I knew scarcely anything about any of them. After four twenty-minute exams, a diploma was placed in my hand. I dared not look at it, but someone said to me—I think it was the chairman—that they had expected more of me, given my good work during the semester, and that they would have liked to have given me highest marks, but I apparently was one of those people who did not perform optimally in examinations; however, I should not be disappointed, for, after all, this was perfectly fine. Finally I glanced at the unfolded paper and said with astonishment: "You mean I really passed? But that is very good of you." This was greeted by great laughter. A bit embarrassed by my remark, I fled the room as fast as possible and waited with my friends for Brunner, who had failed.

The next day, like an old hand, I went to encourage Roessiger and Wilhelm, who were more than prepared for any challenge and needed little encouragement. It was an odd feeling to be plunged again into the atmosphere of the examinations without really being involved, at least as far as grades were concerned. Still, one relived the excitement about the questions asked and answers given.

I spent the last days of the vacation at home, thoroughly enjoying doing nothing. The sky seemed particularly beautiful, indeed, inviting, when viewed through my attic window. And now I had time to gaze at the sky and also to pray. Although the gaps in my knowledge of the propædeutic fields of medicine had become abundantly clear in the course of the exams, I sensed no great need to fill the gaps right then. I had a much greater need to be with God and to repose in him a bit.

THE BROKEN LEG

Winter Semester 1924/1925

Student life was now a firmly established thing, and we no longer expected anything sensational from a new semester—the only real turning point came after the second *propædeuti-*

cum.[1] I lived in anticipation of that point, and it often seemed to me that time was moving slowly, so slowly, toward this destination. To be sure, my impatience did not bother me greatly, for, now that the first set of exams was behind me, medical studies began to acquire a face, a shape. In the second dissection course we would be working on injected cadavers, meaning that their blood vessels had been filled, for the topic of the course was now especially the nervous system and the circulatory system. Bones and muscles were supposed to be old acquaintances to us, included in the course merely as repetition. I was not completely at ease about this, for I saw increasingly how much I did not yet know. Yet despite this feeling of insecurity in anatomy, I did not deny myself the luxury of registering for zoology once again. Following dissection class, I would go to the zoology lab and, under the microscope, study slides I had prepared myself, which delighted me greatly. My friend Portmann was still in southern France, but Obermeyer was present and took great pains with me. I made progress, which, in turn, helped console me about anatomy. The rector of the girls' secondary school had repeatedly suggested to me that I get a degree in natural sciences and then return to them as a teacher. But medicine had always been so important to me that I had not hesitated for a moment. At the most, I thought I would pursue zoology as a luxury field of study so that later I could possess it as a sort of recreation and joy.

At the end of the first week of classes, on a Friday night, I was in the zoology lab and had dissected a rare kind of snail, planning to examine its fresh eggs under the microscope. When I went to the next room to fetch a liquid solution I needed for the slide, I slipped and fell, managing somehow to

[1] The "second prope (= *propæ*)", in student argot—TRANS.

keep the beaker with the solution from spilling. With great difficulty, I managed to stand up and limp back to my place. Zschokke wanted to look at my slide yet that night, and I still needed a few things before it was ready; Obermeyer was helpful, for I could scarcely put any weight on my leg. When Zschokke arrived, the prepared slide was ready; he studied it and, in order to discuss it with me, he looked at me as well. He asked, in a rather fatherly way, "What's wrong?" I confessed that I had fallen. He wished me "get well soon." After he had left, I told Obermeyer that I wanted to go to the hospital right away and have Nurse Bea[2] wrap my leg. I shall never forget that walk. At first I was too proud to accept the arm Obermeyer offered me for support. I walked laboriously alongside him down the Rheinsprung, trying to hop along on my uninjured leg, but that proved impossible, for the jolting made the pain unbearable. Finally we reached the streetcar stop at the *Schifflände* and rode the tram as far as the Totentanz. As we worked our way out of the streetcar, all my pride was gone; I put my arm around my friend's shoulder, and we eventually made our way to Nurse Bea. She refused to do anything until the surgeon was present.

Nurse Bea was and is a wonderful person. For many years she had been a supervising nurse [*Oberschwester*] in the surgical polyclinic. Hélène had worked there for six months, which is how we had come to know her. She was professional, kind, smart. Hélène was a bit afraid of her. I merely admired her. She, too, represented a sort of gateway to the hospital for which I longed so much. I had visited her only

---

[2] With a few exceptions (Sister Marie), Adrienne does not clarify when she is using *Schwester* to refer to a nurse (*Krankenschwester*) or to a deaconess (*Schwester*) who also happens to be serving as a nurse. In the absence of a specific reference to an individual being a deaconess, *Schwester* has been translated as "nurse"—TRANS.

very infrequently, but when I did, I opened my eyes as wide as possible. Simple cases were dealt with right there as ambulatory cases; more difficult ones went through the polyclinic to the wards. The clinic's rooms were totally white and smelled largely of disinfectant, so much so that the air seemed saturated and one's clothes became impregnated with the smell, reminding one of one's visit for days afterward. I loved this so much, for it brought back to me many things from my childhood, even though the smell of the Basel polyclinic was far stronger than that of the hospital in La Chaux-de-Fonds.

When the doctor arrived, he insisted on X rays. Timidly I asked how far away the X-ray machine was. It was on the other side of the hospital. Even more timidly I confessed that I could not possibly walk so far tonight. Hearty laughter interrupted me: I was not going to stand on that leg for a long time to come. I found myself on a stretcher, being wheeled to the X-ray department, passing through long basement corridors with vaulted ceilings, then through a men's ward in which a number of beds were placed in the corridor. I couldn't help thinking to myself: Would these men die here, tonight? I couldn't really tell from their appearance. It pained me not to know, and yet I was so happy finally to be in the hospital. Somehow a beginning had opened up for me, and I almost forgot that I was a patient lying on a stretcher. When the nurse in the X-ray department addressed me by name, I was quite astonished, for it never occurred to me that various departments would be in touch with each other by telephone, and, since my name was no longer unknown to them, it almost seemed like I was already part of the staff. My leg proved to be broken, but it could not be set immediately because it had swollen so badly. Thus I was asked to stay in the hospital. On the one hand, this was a bit disturbing: it would mean the end of all the freedom upon which I laid so much store. On the other hand, what remained of my freedom if I could not even stand up? After a brief moment of hesitation, I decided in favor of the hospital. Since I was part of the student medical insurance program, a bed in a second-class room would not cost me anything, indeed, I had a right to one. The first thing I did, but only after I had firmly made up my mind, was to phone my mother. She was, of course, not exactly overjoyed to hear of my accident, its consequences, my absence from home, and so on. I didn't quite manage to cheer her up. Next came the interminable hospital corridors to the women's surgical ward, where room no. 24a was vacant and became my home. When I was finally alone, with my leg propped up on a stack of sand-pillows, I think the first thing I did was to bawl, and copiously. Suddenly it seemed to me as if there were nothing solid under my feet anymore, as if I might never walk again. I felt as if I had been surrendered to the anonymity of the very hospital I had so yearned for, to the young nurses, and to my own immobility. Then I felt terrible hunger but did not dare say so. A moment later, my mother appeared suddenly, together with Doctor Meyer-Altwegg, a friend of my father's. As a physician, he had access to the hospital at any hour and, despite the late hour, had brought my mother with him. At first she was quite upset, but gradually all of us calmed down. After my visitors left at about ten o'clock, I fell asleep at some point and had a very good night. I saw the chief of staff [*Chef-arzt*], Professor Hotz, for the first time on the following evening. He was a kind and approachable person with whom I soon felt at home. At first he scolded me for having walked on a broken leg, insisting he had never seen such a thing. Then he prescribed all sorts of things: a morphine injection, plaster cast, elevation of the leg. The injection, which made me quite sick to my stomach, came first, followed by the plaster cast in the so-called plaster room. By the time I was back in my room, I scarcely recognized myself, for the morphine produced a sort of dreamy wakefulness that was most unpleasant for me, and I was constantly throwing up. Ever since, in all my illnesses, I have never wanted to have alkaloidal injections. Honest pain is far preferable to me, although that night I began to have the first really unbearable pain. It began about midnight. When I thought I could no longer take it, I rang for the nurse, but no one came. I rang again, every half hour, again and again, but without success. Toward morning I must have begun to groan rather noisily; patients in the next room then rang, with better success than I had had. The night nurse came; they had forgotten to plug my bell into the wall socket. I told her I had terrible pain in the sole of my foot, but she could not see any problem, gave me some ineffective, left-over powder, and admonished me to be patient. Finally, about six o'clock, I managed to persuade her to call the doctor. After he had taken a look at things, he instantly took plaster-cutting shears and removed the cast, which had been applied so tightly that the entire sole of my foot was black and cold. It recovered over the course of the day, and I with it. The whole incident became a real experience for me: in the first place, because I had never realized that pain could reach such an intensity and, in the second place, because I had also not realized that the possibility of committing a technical error remained ever present for the doctor. Yet the most lasting impression was made by the staff's attitude toward pain—when one hears as many complaints as nurses do, one easily becomes inured to them and then often incapable of assessing how genuine and intense the suffering is.

On Sunday morning, toward noon, Doctor Heusser appeared, making, as he said, an official visit; all he lacked was a top hat. He wanted to make the acquaintance of the young woman who had walked on a broken leg. Immediately we seemed like old friends to each other. From that point on, he visited me again and again in between surgeries, to smoke a cigarette and to tell me stories, stories about his studies, about his present life as a staff physician [*Oberarzt*], about the daily events of the hospital. This great friendship lasted exactly two weeks; suddenly one day he did not show up and then never came again. I never learned why, nor did I ask. We encountered each other often enough later in life, either individually or on social occasions, but the threads of those days were never rejoined, we never had a personal conversation again, and our brief friendship was never mentioned. I think this was the only time in my life that a real friendship was taken from me; perhaps it consisted, on my side, more in enthusiasm than in friendship.

During my first days in the hospital, I had quite a large number of visitors, and they spoiled me unbelievably. Then a marvelous change in my daily routine took place. I was busy trying, without much enthusiasm, to read a bit of anatomy one day when Chief of Staff Hotz came to see me and abruptly made the completely unexpected offer to introduce me to surgery. I was to be brought to the operating room each morning, where I would be shown whatever happened to be taking place. I could scarcely wait until the next morning; now the hospital was, as it were, uncovering her very heart to me. The following period was among the richest and most beautiful of my life; it lasted about two weeks, until I was able to walk well enough on my cast to permit me at least to return to the dissection class.

That first morning they wheeled me on a stretcher into

the operating room, and Professor Hotz saw to it that I was close enough to him that I could see the entire operation quite well. As he worked, he explained the anatomical aspects of the operation to me and made sure that I really understood and asked questions. I had to answer his questions in front of the assistants and nurses; my knowledge often came up quite short, or, to put it a better way: the gaping holes of my ignorance opened wide. Playing this sort of anatomy quiz game certainly increased my knowledge, but the human dimension was far more significant. I observed how Hotz dealt with people, with those who were awake and anxious, waiting in the anteroom; with patients on whom he had to operate without anesthesia and who never lacked for encouragement from him even as he operated on them; and with patients under anesthesia: whether undertaking major or minor surgery, he always maintained an attitude of complete respect and reverence for the unconscious human beings entrusted to him. From him I learned what a physician of deep faith could be. I owe to him by far the most of what I attempt to accomplish in this profession. I also observed how he interacted with his assistants and the nurses. He could become impatient, especially when he encountered obvious stupidity, but he was never hurtful, and he never acted like a god, rather always as a man of duty. If, as happened on rare occasions, too strong a word escaped his lips, he never failed to apologize and take it back in front of all those before whom he had uttered it, doing so with the naturalness and humor that characterized him.

In the operating room I also came to know his own sister, dear Nurse Hedi. She was chief nurse for the operating room, and she worked there out of affection for her brother, taking every opportunity to make his job easier. To this day a deep friendship binds the two of us. Nurse Hedi had voluntarily undertaken to be the subordinate of her brother, and she never abandoned this role; while at the hospital, no matter how close and attached she was to him, she never dealt with him on any basis other than as subordinate with a superior. The clear family resemblance in their physical features and the fact that they addressed each other with the familiar *Du* merely served to confirm the voluntary nature of her subordinate position. Their relationship seemed to me reminiscent of that between the Lord and his disciples; such a spirit of love and devotion ruled in the operating room that one felt surrounded by an unfailing atmosphere of prayer and Christian care. All of this seemed to me to be both simple and natural yet, precisely in its naturalness, somehow very mysterious.

I spent several hours each morning in the operating room and, in the afternoons, spent a lot of time with the surgical nursing staff, where I learned how to make the various kinds of dressings, compresses, and swabs. Once in a while a temptation similar to that which I experienced at the Waldau came to me: Why not stay here, work here? Perhaps this would be an opportunity to do on a long-term basis within a more circumscribed framework the sort of service I had imagined for myself. I could live out of and at the same time in the love that reigned in the operating room, while contributing my little piece to the whole.

Crutches had by now replaced the stretcher, but I was still not very skilled at using them, so I slid them both under one arm and hopped around on my good leg.

For a few days I shared room 24a with an elderly woman from Therwil. She was preoccupied with her own death, which she imagined to be very near but which in fact was many years away. She was sick only for a few days. She was preoccupied with her own death because she had been married to a widower who had died a few years earlier. She was afraid that, being single in heaven, he would make advances to his first wife, and she was thus not sure what it would be like to encounter him once again. She was busy making all sorts of plans, none of which really made much sense to her. She was, however, certain of one thing: she did not want to be left empty-handed; she would demand her husband for herself alone.

I was struck by something very curious in my room; the deaconess responsible for us never conducted any worship with us. In the third-class dormitory room nearby, she did so each evening, and she also said a prayer each morning. I asked her once why she did not do that with us, and she explained that it was not permitted for patients in private rooms. I did not completely understand why, but it was acceptable to me.

I also saw a priest around the hospital; it was my first encounter with a Catholic clergyman. He was a Jesuit referred to as Pastor Schnyder. I felt very much attracted by what he represented, that is, I suspected he knew a great many things that I would have liked to have found out. He visited me a number of times, but the conversation always derailed at the decisive moment; every time he would suddenly become a sanctimonious bore, and you could get nothing more out of him, at most a roll of his eyes heavenward and a few vague phrases about the beauty of Catholicism, but never any real information, never anything important. Still, I liked him a lot and was happy when he visited, thinking that the next time I would steer the conversation to something solid. But I never succeeded at this. I think he later visited me at home once, or at least he talked about doing so, though I can't be sure he actually did. He probably did, and the conversation was very likely as insignificant as it had been in the hospital.

One of my teachers, Professor Spiro, visited me once, bringing with him the physiology textbook by Hoeber. It was written in such a romantic and easy manner that I devoured it immediately, but, unfortunately, nothing in it stuck with me.

I had been in the hospital less than three weeks when I suddenly had the feeling that I had to leave and resume my work in the dissection class. My plaster cast felt fine, and I was able to walk quite well using a cane. When I asked Professor Hotz if I could leave, he was initially a bit surprised and asked me if I was no longer happy with hospital life. I assured him that I was very happy with it, but precisely for that reason I wanted to leave. He agreed. And so I left, on a Wednesday evening. I took my little Japanese basket and my cane with me and made my way to the Totentanz. Mama had wanted to come and fetch me in a car, but I had insisted that this would work out fine. Once I was out on the street, however, I was no longer of quite the same opinion; crossing streetcar rails and curbs was quite laborious, and everything was essentially different and more difficult than it had been in the level hospital corridors. My basket and cane were also significant impediments, and in the streetcar there was at first no place to sit down. As we passed the evangelical bookstore at the *Schifflände* a picture with phosphorescent lettering was on display: "Lord, abide with us, for the night is at hand." The saying fit my mood at the time very well, and I repeated it softly again and again. It was still on my lips when I entered our house, and it remained close to me for days, ready, as it were, to help whenever it was needed. It was needed frequently.

I arrived in time for supper, during which I realized how limited my mobility still was. When I was back in my attic room, I was very grateful to return to my solitude, but it was also apparent that I was not completely a match for it. When Hélène came up to see whether I might need something, I needed all sorts of things, especially a metal bow over my foot. Since we had none at home, she went to the hospital to get one and received it from Nurse Bea. Things gradually settled into place, except that sleep refused to make an appearance. During that sleepless night, most of my thoughts had to do with the hospital and the things I had experienced there, with the many patients I knew only from the operating room yet who were by no means anonymous to me anymore. I also thought a lot about the two inexhaustible sources of loving care I had met: Professor Hotz and Nurse Hedi. To me it seemed as if they possessed an incredible secret, into which I wished they had fully initiated me; yet I also realized, even if vaguely, that this secret continually grew out of them and could not be reduced to some sort of simple formula.

It was hard to bear the thought that I would have a long wait before I could be personally involved in hospital work, yet, at the same time, I knew I was really fortunate to have been able to participate directly in so many things. I had to be grateful for that.

The next day it was time for the dissection lab. During the first weeks after I left the hospital, I did not attend any lecture classes but did do a lot of dissecting, sitting down, with my leg on a stool. Despite the vividness of anatomy in the operating room, it had not become any easier. Once again I had trouble synthesizing things and could learn names and interconnections only with great difficulty. I could not envision how the muscles related to the various bones, and the routes of the arteries and nerves remained incomprehensible. Moreover, I ardently wished to know how my cadavers had once lived and where their souls were now; all of that seemed more important to me than anatomy, even though I knew that, in making this observation, I was wrong, at least for now, and that there was nothing left for me to do except to work on my dissections and to do so with the fewest possible digressions. After all, I had required three semesters to prepare for the first *propædeuticum*, and now only two semesters were at my disposal to prepare for the second, if I were going to finish my studies in the minimum amount of time allowed.

My leg slowly improved. Before Christmas I was able to ride my bicycle once again. My lecture classes combined with my tutoring work meant every scrap of time was once again in full use. For the Christmas holidays I traveled to the Waldau. Uncle talked about his impending retirement; he was seventy-two years old but astonishingly robust. It was hard for him to think about retirement. For me the thought was very disagreeable indeed; it weighed me down like a nightmare: to think of losing my home at the Waldau! Uncle's apartment was attached to his official position, and his unknown successor would occupy it, while we would soon become strangers to the entire establishment, including the patients. Adam's expulsion from paradise seemed not entirely unlike what awaited us all. This gave something of a melancholy tone to all my visits to the Waldau from that point onward. When I discussed the matter with Aunt on one occasion, she could not understand me. She had never liked the Waldau and had always felt like a stranger, and even unwanted, so the prospect of putting an end to all that was a happy one for her. She merely hoped that Uncle would make a definitive decision soon and, if possible, relocate in Basel. This possibility had never occurred to me; it consoled me a bit, but only a very little bit, like a tiny ray of hope in the middle of a catastrophe, yet the hope and the catastrophe did not concern the same thing.

At the end of the semester, there was again a *Zschokkefest* and another Professors' Ball also took place. Fortunately, this time I went to the ball with Professor Fiechter again and was free from any unwelcome proposals of marriage. For the first time in my life, I gave a party at my house. I invited the interns[3] from the hospital for an evening of dancing, but I cannot recall which women I invited. I only remember that together we made ten couples and that things grew more and more festive as the night went on, indeed, we danced until morning. Just before the party, I had been tutoring in a house at the end of Leimenstraße, then ridden my bicycle home. It was a very cold night, and, crossing the overpass, I felt as if I would freeze before I got home. I was so horribly chilled that all my happy anticipation for the party vanished; a warm bed seemed to me the most desirable thing. However, by the time I was home again and

---

[3] The German term employed here is *"Assistenten"*, i.e., assistants. As Adrienne makes clear in the chapter entitled "The Death of Professor Hotz," these *Assistenten* have completed their M.D. degrees. Since it is impossible to make the distinctions between residents and interns that are customary in North American hospitals, the word has been translated simply as *interns*, even though some of them may have been closer to what would be called "residents" in North American hospitals. Adrienne's description in "The Death of Professor Hotz" of the solidarity between full staff physicians (*Oberärzte*) and these *Assistenten* suggests that the term "intern" probably carries a lower status than these junior medical staff members actually enjoyed in a Swiss hospital, but no precise North American equivalent exists. Their position is analogous to the assistant professors in other university disciplines: they have completed their highest professional degrees but must spend some time in a kind of apprenticeship to a full professor; in the case of clinical medicine, to an *Oberarzt*, who corresponds to a full professor in other university disciplines. See the note in the chapter "The Beginning of Medical School" above for corresponding practices in the nonclinical natural sciences—TRANS.

had finished the final preparations with Hélène's help, my joy had returned and nothing more could spoil it.

Then there was spring vacation at the Waldau, which began with an odd adventure. The pump for my bicycle, together with some accessories, was stolen from the downstairs hallway. To me the loss was unpleasant because of what it would cost to replace the stolen items, but Uncle was greatly agitated at what had happened: this sort of thing simply must not happen in a mental hospital, for the patients must not be exposed to thieves; it could be the beginning of a crooked path in the lives of many of them. As patients, they ought to be assured of a completely pure environment, especially because of their often striking weakness of will; the illness in itself was not an impurity. The police were notified. A detective showed up and interrogated me first of all. I had to explain exactly what the pump had looked like; my knowledge was no match for the demands presented. Then I nearly had to swear that the pump had really been standing next to the bicycle; I was sure I would have noticed its absence if it had not been, for it was a sense that something was missing that first made me stop, and only after some reflection I realized the pump was gone. Did I have any idea who the thief might have been? Yes, I said. This "Yes" startled me, but since it was already out, it was out; I could not retract it. A few days earlier I had met a young man who had the look of a thief, which is why I said "Yes." So now I had to describe him as accurately as possible, but my description dealt mostly with his eyes. Within a few minutes they had arrested this man. He had been employed by the hospital's administration for several months, and a real warehouse was discovered in his room. He had carried out all sorts of scams and defrauded the institution of thousands of francs by this time.

As they grew older, Uncle and Aunt became more and more touching. Uncle, it is true, rarely said anything about my medical studies, but I had the feeling he was often offering me morsels, that things he said about patients during meals were said for my benefit. I didn't dare take him up on them in conversation, but what he said was not lost on me.

Once I gathered up all my courage and asked Uncle if he would loan me money to buy a microscope; I was not able to cover the cost out of my tutoring earnings but nonetheless wanted to purchase an instrument that would last me the rest of my life, which meant I needed about a thousand francs. Uncle gave me the money without hesitating, and, when I married, handed the note back to me, saying that he did not want me to enter upon marriage owing any debts.

THE SECOND *PROPE* NEARS

Summer Semester 1925

Upon returning to Basel the first thing I did was to buy a microscope, a very handsome one, with all the accessories. I almost believed that my studies would now be easier. One of the difficulties heretofore had been that I was dependent on the various institutes, and I often had to wait a long time for a free microscope.

The semester's work was far from joyful. A major difference from the preceding semester was that my beloved early morning elective class in zoology had to be given up. As a result, my first class, chemical physiology, did not meet until eleven o'clock, leaving the whole morning free. I knew myself and my indolence well enough to fear that I would not accomplish anything without a fixed schedule. So be it: I established a detailed daily schedule that incorporated all the necessary security measures. The first of the security measures was my dear friend Georgine Gerhard. She had to be at the girls' secondary school by seven in the morning, and, since our house was right on the way, we met precisely at a quarter to seven in front of our house and walked happily together to her school; from there I went directly to the library, where all joyfulness came to an end. My seat was next to Ernst Staehelin, who spent most mornings behind mountains of books. My table was completely empty; I brought with me the one book I needed, Hoeber's physiology text; when I had finished it, I started Corning's anatomy. I read without a break, line for line, page by page; made supplementary drawings, calculated calories, and composed chemical equations. After finishing the physiology text, I moved on to Corning, with its splendid and illuminating pictures and concise, very clear text. In the afternoons I regularly worked two hours at home with my microscope and also went to the anatomy demonstration room, where skeletons and portions of skeletons were available for students to study. The air was saturated with smoke from the cigarettes of Polish students who were there in good numbers, loudly and excitably discussing the specimens. Once in a while, if asked politely, they would permit someone else to look at the specimens. However the specimens disappeared very rapidly, until finally the demonstration room was closed, since everything, or nearly everything, had been stolen. All one could do then was to study bones and joints locked up in display cases in other rooms that were open for certain specified hours, which was really of no more use than the pictures in the textbooks. In addition, I was still doing a lot of tutoring. I was very overtired. One day I noticed that the long morning sessions in the unpleasant atmosphere of the reading room were doing me absolutely no good; I was not learning anything; whenever I thought I had grasped something and found a vital thread, it turned out not to be so at all. It seemed like nothing but wasted time. And yet I longed for the hospital, the patients, I yearned to be a doctor. Rationally I knew that this was the only way to reach that goal, and I tried to console myself with the thought. Exams were only a few months away, and then we would doubtless see. But I no longer believed I would pass, and could not think of any better method of study.

On Sunday afternoons, I often went to the hospital to visit Nurse Hedi Hotz. In the tiny workroom occupied by the operating room nurses, I felt happy and free, found courage to face another week, made piles of swabs, and sometimes (rather rarely) encountered a nurse in the corridor with a gurney and could help her push it into a hospital room or into the operating room. These were the high points in my existence; I nourished myself steadily on them. This resurrected the old question once more: Would it not be more sensible to abandon the medical studies for which I seemed so ill-suited and become a nurse or an attendant in a mental hospital? Of course I discussed this with no one and continued to follow the paths that led to the reading room or the anatomy room, doing so with very little hopefulness. Since I had very few lecture classes—I suppose I had taken too many in earlier semesters—now I found myself rarely meeting my friends, who were in any case equally caught up in preparation for exams, preferring to work at home rather than in the library. We sometimes tested each other with exam questions; I seldom knew how to answer them.

My uncle showed up once on a quick visit. I saw him only briefly at midday, since I had to hurry away to a tutoring appointment. He was in some way enthusiastic about my uninterrupted activity; I, on the other hand, would have preferred to complain a little, but my pride prevented me. And what grounds for complaint would I have had? At best, Uncle would have told me that he had always known it would end in a fiasco. He would never have permitted me to become an attendant in a mental hospital; nor probably a nurse. Moreover, at heart I knew myself that both of these occupations were merely temptations for me. I didn't like to struggle; that was at the bottom of it. I not only wanted a path, I wanted it to be broad and comfortable. And so, while I explained the French past participles to Lilly Braun for the umpteenth time, I had to concede the case: there was nothing to do but stand firm and be as determined as possible in learning embryology and the anatomy of the nervous system.

This resolution had to be renewed again and again during the following weeks, although I developed no ability to commit things to memory. Microscope work was not much better; there were few organs that I recognized immediately, and, for the most part, I had to grope my way along slowly and doubtfully until I noted that what I thought was a vein was actually a bit of tendon.

Things were also often difficult with God. I had fallen into a completely mechanical way of praying, and I urgently needed help. I never talked about these things with Georgy, who was probably the friend I saw most frequently. She had an optimistic religion very much tailored to herself— at least so it seemed to me—a religion that knew no problems. Still, Georgy was a splendid person. She was suffering from a slowly growing loss of hearing, which distanced her from many things going on around her, but she put up with it courageously and never complained.

The summer vacation arrived suddenly, but the approaching exams oppressed me. I visited my Aunt Marguerite in La Chaux-de-Fonds first. I felt very close to her. Although we never really talked about serious matters, she had a gift for sharing in an almost wordless yet perfectly natural way whatever was going on. She always seemed to know how you were and managed at the right moment to find the perfect word—or silence. After my stay with her, I was supposed to visit Georgy at Klosters, though I was not very enthusiastic about it, for I was a bit afraid of the other people she had invited, all of whom were about twice my age; I also feared that I would not be able to study in peace. When Aunt Marguerite noticed how much this prospect was bothering me, she suggested that I stay with her for the whole summer, until exams of course. I could not impose on her in that way, since it would have been too great a burden for her very meager purse, but the fact that she made the suggestion cheered me up a good bit.

For the first time in my life, I traveled to Zurich; I had a two-hour stop there, and I was eager to see the city. It was a very humid day, made all the more humid for me since La Chaux-de-Fonds never experiences high humidity. The weather put an end to my sightseeing plans, especially when I noticed a sign in the train station pointing the way to showers. I followed the signs and washed and showered for as long a time as I was allowed. Refreshed, I resumed my journey. I was very disappointed by Lake Zurich—the entire shoreline was dotted with tiny houses, as if all the cottage owners had come together to let their possessions spill over into a pond. This impression has never left me. Georgy was waiting with a cordial and affectionate air when my train arrived at Klosters. With contented chatter we walked together to "Naz", the chalet she rented nearly every summer. I was carrying my suitcase and she a full milk can. It was about a half-hour's walk along an enchanting, slightly ascending path. The house was located all by itself in a forest clearing and was very nicely furnished. The days I spent there were glorious. Miss Iselin, whom I had so feared, was touchingly nice; early in the mornings while we were sound asleep, she would be seeing to things downstairs and preparing breakfast, so that we, scarcely out of bed, could sit down at a fully prepared table. She nearly kept us from tidying our own bedrooms. All the housekeeping tasks were kept as simple as possible, but even so it became thoroughly clear to me then for the first time that I lacked any real aptitude for housekeeping. Unfortunately nothing has changed in that regard since. At the time this insight did not bother me very much; it was only much later that the deficiency became more distressing for me.

A vacation mood reigned at "Naz" from morning to night. All of us lived in this state of mind, which contrasted distinctly with the Waldau and even La Chaux-de-Fonds. We did not have to bring a holiday air with us, for it was already there. For the noon meal, we always went down to Klosters, where we had some fabulous dinner in one of the first-class hotels; we ate our simple evening meals, which closely resembled our breakfasts, in the chalet. We spent the rest of the day outside. Often Georgy or Miss Iselin would read something out loud, sometimes from a medical book by Schleid, which they had chosen for my sake. Each day I spent a few hours studying for exams, this time with ease. Above all I studied the anatomy and topography of the brain and the nervous system and general embryology. Everything now seemed to be connected and was logical and easy to retain. I believe that the little real knowledge that accompanied me into the exams stemmed from these weeks. The library and its lifeless reading room survived in my memory merely as a hazy phantom. Once more I concluded that studying under the firs simply had to be the true way. In any case, I had always loved fir trees, ever since I had read *Heidi* as a child, and I could see them in no way but as they are described there. And "Naz" was as if created to the measure of *Heidi*, especially the rushing winds at night. Everything contributed to a rekindling of my memories of that book from my childhood, except that we never ate cheese that we had melted over the open fire, for we had no fireplace and probably also lacked any suitable forks. Otherwise everything was there, and in later years I often felt homesick for "Naz" just as Heidi longed for her Alps. After spending about two weeks with my friend, I finally ended up at the Waldau.

My efforts to study there were very soon as unfruitful as they had been on previous occasions, so, after several weeks, I returned to Basel, totaled up all the hundreds and thousands of pages I had to read, divided them by the approximately thirty days that remained before the exams, and had to concede in shame that I would never manage all of it. I got myself so worked up over this that I learned even less than before. There has never been a period in my life when I spent so much time in movie theaters; I went nearly every day, sometimes even twice. Once or twice, shortly before it was time for a new set of films to arrive, I found myself standing in front of the theater in perplexity: I had seen all the films, and none of them was worth seeing twice. I especially loved cartoons, but also the big evening receptions with the beautiful gowns. On other occasions I did become a bit bored, but the movies were fascinating enough that for their duration I did not have to think about the terror of the coming exams. I never managed to complete the day's portion of reading, so the amount for each remaining day steadily increased. Still, I never failed to recheck my inexorable figures several times a week, with results that shocked me deeply, yet the shock was fruitless and improved nothing. Using this method, my ignorance never ceased to grow in relation to my knowledge.

One young girl I had known from my school days in La Chaux-de-Fonds, Hélène Gander, wanted to take her exams at the same time as I. She lived in the Baslerhof and was obviously having as little success with her studies as I was. Sometimes we would try to study together, but it did not work out: our questions to each other merely revealed new gaps that seemed impossible to fill. We would soon give up and head for the movie theater, so that we could at least spend some time together.

My mother, my brothers and sister, and my friends had no doubt that I would do well on the exams; this did not bring me any reassurance, for I could scarcely imagine how they would take the fateful news. But I never asked myself what would then become of me; it was simply like the opening into a black hole.

The practical tests began early in September. One morning three of us were standing together in the corridor of the anatomy institute: Sutermeister, Wilhelm, and I. The proctor, who was named Straßer, told us that there were three dissection projects awaiting us: larynx, brain, and hand. When he said "larynx" I felt almost sick; I really didn't know the larynx at all. The other two dissections were tough enough but perhaps not entirely hopeless. Soon Professor Ludwig appeared and held out to me three slips of paper from which I was to choose one. Through the paper, I could see a very short word on one of them and naturally chose that one, thereby escaping the dreaded larynx.[1] I had selected the hand, which was probably the best of the three for me. But my conscience was not entirely clear, and, when the three of us were alone again, I asked my comrades with some anxiety what they thought about my having accidentally seen how short the word was and having chosen on that basis. They judged me innocent, which immediately and thoroughly calmed me.

I spent the entire morning dissecting the muscles, nerves, and blood vessels of my hand, occasionally piecing together with thread something that I had severed. I think that was what I had learned best in anatomy class. Sometimes Professor Ludwig would stride through the room and glance over at us, but he never asked anything. Otherwise the three of us were left to ourselves and had plenty to do.

In the afternoon each of us received a histological preparation, which we had time to study. Then came the oral examinations. I will never forget Sutermeister's oral exam. He gave a proper lecture on the larynx: nothing stumped him; he knew the precise course, axes, planes, and functions of every articulation, whose very existence I had not even suspected up to then. He never faltered; it was almost a lecture; they never had to interrupt him, for there was no diversion or bluffing. He knew everything in detail. I almost thought that I would like to fail the exams in order to learn everything as thoroughly as he had. I could not conceive how Sutermeister, who had spent the same five

---

[1] In German, the three words are *Kehlkopf* (larynx), *Gehirn* (brain), and *Hand*—TRANS.

semesters in preparation as I had, had been able to learn so much. Of course, he had not had to spend hour upon hour tutoring, but he did devote a lot of time to the cello, and he never missed a concert. Yet this was to be his final exam. He scored thirty-six points, a perfect score of six in each unit of the exams. About two years into the clinical portion of medical school, he began to tire and thought he would have to choose between medicine and music. After much hesitation, he finally chose medicine, took an interim position, but was not a success; when the position ended, he took his own life. We all were very fond of him, and his death was a heavy blow.

At the time of the second *propædeuticum*, of course, no one could foresee any of this. My oral exam over the hand followed upon his brilliant exposition of the larynx; it dragged on a bit, but, in general, it went fairly well, as did histology.

The next day the three of us entered upon the practical physiology exam. I was given the topic "sugar", had to perform several chemical reactions, and then write a paper. While writing I shared the room with Hélène Gander, who had been given the topic "protein", over which she was groaning. Professor Spiro came in once in a while. Suddenly he said to me, "You have written enough, certainly more than enough. You may leave." His tone was most definite though not unkind. I was astonished beyond measure and could not make any sense of this. A few days later I learned what had happened. After I left the room, Professor Spiro's assistant, whom Hélène did not know, came in and dictated word for word a proper scientific essay on protein, correcting her faulty German, citing Forscher, whom she knew nothing about, spelling names for her, even having her copy a little table, and then let her go, after she had written about ten pages. At her oral exam, she knew extremely little, but Professor Spiro rescued her in the eyes of the other professors by pointing to the extraordinary quality of her written examination. And so she passed. One day later, according to her, Professor Spiro told her: "Now we are even. You translated my work for me—as payment for that, I have seen to it that you passed your exams." I was a good bit indignant when she told me; she herself was rather alarmed that such a thing was even possible, vacillated for a while about whether she should let it go or not, and finally decided in favor of the former. A few years later she married a Jewish man from eastern Europe with whom she was said to have had a very difficult life. I never saw her again.

A ten-day break followed the practical exams. Despite the fact that I had seen from Sutermeister's examination how it should be done, the time did not do me much good. One afternoon at five o'clock, the three oral exams took place, one after the other. I was paired with another student; one of us was always in the hallway while the other was in the examination room; it was frightful. I made quite a confusing mess of things, knew very little, and was unable to get out what little I did know. When it was all over, I was utterly astonished to hear that I had passed, even with only minimal grades. I had been so convinced that I had failed that at first I could scarcely believe it. Then I waited for Clerc. He had failed, for the second time, and he was completely at a loss. We walked together from the Vesalianum to the Spalentor. He thought I had also failed, and I did not have the heart to tell him otherwise.

As I went home, from time to time I would think: I've got the exams in the bag. Yet somehow it didn't become a reality for me that night. Later, as I prayed in my room, I thanked God for this gift, but despite the thanks, the gift still did not seem like it was mine. Only after awaking at a fairly late hour the next morning was everything real and good, and a tremendous joy filled me. Now I knew with certainty: all my troubles with studies are over, now come the sick people, the clinics, the reality of being a physician, life itself. This was incredibly beautiful, and I lived in this immense, carefree joy until the beginning of the next semester.

If I thought at times about my troubles with faith, it seemed to me that they must now come to an end, for I was going to need to know precisely how to help suffering people, and helping them could only take place in God. I prayed hard and long and felt untroubled. Occasionally, however, it seemed a bit strange that having passed the exams—and by such a narrow margin—should make such a transformation in my life. Yet the exams did mark the opening of a new period.

THE NEERGARD AFFAIR

Winter Semester 1925/1926

The longed-for first day of the semester dawned. It began with a propædeutic surgical clinic taught by Hotz. Only three of the students were Swiss: Wilhelm, Sutermeister, and I. In addition, there were about a dozen Polish students. I was the only woman. The rest of our fellow students had decided to wait a semester or two before attempting the exams. Hélène Gander was in Geneva.

Professor Hotz entered the lecture hall, which was also the main operating room. He brought a woman with him. Right away he called on Wilhelm and me to practice. The case was puzzling at first, and, like all the cases Hotz later introduced to us, impressed itself deeply on my memory. The woman had a large burn on her ring finger, and we had to talk with her about it in order finally to extract the following: several weeks previously she had cut herself deeply on her forearm, severing the *nervus ulnaris*, thus making her insensitive to pain; this made it possible for her to burn her finger without realizing it. We felt our way slowly toward the truth, as in a detective novel. Only this was a living woman, and the wound was quite considerable, deep, and festering. I had already seen all sorts of things, so it did not make me sick, but it was different for Wilhelm, especially since he was decidedly unlucky in answering Hotz' questions. Hotz asked him which nerves served the forearm, and Wilhelm responded with *Ulnaris*, *radialis*, and *medianus* in a single breath. The third of these was a very specialized nerve that was as unknown to Hotz as it was to me; moreover, Wilhelm mentioned the three with a vocal emphasis on the *medianus* that almost eclipsed the other two. It was as if only the *medianus* existed. Hotz heard only that one and missed the other two completely. Then he asked me, somewhat forcefully, "Name the nerves of the forearm, please." I answered as well as my little knowledge permitted: "*Ulnaris* and *radialis*." Wholly satisfied, he turned back to Wilhelm and said in a very loud voice: "Have you passed your second *prope* at all?" For Wilhelm, with his thirty-six points, this was too much when combined with the newness of the operating room and the sight of the wound. He paled, wavered, and had to be helped out of the room. Hotz then said to us, "I don't want anyone in this class who has not passed his second *prope*."

That was the only time in my life that I was aggravated with Hotz, so I had to see him after class was over and tell him that Wilhelm had passed his exams with a thirty-six, something that had not happened for years. He received me with such kindness! It was as if my pride in having a comrade with six sixes had now become his pride in having a student with six sixes.

Hotz gave three classes each week throughout the entire winter semester. He introduced us to many surgical problems, and his entire approach to surgery always centered on the living person in need of help. When he entered the room, he would always greet the patient first, exchanging a few words with him until we all sensed that the patient, too, felt it was only right to be presented, that he was happy to learn more about his own condition or to get to know the chief of staff better. Hotz never established this atmosphere by employing mere clichés; everything was spontaneous, natural, self-evident, and seemed like a genuine give and take, which it was. After the patient had left the room, Hotz would sometimes comment on how necessary this relationship between doctor and patient was, how he considered himself to be the greatest beneficiary, because the patient had given him his trust, the trust that Hotz needed to do his work, for it was from this trust that he drew new strength each day. And we, too, learned how to deal with patients and were glad for all the experiences we were permitted to have in exercising our slowly growing diagnostic potential.

After the class in surgery came one in medicine. It, too, was propædeutic and was taught by Rudolf Staehelin. His style was not helpful for beginners. He would enter the room in a state of distraction, as if he had a thousand other things on his mind, appeared to notice neither the patient nor the students, then suddenly would be so deeply engaged in his topic that no one could follow him. None of us had any idea where the threads of his topic came from or led to. When called upon to assist him, one stood in embarrassment next to him, without any contact with the patient, feeling quite lost. Suddenly he would ask you a question, usually out of a context you had not grasped at all, then you would be left with your own inadequacy. The lecture kept going, and you kept standing there until rescued by the bell. Sometimes, to be sure, there were brilliant insights, an ingenious structure, but we were too immature in our training to grasp it. Only in later semesters did we begin to appreciate Staehelin, to sense and then discover his absolute integrity of character, his great erudition. I don't recall who advised me at the time: "Memorize the formula for Pyramidon; it could be useful." I did that, and not long thereafter Staehelin asked in class: "Does anyone know the formula for Pyramidon?" Since no one answered, I took courage and recited in a monotone: "Dimethyl-amidophenyl-dimethylpyrazolone." "Can you sketch it?" I could. From that point onward, in Staehelin's eyes, I was a gifted student. I was a bit ashamed of my triumph, won by what came close to deceit, for this was to be the only pharmacological formula I ever knew by memory.

Staehelin would have his entire staff of assistants [interns] present when he taught the clinical courses, even the propædeutic courses. One of the assistants was a woman. She seemed a bit embarrassed in the company of all her male colleagues, said very little to them, and, when she did, blushed. I always felt a bit of compassion for her; certainly she did not correspond very well to the image I had of a woman physician. Still, I felt drawn to her in some manner, perhaps at first less in a personal way than professionally. I no longer saw a great difference between a woman doctor and a woman student in clinical training; I thought we could help each other and regarded this help as something thoroughly mutual. That is why I did not think I was being at all presumptuous when one day during a free period I knocked on her door. She received me coldly, thought my interest very odd, and scarcely knew what to make of me. Above all, she perceived me as anything but her equal and took pains to show me the very clear distance between us, since I was so obviously blind to it. Back in the hallway, I felt very disappointed; yet hardly had a year passed before we were good friends, which we have remained to this day.

My momentary disappointment was not powerful enough to trouble me at all, for the hospital as always consoled me very quickly. As I had often done before, I would walk through various stairs and corridors, breathing in the very different smells that characterized various wards. I might hold open a door, help close another one; meet patients, nurses, gurneys, and people with flowers; encounter a hospital coffin or a kitchen maid carrying a pot of boiling soup; all of this was part of hospital life, and the hospital was my homeland, the homeland I had once lost as a child, the homeland I had perhaps lost several times over, but which was finally mine again, mine forever. Whenever I thought about the future in those days, I envisioned it as totally enclosed within the hospital.

Already in my first semester, I took the clinical course in the women's hospital. Professor Labhardt taught in a very clear manner: when dealing with theory, he made a division: there was a right and a left; you always saw what the choices were, this or that. This was good for the students, for a sense of order dominated everything, an order one need only recognize in order to be as though guided by it. Perhaps obstetrics lends itself particularly well to such decisions based on a number of symptoms; in any case, it gives the physician a kind of blind certainty in the event of an emergency, as if everything could only be correct in this way and otherwise would inevitably be wrong. Initially everything took place in the lecture hall. After several weeks I had to attend my first delivery, only as an observer, of course. In those days, single mothers were admitted free of charge to the ward a few weeks before their babies were due; they then had to be available for examinations by students and to give birth in front of four young students. This first birth made a very great impression on me. But it was perhaps not so much the pain the mother had to endure that impressed me as her helpless surrender to the act of delivery: she could do nothing against it and very little for it. Moreover, it seemed to me that her helplessness was increased by our presence; we were just as helpless as she. Beyond that, putting precisely an unmarried mother on display like this pained me, for I feared the young mother might fall into an even greater dissipation. So I tried to console her a bit after her little girl had been born and knitted a little jacket for the baby. I felt attached to the single mother and somehow grateful. My contact with her lasted for a long time.

Among our teachers were two outstanding scholars who were also masters of language: Doerr and Roeßle. From Doerr we had bacteriology and hygiene. His lectures were spiced with delicious humor, and we looked forward from one lecture to the next like little children. Roeßle was less humorous, perhaps even rather dry, but one sensed his intelligence in everything he said and was enthralled by him as a man of research. He guided us into a very special world of meticulous precision as he taught us the rudiments of pathology. If he reached the limits of what was then known, he admitted that in all simplicity and showed us which paths, if necessary, could be followed successfully. He illustrated his lectures occasionally with specimens that could also be viewed after the class. I scarcely had time to study them, since I still had to do a lot of tutoring, which was beginning to become a real burden for me. I found that I had too many things in my studies that were not firm requirements of the program in order to provide enough time for my tutoring. This began to weigh me down more and more, especially since I really should have been spending a lot of time in front of the pathology specimens in order to remember them well. Moreover, once I had become involved with hospital life and begun to work with living patients, my pupils' grades and degree of success in school paled in importance. The stupid ones among them, as far as I was concerned, ought to give up the pursuit of higher degrees, and the others simply ought to put greater effort into their work so as not to need a tutor. My secondary job was losing its appeal. However, for the time being, I had no other source of income, so I could not give it up.

My young pupils often brought all sorts of personal problems to me, the sort of problems typical of their stage in life. It was not difficult for me to give them a bit of counsel here or there, to indicate something that might be an impediment, but let them eliminate it on their own. Such conversations seemed of little weight to me, for my troubles with studying were behind me. I myself had known very few such problems, but where they might have caused me difficulties, as when I transferred into the school in Basel, the rector's sympathy and the kind leniency of my teacher, Burckhardt, cleared most of the problems away long before they could become a real threat.

With the patients it was entirely different. Many of them sought advice, asked me to spend time talking with them, often thinking I was already a fully credentialed physician, appealing to a level of experience that was not present and thereby embarrassing me. Quite often I was not equal to the questions they asked and on the whole had only a remote understanding of what it was all basically about. For that reason I would often make my first words a confession that I was merely a student. But some of them did not let that deter them and insisted that I talk with them. I think that the female patients especially wanted a chance to talk with a woman, a woman who seemed so firmly anchored in hospital life, who must have a certain distance from their day-to-day lives and therefore was called to help them. Very often, precisely because of the imposed distance from their homes, the women seemed inclined to consider their most urgent problems in a different way from before. Occasionally they found themselves confronted by the question of death, which placed the rest of their former lives in question. Often a religious undertone could be detected, yet they preferred to talk with a lay person. At that time there were two chaplains in the hospital. One was Protestant, a frail old man who would read something from the New Testament out loud at each bed but wanted nothing to do with the patients' personal questions. The Catholic clergyman, whom I had met when I broke my leg, had ready answers for all questions but was so impossibly stupid that everyone laughed at him, believers as well as unbelievers.

And so one encountered many patients, above all in the classroom, where they were assigned to us, one for each class session, and we were to try to come up with sound diagnoses. We talked with them and thus, from time to time, found ourselves in the middle of disconcerting conversations I was not equal to. To me it seemed that God alone could make up for my inadequacy by assuming entirely the direction of these conversations. I thought I ought to pray a lot, transferring to God all the concerns that had been revealed to me, and then he could accomplish something despite my ignorance and hesitation. And so I began to pray for extended periods each night, for the most part explaining to God each situation, pointing with my fingers to where the difficulties lay. Then one day I noticed, with a mixture of embarrassment and amusement, that I was placing human limits on God's abilities, as if he needed my explanations in order to manage. From that point onward, I stopped giving God instructions in my prayer, which became more of a conversation with God in which I yielded the direction to him everywhere, and I worshiped in contemplation.

And then it did seem as if he actually took up the direction of conversations with the patients, letting me in some small way become his mouthpiece, which permitted me occasionally to help someone with a word of advice. It became increasingly evident to me that God ordains times of illness so that they can be a time of inner recollection for those who are afflicted by them, an opportunity to recognize better what is going wrong in their lives, to take stock of their daily lives from the distant perspective of a hospital stay, to gain a clearer view of their problems and thereby become better able to master them. To this end discussion is important, which means that the physician ought to be a person of prayer who always has at hand a full supply of possibilities to help. This aspect of the profession made me very happy; it also offered me the opportunity to gain a deeper comprehension of human beings, which in turn would open new possibilities for diagnosis and therapy. When patients revealed their inner nature, the various causes of disease and their symptoms suddenly took on a new relationship and also could be utilized in a new way.

We had a course in medical technique in which the various therapeutic and diagnostic procedures were not only discussed but also performed. When we first practiced giving injections, I sensed that I lacked the courage simply to jab a stranger; I was too awkward. So I first went into an adjoining room and injected myself in the leg; only I did not know how painful the effects of a hypotonic solution could be, so I injected several cubic centimeters of distilled water. I did not soon forget the aftereffects. But the actual injection went very well, so I gained the courage to approach patients with a needle. This course made us familiar with a whole series of procedures, and, over time, I carried them out with increasing joy, until one day something so frightening happened that it left a deep shadow over my life for a long time.

Our teacher was Doctor Kurt von Neergard. As a person, he was neither particularly congenial nor uncongenial to us. We amused ourselves a bit over his vanity but otherwise paid little attention to him. In this course he always gave an introduction in which he not only demonstrated the next procedure but also discussed ethical questions. One theme kept recurring: a doctor is responsible for his actions, he must always make sure, prior to each injection, that the bottle or ampule was filled with the correct medicine. No one can relieve him of this responsibility. Nor should he ever simply relinquish it to someone else, not even the most experienced nurse. Double-checking the work of others was part of his task.

We did not like Neergard's style. Immediately following his course, which took place on Mondays from eleven to one, Adrian Sutermeister and I would always walk to the nearby Blue Cross for lunch. Our usual meal consisted largely of coarse green peas, which were always somewhat overcooked but were well suited to form all sorts of shapes and thereby made our conversation more impressive. We built pyramids and drew paths, spoke endlessly about our future profession, for we both loved it equally. But the peas had disappeared, for our lunchtime was very short that day, since we had to be back in the hospital at one-thirty for a class with Professor Staub, a robust and yet sensitive man for whom we had the utmost respect.

One Monday, perhaps in January, Neergard had loaded me up with a fairly extensive assignment, including, among other things, the draining of an abscessed lung in the lecture hall. Before that, however, I had to undertake minor procedures in various rooms. When I entered the lecture hall, still quite breathless from all my running around, the students were already assembled and the patient was lying down. Neergard said to me that he wanted just to do the injection for the local anesthetic, which was not very interesting, and I could then take over from there. He already had the loaded syringe in his hand and injected it. At the same instant, I saw the patient turn pale, sit up in his bed, and then sink back, dead. The sight was shocking, everything happened so suddenly that at first we saw it without really comprehending it.

Neergard sent all of us out of the room. Terrified and thunderstruck, we stood in the antechamber, watching as Professor Staehelin hurried into the room, followed by Professor Massini and individual assistants. Then someone came out of the room and told us that an accident had occurred and we should just go home calmly. This seemed completely wrong to me. In a loud and determined voice, speaking for all the students (even though we had not agreed on this), I refused to comply. The bed, with the covered corpse, was rolled out, and we quietly returned to the lecture hall, anxious yet sure of our case and of our right to be there. Staehelin gave us a short speech. Neergard had mistakenly injected the wrong solution: a lethal dose of cocaine instead of the novocaine that had been indicated. Death had occurred so suddenly that the antidotes used had been ineffective. We had learned in a tragic way what being a physician could also mean.

I was completely shaken and could no longer comprehend how the profession I had loved so passionately could still have any meaning. At that moment, I would rather have become a teacher or even a cleaning woman, anything except a doctor. Until that point, everything I had experienced, the easy as well as the difficult, had only confirmed me in my profession. Now it was all over, forever, so it seemed. I was just glad that, since it was Monday, I did not have to go home over lunchtime. I did not want to talk with Sutermeister either, for it was impossible to converse, impossible to do anything except despair. I wandered through the streets for a long time, passing from bustling streets to deserted ones and back again. I sat down for a moment on a bench at the St. Johannes-Schanze to think things over, but the cold air soon sent me on my way. And, after all, what was there to think over? Everything looked hopeless. Why study? In order then to kill people out of simple and very human carelessness? I began to wonder if quacks, with their dose of common sense and without any potentially lethal drugs, might perhaps not come out ahead. Was it not really audacious to search constantly for new ways to postpone death if, by a simple confusion of those means one could bring about death? For a few moments I tried to think things through, to make decisions, to pass judgments, then merely stared ahead and inside myself, devoid of thoughts, crushed by the weight of sudden and profound despair. Up until then, I had always been so glad to take responsibility.

Now all I could think was "steer clear of this dangerous game".

It almost seemed as if I could no longer love people who let themselves be killed so suddenly and insidiously, or who at least found themselves precisely in a situation where security ceased, where nothing but error and failure reigned.

In the midst of this, the question of God quietly appeared. But it lacked the power to bring light into my despair.

I encountered children on their way to school, adults with unsuspecting faces. I would have liked to warn them, to warn them about doctors, about science, about the ghastly hospital where death lurked in every corner. But it would not do to start talking openly with people and getting them all upset.

I skipped my class with Staub without realizing it, without any sense of time passing. At one point I was on the outskirts of the city, before long back in the center, then in a suburb. Everywhere people looked the same, whether happy or sad, they all were unsuspecting.

Finally I found myself at the Heuberg, stopped at the door of my friend Pauline Müller's house, and rang the doorbell. She was home. I told her a bit of what had happened, and she did something quite strange. She went to her cellar and fetched a very small bottle of champagne. We slowly drank it together. Our conversation did not become more lively, yet it calmed me, calmed me even though I had drunk scarcely a glass. The oddity of drinking champagne in the middle of the day after the exhaustion from wandering around, the warmth of the room with its painted walls (they were completely covered with pictures of hunting scenes), and the proximity of my friend all helped to dissolve the immense tension within me, or at least to relax it a bit. The pain and despairing mood were by no means evaporated, but one be-

gan to suspect that this fright was not definitive, that it would
be conquered; one simply did not yet know how. I stayed
with Pauline for quite a while, returning home at supper
time. At home everything was as usual, at least outwardly. I
said nothing, for I had a real fear that everything might flare
up all over again, that I might lose what little composure
I had regained, a fear of experiencing the full force of the
terror again and finding it unbearable. I was afraid of fear, I
had a kind of guilty conscience, not much; yet . . .

I slept the whole night in a leaden sleep. The next morning, unlike our usual practice, we all went to Professor
Staehelin's main clinic. All the assistants were also present.
Staehelin spoke about the incident on the day before; he did
so in his awkward way, for he lacked the gift of expressing
what is human, no matter how much he had grasped it. The
whole matter was played down as an occupational accident,
a conclusion to which Staehelin easily managed to come
after an autopsy showed that the man had been much more
seriously ill than had been thought. His life expectancy was
judged to be only a few more weeks. Liability insurance
would accordingly probably pay his widow a few weeks'
compensation. Nothing was said about questions of medical ethics.

Wilhelm, Sutermeister, and I met with Neergard once in
the following days. He refused any responsibility and blamed
the nurse.

In the meantime I had found out about what had gone
on before. The nurse had been old Sister Marie, a white-
haired, conscientious, and much-loved deaconess, who had
headed the medicine department for many years. She had
prepared everything for the procedure. When she brought
him the novocaine solution, Neergard had sent it back; he
wanted to use his own solution, he had one of his own.

Since the only solution of his that she was familiar with was a cocaine solution, she brought that, and Neergard filled his syringe with it without checking it again. People knew that he always found something to complain about when Sister Marie assisted him.

Neergard employed eloquent words to persuade us of his innocence. A physician's responsibility and that of the auxiliary staff were limited and strictly separate from each other; no physician could be expected to second-guess the work of a well-trained nurse. Where would that lead? There was nothing left of his earlier teaching.

This matter left me no peace. Until now I had believed that every doctor became a doctor out of idealism and was obligated to remain true to his ideals. I could imagine changes within one's personal views, but never a complete reversal as a result of naked fear. I could understand cowardice as a momentary reaction, but then one ought to return to the former, better, and now improved principles, and one ought to do so in humility. That someone who had been taken at his word might hastily disavow what he had held as true disturbed me greatly. Somehow I had experienced this disavowal myself for almost a full day; the physician's had seemed like such a heavy, perhaps too heavy, responsibility to bear, even if it were only a future responsibility. To give up this profession would have been cowardice, but this cowardice would never have been able to undo what had happened. A doctor has to stand up to the fact of his malpractice. The possibility of failure is part of being human; this was a hard and new thing to me, something I had never seriously thought about.

I tried to take up the fight against Neergard. I went to him to tell him how great an injustice he had done not only to the nurse, whom he had certainly intimidated in his usual way, but also to us. It was his task to educate us, and he frankly owed it to us to carry out his responsibility like a man. But it did no good. Nothing could shake Neergard's innocence. But this only served to strengthen our demand that one take a stand, that one take one's responsibility seriously.

From that point onward, I met each responsibility in a completely different way from before. In general, I was much more conscious of it; it seemed to me like the possibility of failure lurked behind every little medical or human act. Somehow it no longer seemed self-evident to me that one should step in and help. I had a much more conscious sense of the life of the patient standing before me, of his personality in its unity, of the potential consequences of an intervention in areas of other people that until then I had imagined to be unaffected. The moments when in each case decisions were made emerged more clearly, almost as if analyzed a bit from each other. My friends and I discussed all these things with each other, powerfully affected by what we had experienced and even more by Neergard's unmanly attitude, which we took as a warning for ourselves at a later age. We feared we might also slip into a kind of stupefaction that would make us think our personal unimpeachability was the highest possible good.

Something else was involved as far as I was concerned, although it was difficult to talk about it with my friends because it was not entirely clear to me even though it still was a vague burden to me. It was something like this: If we as physicians were to be witnesses of life and death, birth and parting, and if in the process a significant and, from a human point of view, decisive role sometimes belonged to us, then the patient and those around him must be able to count on us, not only on our knowledge but on our being.

We ought to be there with a sort of transparency, a thorough clarity and purity. We must have a kind of openness that is not darkened by inner contradictions. I did not think that we could ever achieve a personal certainty about this inner readiness, this liberation from our sins, but I did think that we ought to strive for it constantly. Moreover, it seemed to me that, since patients often confessed things to us, including their sins, and since we thereby came into contact with all the problems of guilt, we ourselves ought to be able to lay down our respective sins. I did this frequently before God, but this was not enough for me anymore. I began to yearn earnestly for sacramental confession, from which I expected to receive not only a purifying effect within and for myself but also, above all, a profound effect on my human interaction with patients, so that the distinction between the "mine" and "thine" of guilt and innocence would no longer be very sharp or perhaps distinguishable at all.

But no one in my surroundings seemed to be Catholic, and I thus had no one to talk to about these things.

Yet the questions that concerned us did not burden our interaction with patients; we all maintained an unaffected ease with them. Only once did Sutermeister and I find ourselves inhibited, and that was two or three months before the Neergard incident. We were standing in the examining room of Professor Gigon in the medical polyclinic, where we were to undertake for the first time an examination of the heart and lungs, that is, we were to establish their limits and learn to recognize the sounds of a normal heart and lungs. The subject had first been discussed and explained in the lecture hall, and now each pair of students was supposed to percuss and auscultate a patient in one of the examining rooms. As Sutermeister and I stood there in front of the completely unsuspecting patient, we were at first at a loss.

We didn't know how to proceed to ask him to take off his shirt. And so I began to chat with him a bit in order finally to request that he undress so we could examine him. He complied willingly but was scarcely ready when Gigon arrived to check our results. There were no results yet, and Gigon was a bit displeased, and we were quite embarrassed. The next time we handled things much more skillfully, but our beginning clumsiness seems quite understandable to me even today.

Naturally, we learned a number of different things during this first clinical semester, especially how to grasp the overall picture of an illness in order to perceive the direction that further investigation ought to take; we gathered experience, so to speak, in reading the signposts of illness. We also read all sorts of medical textbooks and introductions to various areas of medicine. But the summit, what was most decisive, even if the least recognized, remained the encounter with the sick as persons. In a way it was as if everything else was secondary, belonging to it but never the most important thing.

On the last day of the semester we went from one professor to another to obtain the necessary signatures in our student logbooks. Hotz was sitting at a small bandaging table in the antechamber. After signing each booklet, he would look at the name on the cover. In my case he said, "Wait a minute." I waited, a bit uneasy, watching as he kept on writing, sitting in his white physician's coat, a bit absently. When finished, he stood up and approached me. "You must promise me something." I was a bit afraid—what did he have in mind? Then he said, "Look, you have to be true to medicine." Softly and a bit embarrassed, I said, "That is what I want to do." "That is not enough for me, I need a promise. Look, some days a person gets tired. I've noticed how the Neergard incident has plagued you but you did not want to interfere. One has to go through that, too, completely and even in abandonment. But other disappointments will come along, and suddenly you will turn your back on the profession, perhaps to marry the first possible man who comes along, whom you take because he just happened to ask you at the right moment, when you were defenseless. So promise me, then, that you will remain as true to the profession as you are now." I promised. I felt a bit of solemnity in the process but not enough to stifle other concerns. And so I gasped out, "I would like to do my clinical training [*famulieren*] this summer in the clinic." Hotz gazed into the distance as if seeing right through the instrument cabinet, almost as if he had not heard me. I was shocked at my own audacity; but it was too late, I could not reclaim my words. Then Hotz said, "This summer?" He was silent for a brief moment, then: "Okay, agreed. But don't forget your promise." He shook my hand, held my hand for a moment in his, and said very quietly, "Be courageous; that's what being faithful means. I have your promise." I never saw him again.

It was a glorious vacation. I had to read a lot of medical material, since I wanted to practice with Labhardt in the coming semester, and my clinical training began in the summer. Everything I read made sense to me, somehow entered into me, and fit with and expanded what I had learned during the winter semester. Several times I visited de Quervain in the clinic and observed him as he operated. I thought he was magnificent, and I also enjoyed the fact that I was permitted each time to join him for lunch. He was very fond of Hotz and had all sorts of stories to tell about him; he was a very sick man; a few years earlier he had had to operate on him on a kitchen table up in the mountains because Hotz had suddenly been stricken with a perforated stomach. This was the illness that had killed my father, and, indeed, probably because no one had fetched de Quervain, who was my father's friend. But I never discussed that with de Quervain. He was always very disconcerting; you never knew where the phrase he had begun might lead him. I found that very charming. And I thought more and more seriously about becoming a surgeon.

Toward evening I often took my bicycle to Bolligen and into the Bantiger area and the nearby valleys. The weather was mild in early spring; it was lovely to pedal for a while and then stop somewhere to watch village life or look around the area.

One Sunday I went to church at the Waldau. It was not a happy experience. I felt totally estranged. Pastor Henzi was pastor at both of the Bernese mental institutions, the Waldau and the one at Münsingen. He was a very well-intentioned, amiable, older man, who seemed to me to lack the power to wrest any validity from the word. To me it seemed as if the word needed some support, but from where? It was not at all clear. After the sermon I went for a little walk with him along the lane, up and down. The meadows were already green, the trees were still bare; there was as if a promise. Suddenly it was clear to me: Protestantism was the opposite of a promise, it was like going in reverse. Something of the fulfillment remained, but as if cut off from the background God desired for it, the word hung in the air, cut off from its union with God. Naturally, at the moment this dawned on me, I was unable to keep quiet, and so I shared it with Pastor Henzi, who was a bit startled by it. At first he was speechless, then he asserted, "What you are missing is prayer; the word is supported by prayer." I contented myself with that and went into the wards until lunchtime. Elderly women patients who had been there for years, who were already ancient when I was still a child, warmed their bones in the early spring sun. One could hardly converse with them, the most that was possible was a kind word, a sign of interest, of shared joy at the approaching spring. Younger women walked back and forth. They formed an almost homogeneous group, yet a group composed of constantly changing young women: psychopaths, thieves, infanticides. It always seemed to me that, despite everything, one could do a lot with them, for they all had moments of insight, though they were simply too weak to sustain it. I gladly spent time with them, always believed a little in their good intentions, was astonished when they lapsed and suddenly found themselves back at the Waldau. We sometimes talked about God, about faith, about the power of faith. The power of faith seemed especially important to me; it could carry them, could help their weakness. Perhaps they would all suddenly become strong and good if they really grasped that they shared in this power and were not limited to their own weakness.

On this day, however, I could not talk with them; there was a void in me, a void that was palpable everywhere, accompanying my thoughts, always there wherever a thought arose, began, and inevitably there, too, wherever it should have been pursued.

The pastor was a servant of the word. But what if this word were no longer the word originally meant?

And yet everything was postponed again. The void in me refused to close, yet my thoughts seemed to learn how to detour around it. It was no longer really an obstacle, only a difficulty that I had become accustomed to.

During those days at the Waldau it happened that I met a priest in the corridor and observed how a woman attendant, not a patient, knelt as he passed by. I asked her afterwards why she had done that. She replied, "He was carrying the Lord." This, however, seemed very strange to me. But there was nothing more to ask, so, as the priest carried the Lord, I carried this attendant's words within me, repeating them from time to time as something significant, doing so a bit shyly but also in joy. It was almost as if one could knock at these words; they were there, echoing, even if not yet with their own tone. To me they were not a source of uneasiness but a soft, friendly, even benevolent admonition to pray more, perhaps even to pray for better understanding.

During the night of Good Friday, a large barn, one hundred meters long and located only two or three minutes from the main building, burned down. I was awakened by hurried footsteps in the garden. When I reached the window, I saw two things that together formed a single, simultaneous image and remained alive within me: a sky that was bright red, with tall, vertical flames flashing through it, and, in the garden, already almost disappearing behind the fir trees, the tall, gaunt figure of my uncle, wrapped in his greatcoat, limping slightly and yet rapidly and nimbly with his cane toward the brightness. Aunt Jeanne, Hélène, and I met each other in the garden and remained there. Aunt said we couldn't help with anything anyway. She said it with such authority that it was simply accepted without argument. And thus we remained spectators and listeners; the sight itself was truly spectacular. The only horrible part was the terrified mooing of the cattle who had been driven out into the night, occasionally accompanied by the cry of a woman patient in the watch station in the new building, who in turn was answered by the howling of a patient from the old building. Such human outcries were, of course, not uncommon from time to time in the institution, but they didn't last as long and, if they merely split the silence in two, were not frightening, but simply belonged to the environment. This night, however, they were scarcely bearable, for they seemed to point to new circumstances; perhaps they had become so understandable that they suddenly made one shudder at the uncomprehended screams of uneventful nights. Never has the urgent necessity of the study of psychiatry been so vitally brought home to me as during that night, for we were also afraid for old Uncle, who might somehow attempt something beyond his strength near the burning barn.

THE DEATH OF PROFESSOR HOTZ

Summer Semester 1926

Death had opened up painful voids in my life when it took my grandmother and, a few years later, my father. Despite this, death did not really belong to my sphere. To be sure, I encountered death frequently, since so much of my life took place in hospitals and institutions; and this was even more true now that I was a medical student. But the night of the fire, death suddenly seemed very different; it lay close to me like a half-concealed threat that would perhaps suddenly announce itself and fetch my almost seventy-four-year-old uncle. We had been so anxious about him that even after he returned safe and sound, although very tired, something of our concern about him remained; we asked more frequently about his whereabouts, checked how long he was away from the house, looked to see if the light in his room was still burning, entered it more readily under the most insignificant pretexts if something seemed not completely in order. We all hid this way of acting from each other, but I noticed how my aunt and Hélène also took advantage of the least occasion to watch over Uncle. I had actually been intended as a present for his fiftieth birthday, but with the sort of willfulness that children often show at their births, I arrived a few hours too late to share a birthday with him. My uncle was, however, my godfather, and thus we had from the beginning a special bond despite my delayed arrival. That also helps explain why Uncle always favored me a bit. Moreover, we would soon be true colleagues. Saying farewell to the Waldau was as difficult at this time as it always was, and the anxiety I had experienced left its trace in an ongoing uneasiness. How much longer would Uncle be with us? I was now, in general, no longer quite so much at ease with the thought of death as I had once been.

Although I still liked living in the Waldau better than in Basel, there was something that spring that helped me through my farewell. In Basel, everything in nature was always somewhat, occasionally as much as three weeks, ahead of Bern, and it was always a joy to notice the difference: if the chestnut trees in the garden at the Waldau were merely covered with swelling buds, in Basel the large, flat, compound chestnut leaves were already fully unfolded, and pleasant smells were to be found everywhere, with each rainfall bringing new fragrances to enchant the gardens or tree-lined walks for a brief moment. The grass shot up suddenly, and a flower began to appear where shortly before there was nothing to be seen. The way to the hospital, to be sure, had little to offer, but the hospital garden was beautiful; even more so was the nearby Rennweg with the splendid trees of its gardens. Then there were the woods, but they were a bit too far away to be easily accessible; city and hospital life kept me occupied. And, finally, the smell of the operating room was particularly dear to me, even though nothing about it would remind one of flowers.

This time, however, a grave concern weighed upon the operating room: in Vienna Professor Hotz had fallen ill with a very dangerous perforated stomach. An immediate operation—it was his third—brought no noticeable improvement to his condition. Hopeful reports alternated with disappointing ones. Life seemed grayer and more routine to me with him absent from the hospital. His staff of doctors tried hard to fill in for him, but we very much missed our teacher, with his kindness and his stimulating nature. Surgery seemed to us to lack the challenges it had before, and this absence spread to the other branches, probably because we had been slowly learning to think in an orderly fashion, and the diagnoses were beginning to arrange themselves nicely into groups.

For our first class in clinical medicine with Staehelin, a new student entered the room. When I saw him, I thought, "How handsome he is." That I took such certain notice of this fact often bothered me later, since he cost me many a bitter hour. He was very tall, nearly two meters [6'6"], with broad shoulders, large and intelligent eyes, and an aquiline nose. His manner was a bit indolent, his smile most captivating. After class he approached me as if we were old acquaintances and ambled with me to the pathology department, where we sat down together. When I was ready to leave with Wilhelm, Guénin (that was the handsome man's name) asked, "You would rather that we not be together constantly?" I replied, "Of course", and paid no more attention to him. I did not avoid him, but never did I seek him out. A few days later, he was assisting Staehelin. Astonishingly skilled and poised, he looked professorially down upon Staehelin, who was quite short, and virtually took over the entire class period from Staehelin. Establishing a diagnosis, suggestions for treatment, chemical formulas—he seemed to know everything. I have never seen anyone assist like that. Staehelin was enchanted; we were rather dumbfounded.

Shortly thereafter I was standing in the lobby of the medical department with a fellow student, Augustin, who was talking about Stifter and his prose; he had, in my opinion, some original views. Suddenly Guénin was standing between us. He needed a private word with me. I accompanied him to a spot a few paces distant; his question was completely insignificant: he wanted to know whom he should contact in order to recommend someone as a hospital attendant. I then returned to Augustin, who was anything but a delicate young man. We had hardly exchanged two words when Guénin—I never knew how—seized him in such a way that he turned him upside down in a flash, held his feet with one hand and paddled his rear end with the other. It all happened with lightning speed and was over before anyone knew what had happened. Guénin told me before leaving, "That's the way it will be each time."

I did not understand what he meant by "each time". Augustin acted as if nothing unusual had happened.

Hotz had been brought back to Switzerland, at his own request. When I heard he had arrived, I rejoiced. But I could tell from his sister's face how bad his condition was. He was in the Andlauer clinic. Nurse Hedi went on with her work in the hospital. Since he was not supposed to worry, he should know that work was going on as usual, even in his absence.

His sister's faithfulness made a lasting impression on me. Perhaps I really saw for the first time what service and sacrifice are. Even the naturalness with which she chose to be true to duty gave me much to reflect on. It seemed to me as if the spirit of the entire hospital were elevated because this one operating room nurse fulfilled her duty. My love for her was now joined by a very conscious respect for her.

I made little jellies out of oranges and lemons for Hotz. It made me proud and happy to hear that he always ate a bit of them.

Early in June, after very painful suffering, he died. It was said that he had been kind to the end and that his humor never left him. News of his death did not, of course, surprise me, but it affected me in a surprisingly profound way. We were at the hospital when we learned about it; it was as if the entire hospital in its deepest sense had suddenly ceased to exist. Staehelin told us of our teacher's death, and we left. I was standing alone on the Petersgraben, not knowing where I was headed, when suddenly Augustin was standing next to me and began to talk about Schiller. We wandered the streets around the hospital for the rest of the morning, making larger and smaller circuits, but with the hospital always reappearing in our sight; we never mentioned it, but it was the center. Schiller and responsibility, his mission as a writer. Doing what one has been called to do, doing it completely; not tolerating half-measures, at least not in one's heart. That was what Schiller had attempted, without interruption, which is what made him greater than Goethe. Next to Schiller: Hotz. Not to mourn. Those who are sent hand their mission on to others. Therefore we were not to mourn, at least not except as was required of us. Schiller, Hotz, and now us. I did not completely comprehend, and yet I comprehended.

Up until then, Augustin had not been especially close to the rest of us; he was somewhat older and already worked steadily in his father's medical practice. His motto was strange: take over anything but then give it up immediately in the event of any uncertainty. His father had begun medical practice at a very young age, probably did not have very extensive knowledge, but was always able to call the Basel medical professors in time or to refer his patients to them. His son did the same, under instructions from his father, and therefore knew most of the professors quite well; indeed, he functioned something like an employer to them and sounded as though he were clapping them a bit on the shoulder when he spoke of them. We knew little about his skills, for, when he could, he avoided assisting. His turn came occasionally, to be sure, but I remember nothing about those occasions except his unusual manner, which was so different from the customary behavior, as if his teachers were a bit embarrassed in his presence, the whole group of them.

And now Augustin was standing very close to me, yet he remained infinitely distant. Had he developed his thoughts without talking about Schiller, it would have been fine with me, as if I could have agreed with everything he said, indeed, as if he somehow had clothed my own unexpressed ideas with everyday language I could understand. But, through the poets, everything took on a foreign tone. Still, I would gladly have acknowledged something familiar, something I could always recognize, in this foreign tone.

Our walk lasted a very long time. Perhaps we placed no limit on it because it represented the shock of the collision of an old world with the future.

The next morning we had a meeting of the clinical students' executive board, at which we discussed various things concerning the participation in the funeral and also speculations about who would succeed Professor Hotz. The practical questions did not interest me very much; indeed, they were perfectly distasteful and seemed tactless to me; probably they were. In my heart I decided to resign from the executive board as soon as possible and, instead, to read Schiller.

That afternoon I went walking by myself. A foehn sky covered the landscape. Augustin and the executive board kept confronting each other in my head as if they were mutually exclusive, as if I was carrying both of them in me and now had to choose between them. I chose Augustin, albeit in a more personal form, that is, I chose prayer, for I ascribed more power to prayer than to action, yet I knew that I could not live from prayer alone, since in Protestantism there is no form of life for that. But mere action as the main purpose of a physician's life or of my life in general seemed impossible to me. Action, yes—perhaps. It was more or less necessary, but only in a secondary way, only after everything else had been surrendered to God to be formed, adapted, placed in his service, with no right of reclamation. A mystery is present in God's giving, even more so in his taking. I thought: Hotz now knows about this mystery; I almost envied him for it, in any case, I no longer sorrowed for him. It seemed to me that everything was good the way it was, and I would now have to try to serve in earnest.

The funeral took place the following morning. At first I could scarcely comprehend that it had not taken place long ago. It was as if one had to go about something once more that had already been taken care of; as if one almost had to breathe new life artificially into it. Yet reality soon swept me into its wake. A huge mass of people assembled in front of the little yellowish house on the Schanzenstraße. Ulrich, another student whose name I have forgotten, and I had to enter the house in order to pay last respects in the name of the clinical students. Everything was precisely planned, including the exact length of our visit, yet the house, which I was entering for the first time, seemed somehow desecrated by the coming and going of so many black-clad mourners, somehow seemed orphaned and enveloped in an ominous chaos, from which we were not exempt. We spoke words that said nothing, shook hands, desperately searched for the exit even though we had scarcely arrived. Once back on the street, it was difficult to find our group again, since everything had moved and the crowd had regrouped. In a well-ordered procession, we slowly walked to the Peterskirche, where the funeral ceremony was to take place. Many people had no place to sit; as students, we were given preference and had reserved seats. I can recall nothing of the speeches; all I could think of was how differently Hotz would have spoken to us on such an occasion; to us, for we counted ourselves among the sorrowful survivors who needed to be consoled but who also needed to be handed something living. But this something living was not to be had there. After that an endless procession made its way to the Kannenfeld cemetery. I was wearing a black dress that my mother had borrowed from a friend, the wife of Doctor Theile. The skirt was so narrow that it was perfectly suited to this slow pace. When I noticed that the narrowness was not constrictive under the circumstance, or that its constrictiveness was precisely right for the occasion, I was annoyed that such profane thoughts had captivated me. For once more I almost imagined that death must determine life from this point onward. Only after we marched past the open grave and saw the coffin lying deep within it did I finally know that death was only to accompany life but was not able to determine it.

Everyday life soon overtook all of us again. The biggest change was that, until a successor could be chosen, Merke and Heusser shared the surgical clinic. Their styles of teaching were decisively different, corresponding completely to their personalities and not yet shaped by any experience. Heusser taught as if he were wooing the students, trying to make his listeners his friends; the subject matter was as if the means toward that end; the patient was a function of Heusser's relationship to us. At first this style of teaching amused me, for it seemed childish but not disagreeable. Before long, however, it disgusted me, and then I attended his lectures very reluctantly. Merke spoke completely differently. For him, the patient and science seemed to be all that mattered; we students were like a necessary evil that he was forced to put up with, in front of whom he simply had to think aloud, without omitting the intermediate thought processes that were familiar to him but strange to us. I loved this aspect of our teacher but did not come any closer to the teacher himself. I was a little afraid of him, above all, it was mostly my ignorance that seemed to be afraid in the presence of his great learning. Several times I had to assist, which did not go too badly, especially because he had a very clear way of asking questions; one could already learn a lot from the very way he formulated the question.

The Neergard story continued. After he had performed so shamefully in our eyes by refusing to take any sort of responsibility, we decided to boycott his class. At the beginning of the summer semester, he announced a new lecture, with a theme that was designed for us and covering material that we really did urgently need to know. But we agreed among ourselves not to take the course. Neergard sought me out once during a break. He had heard rumors that I was the instigator behind the boycott, and he wanted to make peace with me. We talked a bit, back and forth, until finally I took a stand: I would be willing to reconcile our differences only if he would adopt a different stance toward himself but also toward us and toward the court. Couldn't he see the unworthiness of his behavior? He stated that he could not. And so our boycott remained firm, and he could find no students at all that semester.[1]

About the time our teacher Hotz died, we who had witnessed the cocaine incident were summoned to court to testify individually. I had to appear in the morning, which meant missing the last class period that morning. I was surprised that the officer of the court not only wanted a recounting of the entire incident but also demanded my personal opinion in detail and then, point by point, compared it, in front of me and with commentary, with Neergard's opinion, carefully delineating where the two differed. What the court officer thought about this was impossible to know, but I was quite happy to see how attentive he was in noting all differences in interpretation.

When I returned home, the maid informed me that a tall man with a portfolio under his arm had been urgently inquiring for me. I thought it probably had to do with the morning's court session and was eager to know who had been at our house. From the description I could not imagine who it was.

Aunt Marguerite happened to be visiting us then, something that occurred rarely, for she was still running her flower shop and had vey little free time at her disposal. We all loved her a lot and always showered her with questions. Since she had great practical sense and good taste, she was asked to take a hand in all our decisions about clothes and home furnishings. She never tired of coming up with advice or of receiving and giving her opinion about new proposals,

---

[1] Adrienne continued to boycott Neergard's classes until he finally resigned his professorial chair and moved to Zurich—Ed.

and she also knew how to explain well how to make things, how to find inexpensive yet attractive things. In those days I seldom wore a dress with which she was not somehow associated. And Aunt Marguerite was also always willing to help out by loaning her own things.

And so she was with us that day. While we were having coffee in the blue room (since our time in La Chaux-de-Fonds, my mother always had a blue room), she was helping me knit a yellow sweater in a complex openwork pattern for my sister. Suddenly the maid appeared and said that the aforementioned gentleman would like to see me in the parlor. The parlor was next to the blue room, and you could hear every word from one room to the other through the thin wooden doors. I went to the parlor, where I found Guénin, my handsome fellow student. He was more lying than sitting on the sofa, with his legs crossed and extending over the side edge of the Empire couch. Unabashedly smoking a cigarette, he acted exactly as if he were alone and at home. Without rising, he offered me his hand. The whole situation was most bizarre; I sensed that something completely unusual was taking place and was made even more uneasy by the knowledge of the way sound traveled through the walls. I think the first thing I said was "Don't speak loudly." He obeyed and, in apparent total self-assurance, told me he had come to ask me whether we would get married right at the beginning of vacation or not until a little later. Now it was I who had trouble keeping my voice down. I told him as calmly as I could that marriage was absolutely out of the question; in the first place I did not want to marry at all, and, in the second place, if I did marry anyone, it would definitely not be him. He did not let that disconcert him. He knew what he knew, and that was enough for him; I should not keep my feelings a secret; he was happy about my love but had thought that I would have been intelligent enough to say yes without making a fuss about it, for it was perfectly evident that I loved him as much as he loved me. Nothing helped. He was unshakable in his opinion.

As I more or less vehemently threw him out of the house, he promised in the most matter-of-fact way to return that evening. He had chosen this day and no other for our engagement because it had become clearer than ever to him, when I was nowhere to be found at Staehelin's lecture that morning, how much he loved me and that he could no longer bear not knowing where I was at any given time. I forbade his coming that evening but knew that my command would be useless, no matter how firmly expressed. It was utterly impossible to change his mind or his intention. He was so certain of himself that my words made no impression. Their meaning seemed to be lost; he did not hear them; I didn't even know if he perceived their sound.

When I finally returned to the blue room, Aunt Marguerite was most concerned to know what was going on. I was still so shaken that only with great effort could I manage to say that someone had asked to marry me. Immediately Mama became very interested in the story. Although I assured her that the whole thing was absolutely hopeless, she wanted to know as much as possible, so I stood there helplessly and told her what I knew, which was very little, yet Mama found reason for hope even in the tiniest detail. In every way Guénin seemed to her to be the son-in-law she had wished for. Believing that I could stop Mama from perpetuating the state of affairs, for she suddenly seemed to have taken the reins in hand and wanted to follow up on everything personally, I told her about Guénin's poor manners, his lack of principles and his inconsiderateness. These were precisely the sorts of things about which Mama was very sensitive, but not in this instance. She seemed enchanted and was looking forward to meeting him that evening; she was already marveling at his persistence.

That evening I went to visit Georgine Gerhard. Mama received the suitor. I would have preferred not to return home at all. Late in the evening I phoned to find out if he had left. He had, so I returned home. Mama had found him to be very genial and pleasant (I myself never thought he was not genial) and had arranged with him to visit his parents in Delsberg in the near future. Would I like to come along? Certainly not. Next my wardrobe became a topic for discussion. My everyday dress was really too old; Mama wanted to have a new one made for me. I declined. Mama assured me that a future bride had to look more attractive. I wanted to know nothing about any "future bride". A few days later I learned from Mama that Guénin had been happy to hear I had refused the offer of new clothes; I was perfectly right; only inner values mattered to him. "I love her in her blue everyday dress" became a household word. There were days when this was the sole topic of conversation in the house, then there were days on which nothing was said about the matter.

Then Mama actually did go to Delsberg. She came back radiantly happy: the family was charming and was ready to receive me as their daughter-in-law, even willing to wait as long as it took for me to give my consent. Mama and the Guénins had come to the firm conclusion that the wait would not be a long one. Mama was inexhaustible in relating the details of her reception: I learned what the silverware was like, what the pastries looked like; both the white apron of the serving maid and the future father-in-law's mustache were supposed to have an effect on me. All of this meant nothing to me; they were perhaps perfectly proper and nice in themselves, but they could never have anything to do with my life. A marriage with Guénin simply was out of the question. That night I wept pitifully in my attic room; everything seemed horrible, and there was no way to escape. Mama seemed to take no account whatsoever of my resistance; in her eyes it had already been overcome. I considered the wildest plans: running away, serving as a physician on a ship. I didn't see how I would have the strength to cope with all that at home, to fight with Mama again like I had done at the beginning of my medical studies. And then it seemed to me, too, that all my plans for life lacked any real consistency; I had never really taken marriage into account. And yet some element was still missing, something that was not to be found at Saint-Loup and yet ought one day to take some kind of shape and develop into a real path. The more I thought about it, however, the less I was able to figure out what that might be.

Mama changed her tactics here and there in the following days. At the moment when it was farthest from my mind, she might suddenly ask, as if by chance: "What should I tell the Guénins about you? I'm writing to them now." Then there was a day or two of peace and quiet, and suddenly she assailed me with all sorts of questions: Who ought to be invited, whether we ought to have two celebrations, one for the engagement and another for the wedding, whether I had thought about the gift registry, and all sorts of similar things. It almost drove me to despair. And Mama was always immensely surprised when I said I had no thought whatsoever of marrying. She insisted, "That's precisely what all girls say just before they say yes."

Despite all this, time passed. My work as an intern's assistant in surgery began early in July. I had firmly decided to work as if nothing unsettling were in the air. And I looked forward to the work. Actually, it captivated me from the outset, and all the problems and questions associated with this kind of work fascinated me. There was always so much to do that one never kept up, yet it was a peaceful and joyful sort of work, never hectic. I was assigned to Doctor Theodor Huber, who worked in women's ward number one. We had about forty surgical cases to handle, which changed very often, for these were above all cases calling for operations. We spent entire mornings in the operating room, and, since only one operating room was available at that time (the other one was undergoing repairs), the day's work began very early. Usually the first incision was scheduled for about five or five-thirty in the morning, and the youngest assistants, which naturally included me, were blessed with assisting at the earliest. There was no end to what could be observed and learned. All of my family was away on vacation, so I was alone in the house at Sevogelplatz. I would get up about four in the morning and usually walked to the hospital. It took about a half-hour to travel the empty streets, and one somehow felt that one was participating in the city's early awakening. The day was still cool; it lay there like an unimpaired promise; the hospital entrance was peaceful; in the wards everything seemed still to be asleep; the interns' room, where I fetched my white apron, was empty. Precisely the undisturbed emptiness and silence of the hospital showed that one really belonged there; no pretense was necessary. These were happy tokens; it was good to live with them.

The operating room was already busy. Nurses were scrubbing up and preparing the instruments. In the corridor stood an empty bed, whose occupant was in the small neighboring room and had already been anesthetized. Soon all the interns and staff physicians arrived, and then one operation after another took place. My task was above all to keep the operating field clear for the surgeon, using large forceps, and also to keep the blood swabbed away. Often I had small special assignments: a narcotic, a local anesthetic, a suture, a clamp. With each new procedure one definitely felt that the profession was becoming serious; the calling was becoming more and more irrevocable; there was no going back.

In between we accompanied the interns on their rounds, carried out minor assignments, and then returned to the operating room.

After about a week, I assisted for the first time with a goiter operation, and with Doctor Merke, of whom I was more than a little afraid. For me, he was the epitome of the surgeon: daring, always calm, and superior. I was so excited I could not sleep all night. I was afraid I would not insert the hooks properly, would not swab the blood away quickly enough, would not be able to hold my own in the presence of this master, and, beyond that, afraid I might harm the patient. As I made my way to the hospital early in the morning, I quite naturally scolded myself for letting myself get so worked up, not because my confidence had somehow increased, but because I realized that it would have been far smarter to have slept well and to have embarked on the adventure in better shape. But nothing could be done about that now; my realization had come too late. As I was anxiously scrubbing up, Merke came in and, in his calm and matter-of-fact way, well in advance of the operation, gave me instructions about what I would have to do. During the operation, he continued to give his explanations and, between explanations, chatted a bit with the patient. This conversation made it seem as if we were all bound together in common work. My fear had long since vanished; what remained was great trust and a new kind of commitment that strengthened my sense of responsibility for everything that happened to the patient. From that day onward, I assisted Merke almost daily. Each operation constituted a certain high point that always made me very happy.

Another peak experience were the brief private rounds I made from bed to bed on my own in the evening before I went home. This had a human, not a surgical, purpose. Some patients had a great need to talk about all sorts of things and told me about their concerns and joys, their life at home, what they hoped for from their hospital stay. Many of them really perceived this time as a turning point in their lives, and they wanted to learn things from it that would strengthen them later and give them a new perspective for their everyday life and its challenges. For some, their hospital stay was an experience that gave them something as yet indefinable: a first perception of a life consisting of values different from those well-established values of their life at home. These values seemed for the moment to have slipped to one side, but—as they already sensed—they would return all too soon to occupy their customary place. Some patients were surprised that these values were unable to withstand a first and seemingly more serious test from a distance. Others discovered for the first time just what it was they valued. Obviously an accident or an illness, followed by the not insignificant fear of an operation, the embarrassment of suffering, the exposure of treatment, the friendliness of the nurses, the abruptness or the kindness of the doctor, the oddness of living among strangers, the slow adaptation to new surroundings, the acceptance of heretofore unaccustomed practices—all of these deprived the ground of its former solidity. New notions, new possibilities emerged. Generally it did not take long for the person's character, that which really constituted his foundation, to become apparent, and we who were a part of the hospital were often offered an opportunity to intervene and give some helpful clarity.

Two aspects played a role at that time; they seemed a bit odd but were in fact obviously natural and necessary. The first was my incorporation into the hospital. I felt as if I myself were a part of it, that it was a life to which my life belonged. The knowledge that I would only be an intern's assistant for a short time did not affect this. I knew that my three months in this position would pass quickly, yet I really did belong to the hospital. I felt as if I were in my own atmosphere, in my world, a world that was just as present here as it had been at the Waldau or in the hospitals of my childhood in La Chaux-de-Fonds. There was quite simply a belonging.

The second aspect was a deep feeling of responsibility toward all people, toward the nurses and the patients. The interns escaped this feeling. Since they were already trained doctors, they looked a bit condescendingly upon us. With the exception of Doctor Merke, the senior physician [*Oberarzt*]—who really perhaps observed their milieu rather than lived within it—the interns formed a circle that was firmly established more in a human than in a medical sense. New arrivals among the interns had some difficulty gaining access, but, once inside, they soon adopted the curious custom of arrogantly standing apart. Everything was rated strictly according to seniority rather than ability or demonstrated talent. Anyone who had not been there very long was considered a "dunce". And time was measured, not in years, which might have meant something as far as knowledge was concerned, but in months, weeks, and days. As assistants to the interns, we were generally treated with slight contempt, even though individual preferences were shown, whether merited or not. For that reason, we had little contact with the life of the interns and their behavior. We observed all this with silent astonishment. Once you understood it—it was like the rules of a game—you did not need to be concerned about it anymore. In any case, we could have done nothing to change it, since we were not directly involved. Besides, we had plenty of work to keep us occupied—beautiful work that I loved with all my heart.

A very particular disposition to help others had to be developed, something I had no notion of before entering the hospital. I had anticipated the opportunities for surgical training, and I had thought, of course, about the people involved, but about people whose complete helplessness was shown by and limited to their need for a surgical procedure and who needed to be prepared in body and spirit to endure the operation, perhaps a long illness, and even death. I had never imagined that the main problem for many people would turn out to be precisely their convalescence.

The majority of the nurses in my ward were deaconesses. They cultivated a very exclusive form of class prejudice. Not toward me, for they were very nice to me and helped me wherever they could. But toward the other nurses, the so-called "free nurses", they closed themselves off as if behind a wall wherever possible. This was most clearly visible when they had something to eat between meals. Sometimes these snacks were augmented by a cake that a patient or someone else had donated. Regardless whether the food had been given to a deaconess or a "free nurse", it became common property, yet ordinarily the larger pieces went to the deaconesses and smaller pieces to the helpers. I later encountered similar things in other wards and in various hospitals. I was always among the favored ones, and I occasionally dared to protest slightly, but I always felt too much of a guest, perhaps also too young, and never protested energetically enough.

Eating was relegated to one particular place during that period. I was living alone at the Sevogelplatz. On my first day, I ate lunch in one of the restaurants in the city but did not enjoy it; from that point on, I skipped the noon meal and stayed in the hospital to do some laboratory work. Since I never had time to prepare breakfast in the morning, I also did without that. Instead, there was the *Znüni*, the midmorning snack with the nurses, which was often quite hearty, with soup and pudding, occasionally also cake, as I said before, and not infrequently also sardines, since one of the deaconesses' taste for sardines was well known among the patients, and patients who wanted to show their gratitude would donate sardines to enrich the *Znüni* menu. After that I would eat nothing until late in the evening, at home, where I would always cook canned peas with vanilla cream. I always cooked enough of these in a large pot to last for a week or so; when I came home at night, I would place my supper by my bed, take a bath, and then eat while lying in bed, just before falling asleep. I was always tired but also very happy.

As far as I can recall, I prayed very little during that period. When I had time for reflection, I usually thought about the expressed and unexpressed concerns of the patients and tried to deal with them in a larger framework that somehow flowed into God. All through the day I would say innumerable short and fervent prayers to God, but there was no contemplation or sustained prayer. I did not feel estranged from God, but the question of greater closeness or deeper understanding came up seldom or not at all.

Merke was Catholic. This often made a kind of question

arise within me. A touching little Nurse Käthi from the Baldegg nursing school was also there, assisting a deaconess in one of the larger rooms. One morning I suddenly found her in bed in a double room, the very one in which I had lain two years earlier. She complained about tremendous exhaustion, and it turned out that she had a debilitating blood disease that was considered incurable. She was inconsolable, for she wanted so badly to live. She could never make her father understand that, after having spent so much money for her to attend school, now she was going to die. That was what really bothered her. When she saw that her father was far more upset by her illness and with caring for her, she found his fatherly behavior so splendid that she began to hope for a recovery.

The operating room was a special area with its own atmosphere, and that atmosphere was not determined only by the smell of ether. I cannot recall ever having experienced anything like it, and I still do not know whether it was entirely owing to the influence of Nurse Hedi Hotz. I think it probably was. At that time I probably did not even know the word "asceticism", but to this day, when I want to visualize what real asceticism looks like, I think of the example of that operating room, and it proves inexhaustible in the consistent fullness of its essence. Regardless of whether things were quiet or operations were going on in every corner and emergency cases were raining down on us, the nurses were calm and remained calm. The toughest challenges were taken for granted; a doctor might lose his head from time to time, but the nurses never did. The instruments never rattled in their hands. It was as if they had hands made to bring about order, which, even during the most difficult operation, never lost the ability to serve and thereby still to bring order. Even though they stood uninterruptedly in the operating room for six or eight or ten or more hours, in the midst of the most exhausting activity, they never left the room without getting it completely ready again for whatever emergency might come the following moment. There were no moods or tempers, no raised voices and no stubbornness, only a willingness that forgot itself totally in order to serve. If there were a break, the nurses once more revealed personalities with clearly developed characteristics and definite preferences. But once in service, they knew nothing but service. How often did I not see this, as a group sat in the so-called "little room" making swabs as a form of relaxation, and the operating room messenger announced an emergency. Nurse Hedi immediately designated who should answer the call; she knew very well just how much energy each member of her staff had in reserve. Usually she went as well, for she did not know how to spare herself and always was the first to do what she asked of others. There were no sighs or objections. Whoever was designated went, as gracious as always, and no one could tell from her expression that she had been robbed of her rest period.

This manner of being gradually made a very great impression on me. At first I viewed it as a completely natural reaction to the difficulty of this profession, and I may also have thought that the nurse's tasks, even the manual labor and the selection and preparation of the instruments, were sufficiently interesting to implant this attitude in Nurse Hedi and her staff. Over time, however, I noticed that this sort of self-denial was a form of genuine, almost anonymous love. The greatest trustworthiness, vigilance, and calm were all a service of love. Realizing this shamed me not a little. Up to now I had often been very fascinated by the sick, and naturally their illnesses also had their fascination, almost apart from the patient. But that everything was bound up in the unity of the person, not merely the unity of an individual person, but that of all people together, in a genuine bond to which love had its decisive word to say, all of this I understood first through Nurse Hedi. Were it not for her, I would soon have found assisting with chronic appendicitis at second hand no longer interesting but even rather boring. All of this now changed, yet without letting the medically and scientifically important things fade.

One early morning—I was alone in the washroom, wearing a large and heavy rubber apron, with my feet in the very long, broad, and clumsy rubber overshoes, my hands in the wash basin, and my thoughts on some splendid medical problem—Nurse Hedi suddenly came up to me and explained to me how I was not being careful enough with the aprons, was letting sterilized things come into contact with unsterilized things, even sometimes letting the apron's belt drag on the floor before tying it. She said it in a stern, really disappointed voice. I plummeted from the clouds, deeply grieved. She was certainly right about what she had said, but at that moment it was as if I had been expelled from paradise, as if through a bit of inattentiveness I had forfeited all right to work in the operating room, which was among my favorite work. Yet slowly insight dawned. I realized that it was completely useless to admire something from outside, to admire the ordered life in the surgical ward, the perfect willingness of the nurses, and who knows what else, if one did not unconditionally attempt to fit oneself vitally into this existing, constant, yet always living and developing order, indeed, to subordinate oneself to it, so to speak, anonymously, to observe each instruction, each law or letter precisely and with one's entire spirit. This was a new realization for me, but it was in no way a happy one, because I had already acquired bad habits, and it would not be easy, despite Nurse Hedi's precise description, to get rid of them and always notice their recurrence.

At home later that night I was very discouraged. Although the mistakes Nurse Hedi pointed out to me may have been noticed by her alone, they were genuine transgressions against the rules for sterilization. She had noticed them from her sure and experienced superiority, and I had really committed these mistakes, crassly and visibly, despite being an eager and willing worker. How must everything else appear, the things that only God, or perhaps even other people who remained silent, saw? Moreover, if I were to accuse myself of something to anyone in surgery, it would never have occurred to me that I had erred precisely in the inner sanctum of surgery. Suddenly I thought once more about the sacrament of confession, and I longed for it, not only because we are required to search out our mistakes in order then to confess them and thus to seek a path for improvement, but also because God would possess a special kind of presence in confession, a presence that would have to be consoling, encouraging, and purifying, in a sense that was incomprehensible to me yet infinitely vast. In the end I found consolation even in the mere thought of confession. The person of a priest did not bother me at all, for he surely had to be clothed with a sort of anonymity, which would not need to be very different from that of the operating room staff. Nurse Hedi had admonished me in the name of sterilization; the priest would do it in the name of God. And that was certainly good. From the next day forward, I handled the belt of my apron not merely with greater care but with real love. I owed it almost as much as I did the beloved Nurse Hedi.

THE FIRST OF AUGUST

It was a fairly hot summer, with frequent thunderstorms. Often there would be thunder and lightning early in the morning, occasionally a bit of rain, but no relief from the heat. This holiday on the first of August[1] was humid and tiresome. We were doing surgery in the smaller operating room, since the larger one was being renovated over the summer. It was particularly hot in the smaller operating room; the ventilation system had broken down, and we were cramped for space. One often thought of those who were doing surgery in Africa or somewhere else in the tropics; one was not exactly envious of them but did compare oneself with them and had a sense of having shared something of the same experience with extreme heat. But the experience did not bring any new courage along with it.

The first of August was not the only feast day, for the whole city celebrated countless festivals that summer. There was a nautical exhibition, with a festival ship anchored in Little Basel, complete with a bar and dancing. The interns paid it a visit and reported with some enthusiasm about their evenings. I was not particularly attracted to it, although I would not have minded spending a couple of hours there. On this first of August, when the operating room was at its most stifling and no one seemed to be working with much enjoyment, Merke suddenly arrived, and it turned out that we were alone for a moment while we were washing in the room next to the operating room (the alcohol solution that normally seemed so refreshing to the skin was merely luke-

---

[1] Celebrating August 1, 1291, when the original three Swiss cantons formed their "Everlasting League" against the Habsburgs—Trans.

warm that day, but Doctor Merke seemed not to notice). He rubbed his hands vigorously and cheerfully, then folded them for a moment in the washbasin, as surgeons often have a custom of doing, and announced, almost in passing: "Everyone wants to go on the ship this evening. I think that you and I can take care of things by ourselves." I don't think I've ever in my entire life felt so grown-up as when I heard those words. I was anxious—anything could happen!—but also felt honored, as if I already really understood something about surgery. I would have really liked to shout with joy, but neither my new dignity nor the location permitted me that. I forgot to respond. Only after Merke asked "Is that okay with you?" did I murmur a nearly indifferent "Yes". Yet it was a Yes that possessed a meaning, a lasting and forever binding Yes. All my previous experiences, decisions, joys, and anxieties fused together in it and became constitutive parts of a new promise. Perhaps a teacher never knows how much he obligates his pupils. When I later encountered Merke during the most tragic hours of my life and still later, during the most difficult hours of his life, this Yes lived on; it was a certainty in me, a support where no other support seemed to be given. This was in some way the reason I asked him to be my sponsor when I was received into the Church; that seemed to me like a continuation, the natural expression of a very great gratitude and bond.

EDITOR'S EPILOGUE

The story breaks off here, in the middle of the chapter. Fatigue probably removed Adrienne's pen from her hand. Some loose threads remain unconnected and can only be integrated by material from other accounts, notably from the oral autobiography (in volume seven of the German edition of the posthumous works): Guénin pursued her periodically for a number of years and caused her difficulties even after she was married. Her friendship with Franz Merke, which had only begun to blossom, became more firmly established; Merke truly rescued her from the brink of suicide after the death of her first husband; she, in turn, gave him support later when he lost his beloved only child. Her friendship with Adolf Portmann developed harmoniously, whereas contact with other friends from her student days became infrequent or ended entirely.

At the end of the present account, Adrienne was only twenty-four years old. She died at the age of sixty-five. The decisive turning point in her life, the conversion to Catholicism that was to bring fulfillment to the passionate, desperate search she has described here, still lies far off, separated by fourteen years. Her quest continued, through important events that marked the intervening years. A year after the point at which her story breaks off, she received enough money from a relative to take an independent vacation for the first time; but while she was in San Bernardino, her friends from Basel organized a plot to match her with the youthful Professor Emil Dürr, a widower with two small children. After desperate resistance, she finally, so to speak, succumbed to superior forces—out of sympathy for a man

1965

whose goodness touched her and out of perplexity in the
face of the will of God, a will that, to be sure, demanded everything of her but without showing her how. She grew to
love Emil Dürr so much—and her years with him became
increasingly a search for God and for the true Church—
that, as already mentioned, she seemed thrown completely
offtrack by his death. A year after her marriage, she had
passed the exams for government board certification [*Staatsexamen*] and had then taken on various interim positions
until 1930. In 1931 she had opened her own practice in
Basel, which now became the real focus of her activity, even
during the first years of her second marriage (to Professor
Werner Kaegi), just as she also carried out with great care
her responsibilities as wife, mother, and housewife. Much
of what she had striven for throughout her entire youth,
without yet having the proper professional competence to
accomplish it, was now possible: to be entirely at the service of her neighbor and to do so as a mission from God,
out of a bond of prayer with God and in a way that permitted her always to keep the entire personality, the bodily,
spiritual, and religious well-being, of her patients in view,
from God's perspective. Above all the poor were constantly
close to her heart; she took care of many of her patients
gratis.

And yet the synthesis she had always been searching for
had not yet been attained; she had not yet found the locus
toward which all the signs and hints of her youth converged
like dotted concentric lines. She was always aware of some
of these signs: the ones that had pushed her from the outside
in the direction of Catholicism, of which she still had no
kind of inward, intellectual knowledge and which seemed
like an empty spare room; for example the allusions made
by Madeleine Gallet and the Lacroix sisters. Other signs,

which lay much deeper and were positive, seemed at the
time as if submerged, buried alive, although they undoubtedly were at work out of sight: her early encounter with
Ignatius and especially her vision of the Mother of God.
These signs made themselves known very strongly at the
time of her marriage, for was she not as a whole, body and
soul, sealed up for God, preserved for his use alone? A simple "synthesis" of relationship to God and love of neighbor in marriage was not her ultimate goal; it could only
be something temporary, intended for the interim in which
the ultimate solution had not yet come into view. All of
this becomes clear from the pages of her second autobiography. And thus her religious quest continued unabated even
during the years of her most strenuous professional work.
Again and again she sought an opportunity finally to clarify
with a Catholic priest her most basic concerns; again and
again this opportunity escaped her, to her great disappointment.

When I began to instruct her in the Catholic faith in 1940,
the harvest was ripe, almost overripe. Each Catholic truth
that was outwardly new to her proved to be what she had
long expected inwardly and with longing; each truth fit fully
into an already prepared and painfully empty space; directly
after her conversion, on the Feast of All Saints, the heavens
opened up over her soul and poured down streams of the
most extraordinary charisms. Her spirit was led through all
of the heights and depths, for it had been prepared from the
beginning to give an unconditional Yes to everything. The
vision of the Virgin Mary and her encounter with Ignatius
now revealed their existential meaning, the purpose toward
which her life had always been journeying: the absolute Yes
of the Handmaid of the Lord, absolute loving obedience
in imitation of Christ. Even to sketch this unprecedented

1965

1947

profusion of graces is beyond the scope of this epilogue; the books published up to now and particularly the posthumous works to be published later bear witness to them. But it is still important to mention here that the "either-or" of Adrienne's mission as stated by Madeleine Gallet, "either medicine or the monastery", was transcended after her conversion. The synthesis that had seemed impossible was granted her, and she became the foundress of a secular institute that made precisely this synthesis the way of life of its members: to live the evangelical counsels in the midst of secular occupations. It was Adrienne's concern that the unity of the two be achieved uncompromisingly with as much purity and authenticity as possible.

The account of her youth already shows that she was like the young man in the fairy tale who set out to learn fear. Adrienne possessed a natural and religious courage that, despite the great vulnerability of her soul, could not be shaken by anything. And this courage was all the more necessary when the great charisms began to arrive, for now it was not a matter merely of suffering passively but of consciously saying Yes to every fear of the redemption, including the unfathomable mysteries of Holy Saturday, of the Savior's descent into the most extreme forlornness and abandonment that human freedom can ever get caught in. It was to this end that Adrienne's soul for many years was kept open and mysteriously prepared. When all the posthumous works are published, it will be possible to view the present description of her youth as a preliminary negative for all the mysteries of faith that are later printed as a positive image in her existence. These long years of negative imprint were, as a whole, inwardly fragmentary, and their real meaning can only be understood through the later developments of her life. This can perhaps console us for the fact that the present account of her life, which would have had to break off in any case with the year 1940 (after which the administration of Adrienne's mission was placed essentially in the hands of her spiritual director), remains a fragment.

APPENDIX
GRANDMOTHER'S HOUSE

In order to understand the story, one needs to know that I was always horrified by creeping animals: insects, bugs with legs, spiders with their webs, all of these were abominations to me when I was a child. I was afraid they might sting or be inadvertently swallowed. But once, when there were a few such beasts near the window at Grandmother's house, she said, "They just come over from the cherry tree." Suddenly it was as if my fear had taken flight. I thought: if they come from the cherry tree, then they have a special right to exist, they, so to speak, belong to the house, for the cherry tree leaned against the house, and its branches reached right up to Grandmother's window in the summer. After that, whenever I found insects in Grandmother's house I had no fear of them, indeed, I even respected them as rightful inhabitants of the house.

I relate this merely so that one can see by means of this confession what Grandmother's presence and the atmosphere in her house meant to me: even what I disliked was transformed into something precious there. And if by the end of this tale the house seems a bit like something out of a fairy tale, one ought simply to know that it was in fact a fairy-tale house.

First the window requires description. The window where the aforementioned insects were found was next to Grandmother's worktable. Grandmother sat from morning to evening on her chair by this window and sewed and knitted, mostly for the poor but a little also for her grandchildren. While she was still alive, there was a war in Bulgaria, or somewhere in that region, and the massacre of the Ar-

menians, a really hideous story. The orphans of those areas
were completely real to Grandmother, as much present as
we were or the maids' children or the poor children on the
streets.

When she looked up from her work, she always looked
out through the window. And through the window one
could see the peaceful garden, which was a world of its own,
containing everything within it. No matter what the season,
no matter what the mood, it was a very special garden. In
the city we had a very small garden next to our house, but
it was much too small to capture the life of heaven. Grandmother's garden, however, was of one piece with the great
mystery of heaven.

And when it rained or snowed, the garden almost took on
a festive mood, receiving as a gift what had descended from
heaven, placing itself, as it were, at heaven's disposal in order
to make the gift appear more beautiful. For instance, when
the garden received the snowfall, it became very still under
the descending snowflakes, merely holding itself steady so
that the snow would find places to spread out and really be
snow, remaining totally white. The garden's paths, hillocks,
and bushes gradually disappeared completely under the snow
until one could no longer tell where they had once been;
everything was transformed into a still, white plane. And
one always knew that Grandmother also saw this snow. Or
the rain. If it had rained a lot, the paths were eroded and
lakes were left behind for a long, long time. The garden
consisted, really, of two large meadows that were encircled
by walkways in the form of a figure eight. When it rained
hard, it looked as if there were three very elongated lakes in
the garden. They looked like the Walensee on the geography map that hung in the hallway. When the rain stopped,
the sun came out and was mirrored in these lakes—which

were really just large ponds—making everything shimmer. But we always had the feeling that everything looked especially beautiful when viewed from Grandmother's window.

Once I came to Grandmother with a large bump on my head. Grandmother was very frightened because she had heard me fall down the steps and thought something terrible had happened. So now she was quite happy, seeing that it was nothing serious, and wanted to give me a big present; I was to choose. I made up my mind very quickly but did not dare say it. So she said she would like to guess. First she asked, "Do you want a new doll?" (But she knew very well that I did not want any new doll.) Then: "Do you want the whole chocolate that is in the drawer?" (She had a certain drawer where she kept chocolate for the grandchildren and for the poor children.) But that was not what I wanted either. Grandmother knew from the first what was important. So she finally asked: "Would you like to sit all afternoon at my table and have the window to yourself?" And that was exactly right. It happened to be an afternoon when it was snowing. So I looked out the window all afternoon, from time to time reading or knitting a little. But that was unimportant, for I could not get my fill of watching how the snow fell and fell and fell. Finally one could see how night was very slowly approaching; and, like the snow, the night came down from heaven. Then Grandmother went out to the veranda and lit a lamp, just for me, so that now one corner of the garden was illuminated, and one could see how the snow continued to fall during the night.

But now something must be said about lights at Grandmother's. For she had gaslights in her living room, where she spent most of her time, and these lights always sang a bit. And it was always an event when it began to grow dark and

Grandmother would say, "Now I'll light." For us at home this was nothing very important, since we had electricity. But here it was very mysterious, for one had to produce the light with a match, and afterward one could never forget the light, since it constantly hissed and hummed very softly, but never on the same pitch, rather, up and down like a little melody. Lamps were lit in the other rooms, lamps that the maid had to spend a long time cleaning each morning. And when, at age seven or eight, we were permitted for the first time to carry one of these lamps—while it was burning! —from one room to another, we knew that now we were grown up!

Grandmother, sitting day in, day out at her window, was like someone who was constantly waiting for something and was inwardly totally ready for whatever she was always waiting for. She was so prepared that, when someone came to her with some sort of concern, with something on his conscience, or to ask a question, she always knew precisely what he wished to express and also what she wanted to say to console him and restore peace.

And she also told stories. Her stories were always of the sort that afterward your heart was light. It was always as if you had been waiting for exactly this story, anxious for this one and no other. She told stories from her youth or recounted the story of the house or told many stories about God. And when she spoke about God, you knew that she knew him very well. She knew exactly what God liked and what God did not like, so precisely that she could speak in God's place. And if she found it necessary to scold you because you had done something wrong, she would say, for example, "the Christ Child would not have done that." Or she would say, "When Jesus says, 'Let the little ones come to me', of course he meant children who are well-behaved, who have already told the foolish things they have done and don't want to do anything so foolish again."

Whenever Grandmother finished something—and nearly every day she finished two or three items—she always carried it into an anteroom. Three large cupboards were to be found there in which she placed the things that were to be given away. And then, on special occasions or when a collection was being taken or when Christmas was approaching, she would make up large packets out of the things she had made and give the packets away. But one shelf belonged to us. On this shelf was a large white box in which Grandmother placed the things she had knitted and sewed and crocheted for our dolls. And she always found some pretext to distribute a reward, which meant that we could choose one item from the box. In a cupboard next to it were the fruit preserves, a huge collection of jars. If one asked, "But Grandmother, do you really eat all that jam?" She would answer, "No, but whoever can eat jam himself must also have some to give to the poor." She often visited the sick, and, when she did, she would take along some of her jars of jam for the sick and the poor. A light fragrance of fruit preserves would spread from this cupboard throughout the whole house when she opened it, which she did frequently. And beside the preserves she had tiny green oranges and all sorts of exotic fruits preserved in sugar, fruits that she had received from foreign lands like Japan. For, as a young wife, she had made a world tour with Grandfather, so she had friends everywhere, and they would send her all sorts of things. She had preserved the green oranges in a sweet-sour syrup according to a detailed recipe from Japan, the oranges' place of origin. Once when I was permitted to taste these green oranges and remarked that I did not think they were good, Grandmother said, "I don't either, but, you know, the

Adrienne being embraced by her grandmother

woman who sent them to me did so with such great love, as if they were something very especially good, that you just have to eat them as if they were something very especially good." With those words she explained how attitudes can transform things.

When staying with Grandmother, one left the living room in the evening to go to the dining room at the back; this was very dark and much less well heated than the living room. It always seemed a bit peculiar to pass into this room. Something else was quite different at Grandmother's from at home: you were permitted to eat supper at the same time as the adults and to eat the same things. At home, supper was always gruel and prunes that had been softened by soaking. At Grandmother's, there were all sorts of things that one was unaccustomed to, perhaps even a bit uncanny, and certainly not particularly good. The nicest thing was when you could go back into the living room after supper for a moment, for it was warm and cozy there.

But in the summer, when for once we had a nice warm day (which was fairly rare in La Chaux-de-Fonds), we spent a lot of time in the garden. Grandmother always pulled the weeds from the pathways herself. If it had rained previously, the gravel would be covered with thin, green, moist membranes. This happened several times each summer, more in some places than in others. To remove all of them required hours of work from Grandmother, and we were permitted to help her. When I was very small, I was afraid of these little membranes, for they were like limp balloons.

I think I need to say something about this fear. When I was very small, I once received a real balloon. I fastened it to the doll cradle with a string. But during the night the balloon burst or lost all its air in some other way, and, when I went to fetch it in the morning, the string hung straight down to the ground, and at its end was a ghastly violet skin. A terrible fear came over me: something that had looked so beautiful the day before . . . and now. . .! The more people tried to make me understand that all balloons must end up this way, the more my fear increased. This was perhaps the only time in my entire childhood that I suffered such awful fear. It was probably the first time I encountered transitoriness and, with it, death. I cried at the sight, yet at home I did not dare reveal the depth of my fear. I was simply incapable of expressing it. But that afternoon I went to Grandmother's, and when she asked, "Didn't you bring your balloon with you?", I had to say "No" and began to cry again. Thereupon Grandmother explained to me at length how things are in the world and that they wouldn't be at all the same in heaven. In heaven, balloons would always stay as they were. In the world, however, there are many things that one day simply pass away. That makes people feel sorry, but it is simply a sign of the world. It is as if God wants to show us that as long as all people are not nice, he cannot let the things that give us joy continue. Now I felt as if I understood very well, but I still always felt a little bit of anxiety when I thought about the balloon. And, whenever the algae appeared in the garden after a rain, I could not help thinking about the balloon.

In the garden stood the cherry tree. At best it yielded two to four cherries a year. They were large, plump, white, and red, but we never were permitted to taste them. They were reserved for Grandfather. Once I asked Grandmother whether she wasn't sorry that she had never had one of these cherries. She said, "No, no", and added that she was just as happy as we were that the cherry tree blossomed and then was so especially pretty; and that she enjoyed seeing the tiny green fruit growing larger from week to week; and that she enjoyed seeing how in the end there were in fact a few ripe cherries. And when one has had so much joy at the beauty of these cherries, it is not hard at all to leave the joy of eating them to Grandfather, who, after all, does not have so much time during the day to enjoy their beauty.

Besides the cherry tree there were other kinds of fruit in the garden: the berries, black currants and gooseberries. These were present only in limited quantities. There were one or two bushes of each, and they did not bear fruit every year. Still, whenever possible, Grandmother waited to pick them until we were present, so that we could pick them with her. Yet the care and love with which she picked them made clear to us that there were only a few and that we dare not be bold enough to eat any on the sly. So we picked them together with her and, when the basket was full, she weighed it and then parceled out a few berries to us. We ate these berries with a sense of having received something very special.

Flowers were few, but grass was plentiful. And Grandmother often showed us how beautiful a single blade of grass is, for example, when a single, round, shining drop of rain hangs from it or when a bit of dew lies on it in the morning. It seemed to us as if Grandmother also loved the garden most when it bore traces of heaven, traces of something that had come down from above. I don't know *how* often Grandmother told about heaven. But you felt that it was something very present in her life and that every time she caught sight on the earth of a trace of heaven, she would tell about *all* of heaven. The birds were most beautiful when you could not see them. They were most splendid in the winter, when they left the first traces of their steps in the newly fallen snow. Occasionally Grandfather would come and explain: "Here you can see the tracks of a titmouse or a sparrow or the trail of a raven." But I never learned to tell them apart. Everything was beautiful enough as it was, and the tracks had been so neat, softly, and unobtrusively impressed on the snow that you were happy about the marks that were left behind. Only rarely did you catch the moment at which the bird made the tracks; usually they were simply suddenly present. In contrast, you often saw how the birds came to peck at the little basket full of nuts that Grandmother had hung in the window. The birds were then so close to you, separated only by the pane of glass, that it seemed a bit unsettling. It was nicer when they simply ran across the snow.

And then there were the leaves. Down in the garden there was a tree, I no longer know exactly . . . yes, I do: it was a birch tree that Grandmother had received from Grandfather for her twentieth birthday, for when they were married, their combined age was less than forty years. The climate in La-Chaux-de-Fonds was a bit raw for birches, so they sought out a particularly sheltered place in the garden for this birch. When the last snow had vanished in the spring and you could walk freely again, Grandmother's first walk was always to this birch tree: Had it survived the winter in good shape? Was it already budding? Then you noticed that its leaves were shining and trembling, even when you could hardly feel a breeze. The birch made an infinitely delicate and shining contrast to the other darker trees, which were largely firs and beeches. And so you visited the birch frequently, checking to see how the leaves were growing, something you could follow easily. Because they trembled the way they did, you felt as if they were particularly alive. Even the trunk, which was white and gray, and so shining, seemed especially elegant to us.

It was also wonderful to be able to play with dolls in

the garden. We took care of them in their doll carriage and pushed them through the long pathways, completely free of the governess, free of any supervision. The governess accompanied us only as far as Grandmother's house. Once she had helped us remove our wraps in the entrance way, she left. And so, once alone with one's dolls and the little doll carriage, perhaps even with provisions in it—for we often received our afternoon snack right away at the beginning of the afternoon so we could take it with us into the garden —once one was alone, it seemed as if the garden was the entire world and that it belonged to oneself alone. No kind of noise could be heard in the garden, any more than in the house. Everything was totally quiet, distant, and separate from the other residences, far from the street with its traffic. At our home, we always heard the street noises and the many children playing outside. And so one was never without contact with this almost unknown world, which was so noisy and whose voice one always heard. At Grandmother's, stillness simply reigned.

When the onset of darkness or evening's chill caused you to reenter the house, you entered a completely new stillness, and it seemed as if each room had its own peculiar sort of peace and quiet and light. The stillness of the living room was permeated by Grandmother's gentleness, whereas in the room where I slept when I stayed at Grandmother's, stillness and solitude united. In the antechamber, stillness merged with the fragrance of fruit preserves. It was actually almost as if stillness possessed all kinds of different colors. When I was a bit older and had already begun to attend school, there were occasionally periods when I stayed with Grandmother for days at a time, for example, when my little brother was born. On those occasions there was a very special arrangement at the end of the hallway. It was a long corridor, and at the end stood a wood stove, and in this wood stove was a large opening, and in this opening were apples and linden-blossom tea for us. And the teakettle always sang, and the stove always hummed. It was not the crackling of the firewood that you heard, but real music, a real humming in the stove. When, for example, you came home from school (the school was located on the other hill in the town, in Crettez, whereas the house was in Les Tilleuls), you had a good half-hour walk. And if the streets were covered with a wet spring snow, you arrived home thoroughly soaked. I had a red knitted cap that always became wetter and wetter when it was raining, until finally the cold water ran down my neck and back. That was quite unpleasant, and when it was already starting to turn dark after the afternoon's classes, the darkness and the cold wetness could be a powerful experience. You would therefore be looking forward to arriving soon at Grandmother's and, when you did arrive, the light would already be burning and the entrance hall would be really hot and you were permitted to help yourself to what was ready on the stove, and there would also be something to eat on the table: bread spread with jam; and so everything turned into something of a festival, a celebration of arrival and security. First you warmed yourself, and, if it was particularly cold outside, you were permitted to take one of the warming stones from the stove and hold it against yourself. There were also bags filled with cherry pits that served as warmers, but they were usually in Grandmother's room, whereas the warming stones were found in the hall. Next Grandmother came out to see if you needed to change clothes. Next we had homework to do, and only after it was finished were you permitted to go see Grandmother. For when we were actually living with her, the day was divided up differently from when we were merely visiting. She also had adult visitors. When we had finished our homework, we went to see her and also greeted her visitors. Often Cousin Clémentine was there. She was incredibly ugly, so much so that she filled one with fear. Her voice was completely masculine, the purest bass. And she always wanted a kiss. She had a trick to help overcome that fear in us: she would say, "Je te donne un baiser á la menthe [I'll give you a peppermint kiss]." Then she would take a small peppermint drop out of a tiny silver box in her large black bag and pop it into her mouth. If you then gave her a kiss, she would breathe it on you. It was terrible. But there was no way of escape, for she was Grandmother's best friend.

Grandmother owned a golden thimble. On its outer edge, very fine engraving read "*Ora et labora.*" She showed this to me one day and explained that *ora* meant "to pray" and *labora* meant "to work". I noticed that *ora* was repeated within *labora*. I talked about that with Grandmother, and she said that prayer was contained in all of life, in everything one did. Grandmother knew no Latin.

About the time she showed this to me, it snowed very heavily one day, and right on the window, as it often did. A good number of flakes stuck to the lower part of the window, so that the view grew steadily smaller, in fact, twice as small, since the window had a horizontal crossbar. Ever smaller and smaller. And the room grew darker and darker, although it was not yet time to light the lights. I no longer know what we were talking about. But finally I asked Grandmother: If life can turn into prayer as she had said, does God in fact send the snowflakes so that one might fill each flake with a prayer? Is it as if each individual snowflake were a desire, an invitation from heaven to prayer? It is hard to say exactly what I imagined at the time, but somehow I thought that God was sending us his wish-list before Christmas, and we are supposed to pray, to answer each snowflake in the entire world with a prayer. And I also thought: when the snowflakes end up creating a mass of snow, then one would know how much remained to be prayed until such a collection of prayer were built up. Grandmother said: Yes, but one should not think that, once the snowflakes had vanished, everything was then all right. On the other hand, neither need one think that each individual flake was an admonition or a requirement. For not only snow but also rain could be received as coming from God. And when the weather was nice, one need not think that God was no longer sending anything from heaven. One was united to God even when one could not see it.

Nightfall under a blanket of snow is something especially beautiful, and not merely because it is nighttime. It is almost as if God wanted to wall a person in. It is not at all dreadful but rather cozy: to be walled in by God's prayer wishes. Later, when Grandmother lit the gaslight, the famous gaslight, it seemed to me as if this was a direct reply to God: Yes, yes, we are here. He ought to be able to see that a light burns in us, too.

There was one problem for me: when it rained, the raindrops did not really cling to the window. Of course, Grandmother said, but the raindrops do knock on the window. It's simply another way to announce oneself. The rain knocks and then falls deeper, into the ground, where it gathers together. And, she said, in that we see that much, much, much prayer is needed very much deeper, in a place one may never come near. I had the feeling that perhaps this deep place would be the place of many sinners, or the place of raw sin . . ., which one can't see, so to speak, from the window, a place into which one must descend as if to enter a completely different place. Later, when it rained once, one could see how little rivulets formed in front of the house. They were completely bright and transparent and flowed downhill, but from the window one could see how they became even murkier and browner, picking up ever more soil. Grandmother said: "It is as if God wanted to clean down there with his rain." At first I thought that this was not at all necessary, but when one saw how the clear water become browner and browner, one had to admit that there certainly was a lot of dirt in it. Of course it was no great stream, merely a little rivulet. . . . Later in life, when it rained hard against the window, I would often think of Grandmother and how she would say that one must be grateful not only for the pretty snow but also for the rain. . . .

Once Grandmother visited us at home. At that time I really loved rain. It was raining, and I happened to be outside, knowing full well that Grandmother was visiting at our house. But I was in no hurry whatsoever. I had been sent to buy something; I was five years old. Slowly and blissfully, I wandered in the rain toward home. All at once I glimpsed a roof gutter. One can imagine what followed. I stood under it; I had my large Red-Riding-Hood cap, the knitted one, on my head. The raindrops collected in it and ran all the way down my body. When I came home, the maid saw immediately what had happened. Grandmother was with Mama. Mama was not at all pleased. I said: "It's like in the *Trials of Sophie* [*Malheurs de Sophie*]." And I knew that Grandmother would understand that this had very little to do with Sophie and that standing under the gutter really meant: "Dear God, I want to collect as many of your wishes as possible" —something that never would have occurred to me, for example, when taking a bath or when drawing water from a faucet. . . . From that day to this, it has always been something of a struggle for me not to stand under a gutter that is going full force. I have a great affection for gutters.

Grandmother's hands were wrinkled a bit. I liked to play with the wrinkles. She said that *her* grandmother had had very wrinkled hands, so that one could make a crown out of the skin, a crown that would stay there all by itself. One could do that with my grandmother's skin, but only a little bit. She said that it was always like this when one is going to die soon: God begins to loosen one's skin a bit so that one learns gradually to loosen oneself from the earth and to think more about heaven.

The bathroom at Grandmother's was completely different from ours at home. At Grandmother's, there was a gray tin bathtub—a bathtub that resounded, you understand? If you tapped on it, it emitted an incredible echo. You could tap out a whole melody on it. It could produce almost an entire musical scale—approximately from *do* to *fa* sharp. Naturally that was glorious. When the water ran into it, that too echoed loudly. We had nothing like this at home, none of this fantastic echo. But it was very difficult to heat the bathroom at Grandmother's, so it was not used very much during the winter. Instead, it held the jellied quince. Grandmother would make entire plates of them in October or November. But it was the tradition that one not even *taste* them before Christmas. One could only see them sitting there, some on large plates, the rest in little molds, but in the latter case one could not see the contents, for the jelly was under the mold. Before Christmas it was out of the question even to touch them. But after they had been given away at Christmas—usually with very little left over—then one might ask whether any were left over.

Grandmother understood completely that one simply

needed some quiet now and again. I would arrive at about two in the afternoon, and Grandmother usually handed me provisions for the entire afternoon right away. At home we usually had milk and bread with jam at four o'clock. At Grandmother's, on the other hand, there were nothing but unusual things, for instance, the *biscômes*, which were a sort of gingerbread with an almond in the center, or perhaps bread with a very tough crust. And the chocolate was in a wrapper with a squirrel on it. Grandmother might then give me a little basket with two slices of bread, a *biscôme*, and a small bar of chocolate and ask: "Do you think this will be enough?" After that I could go and hole up somewhere, in any of Grandmother's rooms or in the entrance hall or in the garden, taking my knitting or my favorite book. I would spend the entire afternoon on an island of this sort. I don't know if Grandmother herself had such a great need for quiet or whether she merely figured out that I did. As far as I was concerned, she was certainly correct. She often said that we were like Robinson and Friday, except that we had not yet encountered each other: there were two of us on an island. There was, however, nothing at all extravagant in that, rather the greatest simplicity. Occasionally there was a tea at four o'clock. It would be ready on the stove in the hall, for example, tea of linden blossoms from the garden, already sugared. You could help yourself and felt marvelously free in so doing because you did not have to drink that awful milk.

Whoever entered the house had to go through a small wooden vestibule that had been added in order to shelter the entrance in winter; it kept off the snow, wind, and rain. Next one entered a dark antechamber, which, however, was incredibly alive and as though populated. From here steps led up into Grandmother's residence.

There was, however, another door, to the right. If you opened it, there were three steps down; but you always forgot that the steps were there. From there you reached the bright gray hall where all the apes were assembled, on branches in glass display cases. It was something absolutely horrible. Entire trees were inside these cases; in addition to the apes, there was a fox. The cases were tall and stood opposite each other. The rest of the hall was filled with deer antlers and other hunting trophies. They were to be found even in the windows and between the display cases. Grandfather had shot most of these animals, except for the apes, which came from America, from a great-uncle. Sometimes it smelled like wild game in here, and one sensed that this must make the animals miserable; it was when Grandfather had returned from hunting and was cooking the deer himself.

From the main door in the antechamber, one would enter the parlor. This was a very large room filled with Louis XV furniture, not at all beautiful. It seemed totally uninhabited. There were also vases there, by which you could measure your growth. At first, you looked at them from below; in the end you could look down from above them and see what was inside. These were genuine Japanese vases. And if you were to knock into one of them with your shoe, you would have lost as much money as if you had set the entire chalet on fire, according to what Grandfather said. I hated this parlor; nothing in the world could have persuaded me to enter it by myself. Mama always said that when she was living at home she had to dust the parlor every morning. Whenever she said that, I would think: "What a penance!" All I can remember is that Willy was baptized there. On that occasion, we were brought in coaches. I was supposed to climb into one of them, but instead I went wild and started hitting out around me and said that I wanted to go to the baptism, not to Pouierelles. They had all they could do to convince me that that was where the baptism would take place. I remember nothing from the ceremony, only from the meal: that there were a host of paper sleeves that held fish and poultry, and everything was so weird.

Right next to the parlor was a very dark room with equally dark wallpaper: the music room. It was usually cold in there. It held a piano, and there was music. From time to time someone would rush into this room to fetch some music. This room was also a little frightening to me until one day I heard Grandmother playing. To me, her playing sounded unimaginably beautiful. When Hélène was small, she had taken piano lessons from her. I asked Grandmother how these lessons were going. She said that she would never make a virtuoso out of Hélène, because she herself knew so little. When Hélène came back from her first lesson, I was frightfully excited and wanted to hear immediately what she had learned but was very disappointed that she did not know how to play any scales. I told Grandmother that Hélène still could not do very much on the piano. Grandmother said: Yes, she was probably a poor teacher. Moreover, she did not want to teach piano very long, or she would end up having to give piano lessons to all her grandchildren, and she could not do that.

Next came the dining room, about which I have already spoken. From there one entered the veranda. During the winter, the veranda was always closed off but was connected to the dining room through a window that had no curtains. The dining room had no other windows. I never understood how this veranda, which was so terribly cold and lifeless during the winter, could be so inhabited and cheery in the summer. How could a room transform itself like that?

A large number of pillows were to be found on the veranda, all of them white and blue and all of them embroidered by Grandmother. The kitchen, however, was unspeakably cozy. In the center stood a very large table, scoured white. Then there was the wood-burning stove, which was always so full of life. Occasionally the maid would open its door, and one could gaze into the fire. A fire like this was an awful lot more beautiful than the gas stove we had at home. The entire wall of the kitchen was hung with copper vessels, with pans and lids and pudding molds, including three that were shaped like fish. And then there were deep bundt cake pans. I never could understand how people could need so many utensils. I always thought that one would place all one's utensils on the stove at the same time. That would, of course, be the most beautiful way to do it, but it never happened.

From the kitchen you went directly into the open air. There were then several possible paths: either up some steps to a large terrace behind the house, leading back into the second floor of the house, or to the garden gates. Or you could go to the chicken coop, for Grandmother had a large poultry yard, surrounded by a fence, with a pond in the middle for the ducks. The most amusing thing was when you would give duck eggs to a hen to hatch, and the duckling would then enter the water cheerfully while the shocked hen remained standing on the bank. The chickens had a multistory chalet constructed of wood; a porcelain egg lay in each nest to encourage the hens to lay. From time to time we were permitted to hunt for eggs in the chicken house. The porcelain eggs were much colder; but often one laid hold of an egg that was still warm from the hen. Naturally, the most exciting thing was to be present when the chicks hatched out of the eggs, something I witnessed two or three times. My grandmother had been present when I was born, and I had always been told that it was an atrocious birth. Grandmother said: "You simply did not want to come." I thought: "I just didn't want to break the eggshell."

After the chicken coop came the dog house, where Tell was. He was a large, brown dog, whom I liked very much. When he died, Aunt Annette was very sad that I did not cry, too. But no. People always compared him to Médor, whom I had never known and who must have been the perfect dog. So Tell always seemed to me to be inferior. Still, I had no pity on him; to me, he was fine as he was.

It is not very seemly to talk about the lavatory. Yet it was marvelous. For opposite the seat was a splendid bowl, which was decorated with blue flowers just like the basin. A pewter pitcher filled with water was poured into the bowl for the purpose of washing your hands. Naturally you did not wash your hands so readily here, since the maids had to refill the pitcher with water daily. But next to the pitcher was a bottle with *eau de cologne*, not an ordinary bottle, but a carafe. You might pour a drop from this carafe into the washbasin. The entire place smelled gloriously of *eau de cologne*. I would be most insulted if someone suggested that any other smell ever arose there. Even upon entering, you were surrounded by this pleasant odor. It was a large room and very bright.

The house had no real attic, at least I never knew of one. On the other hand, the coach house contained the garden tools and a great many cobwebs. This space was thoroughly cleaned each year, but by autumn it was full of beasts again. This was also where the large straw hats, the ones we wore when we were in the garden, were kept. There was one other weird thing there: an invalid chair, which took the form of an armchair on wheels. In it a family member could be carried for a walk in the garden and lie in the sun.

At Grandmother's you always encountered ladies who seemed utterly ancient. It took me a long time to understand that Grandmother had once been a child too, so it seemed like a joke to me when these ladies talked about having been at school with Grandmother. I did indeed have a sense of my own growth, but I thought adults existed in an immutable and stable condition. I also assumed that their relationship to me was stable. Adults were eternally adult, and the elderly among them were eternally elderly. Once when Grandmother was celebrating her birthday, I asked her: "How old are you?" She smiled and answered: "One year older than last year!" It seemed extremely funny to me to think that she also was growing older. The main person I met at Grandmother's was the aforementioned Cousin Clémentine, who was so ugly and had a mustache. Yet she had a special affection for me and always told me the same story, which, after a while, annoyed me a little. Only much later did I appreciate her. Her story was that once, when I was two or three years old, I had visited her. She received us in the parlor, we sat down, and she had begun a conversation with Grandmother when suddenly I stood up and in horror said "Bonjour, Madame" to a doll that was sitting in a chair. It was an ugly doll with a genuine kimono and real black hair and a Japanese face. The constant retelling of this story always left me feeling a bit humiliated. But when people spoke about Cousin Clémentine, they always praised her. Much later I learned that her husband had continually been unfaithful to her, once with a young sales clerk employed in Cousin Clémentine's jewelry shop. She had actually taken in this young woman with her illegitimate child as if she really belonged to the family. She was ancient when she died, somewhere between eighty and ninety, and was touchingly cared for until her death by this unmarried mother.

Clémentine and her husband did what many older people in La Chaux-de-Fonds did: they moved back to Geneva, into a large house in Conches, surrounded by spacious grounds. The young woman and her child accompanied them.